STICE, LORD DENNING AND T

ustice, Lord Denning
nd the Constitution

Edited by
PETER ROBSON
Law School, University of Strathclyde

and

PAUL WATCHMAN
Faculty of Law, University of Dundee

ower

Published by
Gower Publishing Company Limited,
Westmead, Farnborough, Hants, England

ISBN 0 566 00399 6 Cased edition
ISBN 0 566 00454 2 Limp edition

British Library Cataloguing in Publication Data

Justice, Lord Denning and the constitution.
1. Denning, Alfred Thompson Denning, Baron, b.1899
2. Law - England - History and criticism
I. Robson, Peter II. Watchman, Paul
340'.092'4

Printed in Great Britain
by Biddles Limited, Guildford, Surrey

Contents

Contributors

Ian Duncanson, LL.B., B.C.L.	Lecturer, University of Keele
Ray Geary, LL.B., LL.M., Solicitor	Lecturer, Queen's University, Belfast
Tom Guthrie, LL.B	Research Student, University of Glasgow
Sheila McLean, LL.B., M.Litt	Lecturer, University of Glasgow
Ken Miller, LL.B., LL.M.	Lecturer, University of Strathclyde
Peter Robson, LL.B., Ph.D. Solicitor	Lecturer, University of Strathclyde
Paul Watchman, LL.B. Solicitor	Lecturer, University of Dundee
Eric Young, M.A., LL.B. Solicitor	Senior Lecturer, University of Strathclyde

Foreword

The judges of our superior courts, for all their authority, are retiring individuals. Except when caught in the limelight of major criminal trials, they carry on in decent obscurity their essential work of settling disputes. If, in justifying their decisions, they make new law, they do not proclaim it to be such, but leave it to those who come after them, advocates and judges, to tease out the new rules and apply them to fresh circumstances.

Lord Denning is the exception that throws this practice into relief. With the serenity of the very old who still command all their faculties - and his are of the sharpest - he uses each case as an opportunity to proclaim what the law is, or what it should be and shall be from thenceforth. It is the performance of an oracle, but a kindly and approachable one who expresses himself in no Delphic utterances, but in English of the most pellucid clarity, as if to ensure that none should fail to receive his message. To some of his brethren he is a *vieillard terrible*, but young lawyers for several decades now have given him their hero-worship as a Mr. Valiant-for-Justice.

The celebrity of this Master of the Rolls extends far beyond England and beyond the legal profession. In this work some sceptical academic lawyers, Scots most of them or working in the astringent air of Scotland, pose like Hans Christian Andersen's embarrassing child, the awkward question, does this judicial monarch wear any conceptual clothes? Are his judgments based on anything more than hunch, whim or even prejudice and thus an affront to true law, which forms a cohesive system, is consistent in application and so predictable in its future effects? Is the justice which he so often invokes as his guiding-light amid the encircling gloom of bad precedents not a fitful and wayward torch? And how can this brazen judicial law-making be reconciled with the assumptions of parliamentary democracy?

It is right that academics from their standpoint of detachment should raise these questions, but that they should do so when at 81 their subject seems to be ever bolder and more inventive in his judgments is in itself an acknowledgement of Lord Denning's greatness. May his ability to personalise these profound questions of jurisprudence and politics and theirs to formulate them work together to generate an informed debate.

I.D. Willock

University of Dundee

Acknowledgements

We are especially grateful to Janet Watchman for help over the years with illustrations. Our other technical assistance from Elaine Smith in typing the draft and final versions of these essays is greatly appreciated. Thank you Elaine. Many thanks to Tom Guthrie for all his work on the Index and Case Index, and to Mick Kemble of Manchester Polytechnic for his encouragement and comments. Our gratitude, finally, to our parents, spouses and others for their support and interest.

This collection of essays was originally conceived and written for the journal <u>Law and State</u>. However, the length of the essays dictated that we seek an alternative channel for our comments. Our appreciation to all our subscribers who have supported our ventures into alternative legal discourse. The proceeds from this work will go to the financing of improved production and distribution of <u>Law and State</u>. For details of <u>Law and State</u> contact the editors of this collection.

Select Bibliography

The Meaning of 'Ecclesiastical Law', 60 Law Quarterly Review (1944) 235.

The Divorce Laws, Lecture at King's College, University of London (London, 1947).

Freedom under the Law, Hamlyn Lectures (London, 1949).

The Independence of the Judges, Holdsworth Lectures (Birmingham, 1950).

The Equality of Women, Lecture delivered at the Annual Conference of the National Marriage Guidance Council (London, 1950).

The Spirit of the British Constitution, 29 Canadian Bar Review (1951) 1180.

Recent Developments in the Doctrine of Consideration, 15 Modern Law Review (1952) 1.

The Need for a New Equity, Address delivered before the Bentham Club by its President, 5 Current Legal Problems (1952) 1.

The Changing Law, (London. 1953).

The Rule of Law in the Welfare State, Haldane Memorial Lecture (London, 1953).

The Influence of Religion on Law, Earl Grey Memorial Lecture, King's College, University of Newcastle (Newcastle-on-Tyne, 1953).

English Law and the Moral Law, The Listener, 25 February 1954.

The Christian Approach to the Welfare State, Shaftesbury Society (London, 1954).

The Independence and Impartiality of the Judges, 71 South African Law Journal (1954) 345.

The Road to Justice, (London, 1955).

Law in a Developing Community, 33 Public Administration (1955) 1.

From Precedent to Precedent, The Romanes Lectures (London, 1959).

'The Way of an Iconoclast', 5 Journal of the Society of the Public Teachers of Law (1959) 77.

Responsibility before the Law, Lionel Cohen Lecture, Hebrew University (Jerusalem, 1961).

Borrowing from Scotland, The David Murray Lecture (Glasgow, 1963).

Gems in Ermine, English Association, Presidential Address (London, 1964).

'Let Justice be Done', Oration delivered at Birkbeck College, University of London on 3 December 1974 (London, 1974).

Giving Life to the Law, 1 Malaya Law Review (1976) C.III.

The Freedom of the Individual Today, 45 Medico-Legal Journal (1977) 49.

'A Life in the Day of Lord Denning', Sunday Times, Colour Supplement, (1978).

The Discipline of Law, (London, 1979).

Due Process of Law, (London, 1980)

Introductory Note

Lord Denning is a major figure on the political landscape. He has occupied an important place in the state for over thirty years. His political significance stems from the possibilities he opens up for alternatives to democratic institutions in the state. He is, however, a judge. The work of the judiciary is to a large extent hidden from public view. Even when a case is publicised the language used often means that laymen have difficulties in assessing exactly what is being done in the legal process. The judiciary have only recently begun to emerge as possible 'honest brokers' in the struggle of politics as operators of a Bill of Rights. The judicial image has been refurbished largely at the hands of Lord Denning. His style and his approach have provided a possible taste of the future now.

He has consistently stressed the importance of justice at the expense, if necessary, of the rules of the law. Overriding principles have appealed to him more than the constrictions of the law. He has acted more like a judge operating a written constitution. His approach may be typical of what is in store with such a constitutional development.

It is important, then, that this branch of state power is examined critically. Lord Denning has already provided extensive accounts of how he sees this work. His version of what he has done and why can be gleaned from his writings in the Select Bibliography and more recently in his two books The Discipline of Law and The Due Process of Law. We feel that this view does not tell the whole story. In some instances, the rhetoric and the reality do not seem to fit. We have attempted to provide an alternative view of the achievements of Lord Denning.

Our approach to the topic of Lord Denning's work has been to adopt a series of simple criteria. Most typically, we have tested Lord Denning's performance by the goals which he sets. His own standards are taken as a major reference point. Lord Denning talks of working to curb abuse of power. He talks of the rights of the underprivileged.

He has certainly worked to limit the effectiveness of trades unions. He has led the expansion of the property rights of deserted wives and lovers. How do other areas where power is wielded fare under Lord Denning? What has happened to other groups with limited resources in the welfare state?

In addition, we have looked at the operation of Lord Denning's approach to Parliament's statutes. Insofar as these represent a democratic test, it is possible to see to what extent Lord Denning subscribes to a belief in the 'rule of law' in his own work.

We attempt to relate Lord Denning to the society in which he works in the opening and concluding parts of the book. In the first section, we situate Lord Denning in his judicial context. Paul Watchman suggests in Lord Denning, Palm Tree Justice and the Lord Chancellor's Foot why it is important to recognise the power of the Master of the Rolls and how Lord Denning's work has fared at the hands of academic and judicial critics over the years. The inaccessibility of much of the work of the courts has meant that this sustained line of doubt has gone largely unnoticed. Peter Robson links this in with the restricted nature of work on the judiciary in Problems of Judicial Study where he points out some of the limitations and difficulties of such studies. This, Peter Robson suggests, in Media, Politics and the Judiciary, has allowed a situation to emerge of uncritical admiration for the judiciary in general, and Lord Denning in particular, in the 1970s.

Part Two of the book contains substantive essays on the work of Lord Denning. In Lord Denning and Morality, Ray Geary deals with the strong strain of morally directed policy within the work of Lord Denning. His own views on morality have vied with the provisions of the law.

Tom Guthrie points out in Spies, Subverters and Saboteurs that the early espousal of the notion of open government by Lord Denning has been reversed with the Master of the Rolls reposing absolute trust in the wisdom of the Executive and abandoning any attempt to impose any test of reasonableness on the Government; the espousal of the cause of the medical profession by Lord Denning is noted by Sheila McLean in her essay Negligence - A Dagger at the Doctor's Back, which demonstrates the way the concerns of Lord Denning for the reputation of professional men and the interests of patients have been weighed in a series of leading decisions during his career; Peter Robson and Paul Watchman discuss the lead Lord Denning has given in his dealings with claimants and the homeless in Resisting the Unprivileged; in The Labours of Lord Denning, Kenneth Miller looks at the performance of Lord Denning on the issue of trade union immunity in the face of a resolute legislature and a House of Lords determined to give effect to the intentions of Parliament; the obstructive role of Lord Denning in the field of rationalising judicial review and introducing a degree of consistency to interventions by the courts in administrative matters forms the core of Eric Young's essay, Developing a System of Administrative Law; the leadership of Lord Denning in adopting special criteria to limit the rights of tenants in the welfare state is examined in Sabotaging the Rent Acts by Peter Robson and Paul Watchman. As already indicated, the consistent message of all the essays in Section Two is that in the areas which we have examined, Lord Denning has failed to carry out his own stated goals of limiting the potential for abuse of power or respecting the democratic process. He has introduced inconsistency and uncertainty. The criteria he will adopt on any issue are unreliable and idiosyncratic. It is this Section which exposes the limitations of his method. It is perfectly capable of protecting deserted wives at the one moment and leaving the homeless in the streets at the next. Whether, on balance, the advantages outweigh the attendant problems depends on one's own weighing of the merits of such groups as claimants, trade unions, deserted wives and various entrepreneurial agencies.

It does not matter how one assesses the judicial performance on specific issues from one's own individual or sectional view point. The problem with the Denning approach would seem, from this work, to be that on some issues the judge may be prepared to intervene and 'bend' the rules as Lord Denning freely admits he does to achieve a specific policy purpose. When this does not coincide with either the individual's standpoint or when it conflicts with purported legislative intention, the Denning approach loses something of its attraction. In so far as politicians rely on the judiciary to give a seal of approval to certain of their policies in the courts, the judiciary have the possibility of exploiting the free space which their role gives them in return. Politicians cannot be relied on to 'pull up' the judges when they 'step out of line'. This will depend on the issue. This is the real challenge to the 'rule of law' in our society. Only those with confidence that the judiciary will, on balance, favour their interests, are likely to look with confidence on the enhancing of the judiciary's power with a Bill of Rights.

The collection concludes with Ian Duncanson's Digression on Denning which examines how the current judicial role fits into the developments in the political economy. The predilections and goals of the judiciary do not spring ready formed from their owners, but represent a specific way of treating social, economic and political issues. Whilst it is important to test Lord Denning's work by reference to his own avowed goals and in terms of legislative purposes, it is necessary to recognise that to appreciate the totality of the judicial position and potential, a wider view needs to be taken. Ian Duncanson begins this movement from the particular to the general in his essay and we hope to publish in the future on this to provide a clearer picture of the judiciary in general within the political economy. We feel our examination of Lord Denning is necessary because of the unique power and symbolic aura attaching to Lord Denning which requires him to be taken very seriously within debates on resolving issues of political decision-making within the state. This collection, we trust, goes some way to extending a debate on this hitherto specialist topic.

Lord Denning

Alfred Thompson Denning, Baron Denning of Whitchurch

born 23 January 1899

education: Andover Grammar School and
Magdalen College, Oxford

Firsts in Mathematics and Jurisprudence

Eldon Scholar 1921

Prize Student Inns of Court

Called to the Bar 1923

King's Counsel 1938

Judge of the High Court of Justice 1944

Lord Justice of Appeal 1948-1957

Lord of Appeal in Ordinary 1957-1962

Master of the Rolls 1962 to date

Club: Athenaeum

PART I
Lord Denning in Context

Palm Tree Justice and the Lord Chancellor's Foot

With the possible exception of the Lord Chancellor, the Master of the Rolls occupies arguably the most powerful and influential position in the English legal system.[1] Presiding over and controlling the flow of work within the Civil Division of the Court of Appeal,[2] there can be little doubt that the Master of the Rolls is best positioned to influence the development of the law. For, as the present Master of the Rolls, Lord Denning, is keenly aware, the Court of Appeal is in many respects a more important appeal court than the House of Lords.[3] In terms of the sheer volume of cases with which the Court of Appeal deals, this is certainly the case. Stevens, for example, notes that whereas the House of Lords deals with an average of fifty to sixty cases annually, the Court of Appeal deals with an average of eight hundred.[4] Given the very small number of appeals which are taken to the Lords and the fact that the Court of Appeal seldom does not have the last word in cases of great urgency one can agree with Lord Denning's observation that 'the Court of Appeal really does lay down the law in the civil cases in this country'.[5] Under the leadership of Lord Denning, I would argue, the advantages which the Court of Appeal enjoys over the Lords have been assiduously increased. For Lord Denning combines a legendary distaste for precedent which does not accord with his intuitive and idiosyncratic sense of justice[6] with a prediliction for policy-making[7] which at times has given the Court of Appeal the appearance of a legislative rather than a judicial body. Lord Denning, to be fair, is refreshingly candid about his beliefs. A trenchant opponent of substantive formalism, Lord Denning has declared that the role of the judiciary should be to mould and shape the principles of law laid down by the judges in the nineteenth century to the social necessities and social opinion of the twentieth century:[8]

> 'Some people seem to think that, now there is a Law Commission, the judges should leave it to them to put right any defect and to make any new development. The judges must no longer play a constructive role. They must be automatons applying the existing rules.

> Just think what this means. The law must stand still until the Law Commission has reported and Parliament passed an Act on it; and, meanwhile every litigant must have his case decided by the dead hand of the past. I decline to reduce the judges to such a sterile role. They should develop the law, case by case, as they have done in the past; so that the litigants before them can have their differences decided by the law as it should be and is, and not by the law of the past'.

THE WAY OF AN ICONOCLAST[9]

John Mortimer has recently described the Master of the Rolls as 'A St George of the law courts'.[10] For, like St George Lord Denning has slayed a number of dragons. In the name of justice Lord Denning's clean and bright sword has cut a path through seemingly impenetrable thickets of precedents and legal fictions. The creation and development of the concept of promissory estoppel,[11] the attempt to introduce a *jus quaesitum tertio* into English law,[12] the proposal of a 'just and equitable' approach to frustration of contract,[13] the campaigns against exemption clauses and penalty clauses,[14] the rapid extension of the boundaries of tortious liability,[15] the limitation of Crown privilege,[16] the increased accountability of local authorities for their officials,[17] the greater willingness of the judiciary to scrutinise administrative actions by the application of natural justice principles[18] and by way of judicial review,[19] and the rebellion against the principle of *stare decisis*[20] all bear the *imprimatur* of the Master of the Rolls. The influence of Lord Denning on the development of law is pervasive. As Michael Beloff points out, Lord Denning defeated is merely the prelude to Lord Denning triumphant.[21] For in a number of instances where Lord Denning has been overruled by the House of Lords, parliamentary intervention has given statutory effect to reforms advocated by Lord Denning. The limitation of state immunity, the extension of property rights to deserted spouses and mistresses, and the control of secondary picketing are examples of such intervention.[22] As an activist in a profession renowned for restraint, Lord Denning has his admirers. Clive Schmitthoff has written that 'the contemporary scene in Great Britain is unthinkable without Lord Denning of Whitchurch ...'[23] and Lord Scarman has characterised the postwar era as the period of legal aid, law reform and Lord Denning.[24]

The appearance of both The Discipline of Law and The Due Process of Law in The Sunday Times bestsellers lists indicates that admiration for Lord Denning is not confined to the Inns of Court and the Law Faculties. Yet, if the apparent ease with which Lord Denning can impose order on difficult areas of law has earned him praise, the approach of the Master of the Rolls to judicial decision-making has been criticised as unsophisticated, dangerous and unconstitutional.[25] Before turning to look at these criticisms in some detail, it is perhaps useful to note the assumptions and implications of Lord Denning's method of legal reasoning:[26]

> 'He [Lord Denning] looks at law as an instrument of doing justice, doing justice now in the case before him, justice which is founded on what the majority of right-thinking people regard as a fair solution, justice which the common people understand and which gives them confidence that those occupying the judgment seat do not live in a different world of ideas from their own and understand their hopes and anxieties.
>
> The belief that law is an instrument of doing instant justice, is the explanation of Lord Denning's often misunderstood radicalism. His approach is teleological. He thinks of the result before he considers the legal reasoning on which it has to be founded. If the result to which established legal doctrine leads is obviously unfair or out of touch with what ordinary people would expect to be the law, he will examine first principles in order to ascertain whether they really compel an unjust solution and often this method will enable him to arrive at an answer which is more adequate to modern needs'.

It is argued, then, that Lord Denning is a populist judge who dispenses justice on the basis of pragmatism rather than principle. In fairness to Lord Denning, it should be noted that the pressure under which the Court of Appeal is forced to operate in part inclines the members of that Court towards the teleological method of decision-making.[27] The dangers and limitations of this approach are the subject of this volume of essays.

Palm Tree Justice and The Lord Chancellor's Foot

In this essay it is proposed to look at the assessments of the work of Lord Denning by two different groups of lawyers. Whilst the style and language of Lord Denning have commanded the attention and approval of the media, his reception by academics and the House of Lords has been less enthusiastic. Other essays in this collection examine various specific legal issues from a critical perspective. What is done here is to indicate that in a variety of other areas, there have been individual doubts over Lord Denning's method of law-making in both academic and judicial circles. Even where the result is deemed satisfactory, the way in which Lord Denning reaches his conclusions have in the past given rise to disquiet and concern.

This essay documents the ways in which criticisms have been levelled in the past at the approach of Lord Denning over a variety of areas from both academic and judicial sources. As this essay makes clear, the problems raised by Lord Denning's quest for 'justice' at the expense of the 'law' is not in itself a novel issue. The criticisms have been a feature of Lord Denning's whole judicial career. The range of critics has been extensive and whilst they may not have common political or social goals their concern about Lord Denning is shared. He is the unlikely poser of a real threat to the rule of law and the social democratic political process.

ACADEMIC CRITICISM

Legal academics 'judge' the judges. The function of the judiciary is to do justice according to the law. This entails the interpretation of laws passed by Parliament and the adherence to precedent. An important part of the function of legal academics is to analyse judicial decision-making, to examine the reasoning of the judges for flaws and defects, and to assess the contribution made by judges to the development of the law. Judges and academics therefore come into conflict. Given the length of Lord Denning's tenure as an appeal judge, it would be remarkable if the decisions of the Master of the Rolls had escaped academic censure. Criticism of Lord Denning, however, is not limited to the merits or demerits of individual decisions or technical issues of legal method, but relates to matters of fundamental importance, such as the proper and constitutional function of the judiciary, legal reasoning, statutory interpretation and the doctrine of precedent. While it is not possible to give a comprehensive account of the criticisms levelled at Lord Denning within the space of an introductory essay, it is perhaps sufficient to give a flavour of those criticisms by selecting specific areas of law for study. As some of the areas chosen are the subject of bitter political controversy, I have attempted to balance criticisms of Lord Denning in areas such as trade union immunity and immigration with criticisms from less politically controversial areas such as the interpretation of testamentary deeds and frustration of contract.

Frustration of contract and limitation clauses

In 1967, the House of Lords rejected the doctrine developed by the Court of Appeal that if a person was in fundamental breach of contract, he could not rely on an exemption clause. In the leading case of Suisse Atlantique[28] the House of Lords held that the problem was simply a question of construction and if an exemption or limitation clause was designed to cover events which in fact did materialise the party for whose benefit the clause was included in the contract was entitled to rely on the clause to limit or exclude his liability. Three years later, this issue was raised again before the Court of Appeal in the case of Harbutt's 'Plasticine' Ltd. v Wayne Tank & Pump Co. Ltd.[29] In this case, Lord Denning, in the face of clear authority from the House of Lords specifically disapproving the applicability of the frustration doctrine in the case of limitation and exclusion clauses, re-affirmed that doctrine and held that fundamental breach ends the contract and exposes the party who attempted to limit or exclude his liability by way of such a clause to unlimited damages. J.A. Weir, writing in The Cambridge Law Journal was in no doubt that the judgment of the Court of Appeal was bad law:[30]

> 'This unhappy doctrine was not necessary ... The present doctrine of frustration being unsatisfactory, it is a pity that Lord Denning has invoked it in connection with limitation clauses. But its invocation is not only regrettable with regard to limitation clauses; it is wrong with regard to frustration. If the limitation clause, properly construed, covers the events which occur, then the

> doctrine of frustration cannot apply, since frustration occurs only when the parties have not regulated the legal consequences of the catastrophe ... [the common law] ... would not frustrate a contract, if the parties had made their own provision and the rule, lately reasserted, that a limitation clause would be given its intended effect notwithstanding a fundamental breach. Lord Denning has trumped both rules, and it must have been a double gratification for him to subvert Suisse Atlantique by perverting the doctrine of frustration. Masterly indeed'.

Weir's analysis of the law has been supported by the House of Lords in the recent case of Photo Production Ltd. v Securior Transport Ltd.[31] Here the House of Lords affirmed the principle laid down in Suisse Atlantique and held that there was no rule of law by which an exception clause in a contract could be eliminated from a consideration of the parties' position when there was a breach of contract (whether fundamental or not) or by which an exception clause could be deprived of effect regardless of the terms of the contract. It held the parties were free to agree to whatever exclusion or modification of their obligation they chose and therefore the question whether an exception clause applied when there was a fundamental breach, breach of a fundamental term or any other breach, turned on the construction of the contract as a whole, including any exception clauses.

More important for our purposes, however, is the speech of Lord Wilberforce. Dealing with the judgment of Lord Denning in Harbutt's 'Plasticine' Lord Wilberforce supported Weir's view when he suggested that Suisse Atlantique was by the Master of the Rolls misused:[32]

> 'My Lords, whatever the intrinsic merit of this doctrine ... it is clear to me that so far from following this House's decision in the Suisse Atlantique case it is directly opposed to it and that the whole purpose and tenor of the Suisse Atlantique case was to repudiate it'.

Indeed, Lord Wilberforce concluded that:[33]

> '... there are ample resources in the normal rules of contract law for dealing with these without the superimposition of a judicially invented rule of law'.

Immigrants and personal freedom

> 'Every man who comes into England is entitled to the protection of English law, whatever oppression he may heretofore have suffered and whatever may be the colour of his skin. The air of England is too pure for any slave to breathe. Let the black go free'.[34]

Lord Denning's concern for personal freedoms was expressed initially in the series of Hamlyn Lectures delivered by him in 1949. In Freedom under the Law[35] Lord Denning enunciated what he described to be the fundamental principle that 'where there is any conflict between the freedom of the individual and any other rights or interests, then no matter how great or powerful those others may be, the freedom of the humblest citizen shall prevail over it'.[36] It is clear that not all individuals could expect such protection as the American scientologist, Andrew Schmidt found. In the case of Schmidt v Home Secretary[37] Lord Denning declared that 'the Minister can exercise his power for any purpose which he considers to be for the public good or to be in the interests of the people of this country'.[38] The years which separate the Hamlyn Lectures and Schmidt mark the re-emergence of racism in Britain and the growth of public concern about the problem of black immigration.

Prejudices and fears about black immigration reached their zenith in 1972 with the expulsion from Uganda of some 40,000 British Asians. The press reported floods, deluges and tidal waves of immigrants on their way to Britain. Two years later the Court of Appeal heard an appeal from a British Asian claiming a right under international law to settle in the United Kingdom. The Court of Appeal held that there was no rule of public international law that a British protected person who had never lived in the United Kingdom was entitled to settle in the United Kingdom on being expelled from his own country. In refusing the appeal of Pravinlal Amarshi Thakrar a Ugandan Asian possessing a British passport who had been expelled by Idi Amin, Lord Denning stated:

> 'In 1972 a sword fell on the Asians living in Uganda. It was the sword of the President, General Amin. He declared that all Asians who were not citizens of Uganda must leave the country within 90 days. The declaration placed thousands in sore plight ... To support [his claim that Pravinlal was entitled as of right to come into the United Kingdom], counsel quoted Oppenheim: 'the home State of expelled persons is bound to receive them on the home territory'. ... But that rule does not apply when the home state is an outgoing country with far-flung commitments abroad, such as the United Kingdom has or recently did have. Take the class of persons with whom we are here concerned - British protected persons. They are said to be British nationals, but they are not British subjects. These number, or used to number, many millions. They were not born here. They have never lived here. They live thousands of miles away in countries which have no connection with England except that they were once a British protectorate. Is it to be said that by international law every one of them has a right if expelled to come into these small islands? Surely not. This country would not have room for them. It is not as if it was only one or two coming. They come not as single files but in batallions. Mass expulsions on this scale have never hitherto come within the cognisance of international law. To my mind, there is no rule of international law to which we may have recourse. There is no rule by which we are bound to receive them'.

Michael Akehurst thought it likely that the Court of Appeal's decision in R. v Secretary of State for the Home Department, ex parte Thakrar would arouse some anxiety among public international lawyers. Writing in The Modern Law Review in January 1975, Akehurst argues that Lord Denning appeared to be making three distinctions simultaneously. First, a distinction between individual expulsions and mass expulsions; second, a distinction between a self-contained country and a country with overseas colonies or protectorates; and third, a disinction between British subjects and British protected persons. These distinctions Akehurst argued were based on policy considerations, unnecessary and dishonourable.[40]

In 1972, the British Government waived the restrictions on immigration imposed by Parliament and accepted tens of thousands of Asians expelled from Uganda, on the grounds that international law required the United Kingdom to receive its nationals if they were expelled from other countries. To decide a question of international law without paying attention to the practice of the British Government (and of other governments), Akehurst adds, is to run the risk of producing a judgment which constitutes a very distorted picture of international law and Akehurst submits that the Court of Appeal mis-stated international law in Thakrar simply because it disregarded crucial evidence of international law.

More recently, the Court of Appeal has been exercised by the question of the detention of immigrants under the Immigration Act of 1971. Under this Act, immigration officers are empowered to examine any person arriving in the United Kingdom for the purpose of deciding whether he is a patrial, whether he may enter the United Kingdom without leave, and if not whether he should be given leave. Further, immigration officers are empowered by the Act to detain any person who is required to submit to such examination, pending his examination and a decision whether leave to enter should be given. And if such a person is refused leave to enter or if the person is an 'illegal entrant', he may be detained pending his removal from the United Kingdom. The Act provided a right of appeal against removal, but the remedy is not thought to be very beneficial because it is seldom exercised until the person has been removed from the United Kingdom. Given the ineffectiveness of the appeals procedure under the Act, detainees have resorted to the writ of habeas corpus, described by Lord Denning as 'our great writ which guarantees a personal freedom'.[41] Habeas corpus is the best known of the prerogative writs. This writ lies to bring up the body of a person imprisoned on a criminal charge or in civil detention. On an application for habeas corpus, the court is entitled to examine the grounds of detention. Such is the importance of this writ to the protection of human liberty that applications for habeas corpus have priority over all other court business. The burden of proof lies on the respondent. It is for the respondent to prove lawful justification for the detention, not for the applicant to prove that his detention is unlawful. In the case of immigrants, however, the Court of Appeal appears to be very reluctant to apply the protection of habeas corpus. For example, in the case of

R. v Governor of Pentonville Prison, ex parte Azam[42] Lord Denning viewed the question of the lawful detention of immigrants as non-justiciable:[43]

> 'If the men are allowed to remain, it will be difficult to refuse the wives and children. If this were allowed, the numbers of immigrants would be increased so greatly that there would not be room for everybody. Again, if an amnesty were granted, it would be an encouragement to others to follow their example: and that simply cannot be permitted. By sending back illegal immigrants, it will help to deter others from trying to do the same ... It is an administrative matter for the Secretary of State. It is very like his discretion to remove aliens, which has never been questioned in all our long history'.

J.A. Wade had harsh words to say about the reasoning of the judges in Azam.[44] On close inspection of the speeches of the judges who heard Azam's application for habeas corpus in the Divisional Court and his subsequent unsuccessful appeals to the Court of Appeal and the House of Lords, Wade detects a cloudiness of thought as to the interpretation of the Immigration Act of 1971. The case, Wade points out, turned on whether Azam was 'settled' in the United Kingdom at the commencement of the Act. The judges, in Wade's view, misused basic concepts in an attempt to promote the policy of the Act in spite of the words of the statute.

In 1978, the Court of Appeal imposed further restrictions on the availability of the writ of habeas corpus to immigrants. The burden of proof where a person applies for habeas corpus, as I have already pointed out, lies with the respondent. It would appear to follow that where an 'illegal entrant' applies for habeas corpus the burden of proof rests with the Home Office to prove lawful justification for the detention. However, in the case of R. v Secretary of State for the Home Department, ex parte Choudhary, the Court of Appeal placed the onus of proof on the applicant. For in that case, Lord Denning stated:[45]

> 'The return on the face of it, affords sufficient justification for his detention and removal from the United Kingdom. It is prima facie good. If that return is to be challenged, it is for him

> to challenge it. The burden of proof is upon him to show that he is being unlawfully detained. If the immigration officer acts honestly and on reasonable grounds, that is sufficient and the court will not further inquire into it. If the applicant is dissatisfied, there is a remedy by way of appeal. There is not a remedy by way of *habeas corpus*'.

However, that remedy, as the Master of the Rolls pointed out in *Azam*, is not a very beneficial one if a mistake has been made. The effect of the *Choudhary* decision, David Lloyd Jones argues, in *The Law Quarterly Review*,[46] is to impose on the applicant a burden which is impossible to discharge. Firstly, an immigrant required to prove the negative that he is not an 'illegal entrant', and secondly, he has to show that the Home Secretary or the immigration officer acting on his behalf did not have reasonable grounds to believe that the applicant was an 'illegal entrant'. The practical effect is to deprive the immigrant of recourse to the English courts.

Interpreting wills - palm tree injustice

> 'Were I a cadi dispensing justice under a palm tree ...'[47]

Few areas of law can be less politically contentious than the interpretation of wills and settlements. Yet the case of *Re Jebb*[48] rudely disturbed those academics who work in this specialised area of law. For prior to this case the paramount need for certainty in ascertaining the intention of testators had been universally recognised. After all, it had been thought, the testator can hardly be afforded the opportunity to re-cross the Styx and explain to the court what he had actually intended by the use of certain words in his will. The Chancery Court, therefore, adopted the practice of ascertaining the intention of the testator by giving the words used in the will their literal meaning. By this means, words and phrases took on a more precise meaning than are ascribed to them in everyday usage. These words and phrases are known as 'terms of art' and have been developed through an interaction between the courts and draftsmen to guide those who draft such documents on how to give legal effect to their intentions. Admittedly this approach has caused injustice but it is generally agreed that the advantages of the literal interpretation of wills clearly outweigh the disadvantages.

However, in Re Jebb, the Court of Appeal departed from this established rule of construction and brushed aside a great body of authority to impose a new rule of construction which in effect enabled the court to re-write the will of the testator according to what the court, in the light of the surrounding circumstances, believed the testator's intention to be:[49]

> 'In construing this will, we have to look at it as the testator did, sitting in his armchair, with all the circumstances known to him at the time. Then we have to ask ourselves: 'What did he intend?' We ought not to answer this question by reference to any technical rules of law. Those technical rules only too often led the courts astray in the construction of wills. Eschewing technical rules, we look to see simply what the testator intended'.

On the face of it, Lord Denning's view in Re Jebb is extremely attractive. In the name of justice, legal jargon is banished and common sense imposed. However, reaction to the 'armchair rule' of construction was extremely unfavourable. Commenting on the decision of the Court of Appeal in Re Jebb in The Law Quarterly Review, J.H.C. Morris condemned the cavalier treatment of clear and binding precedent in the judgments of Lord Denning and Danckwerts L.J. and concluded:[50]

> "By departing from the established rules of law the Court of Appeal seems to have usurped the function of the legislature. The decision will require the rewriting of the whole of the chapters on gifts to children in the textbooks on wills, unless the editors have the courage to say that it is manifestly wrong ... Nor is this all ... If this new attitude to the construction of wills comes to prevail, it will not be sufficient just to rewrite the chapters on gifts to children in the textbooks on wills. The textbooks themselves will have to be scrapped and construction reduced to the level of guesswork. It is submitted that rules of law binding

> on the court cannot be evaded merely by calling them 'technical'".

The new attitude, however, did not come to prevail. For in the following year, the Court of Appeal was given the opportunity to reconsider Re Jebb. Sydall v Castings Ltd.[51] turned on the meaning of the word 'descendant'. The majority of the Court of Appeal in this case construed that word to exclude illegitimate children and thus held that a three year old baby girl was not entitled to benefit under a group life assurance scheme for the dependants and relations of members. Lord Denning viewed the construction put forward by the majority of the Court as anachronistic and based on nineteenth century moral standards:[52]

> 'The judges in those days used to think that if they allowed illegitimate children to take benefit they were encouraging immorality ... In laying down such rules, they acted in accordance with the then contemporary morality. Even the Victorian fathers thought they were doing right when they turned their erring daughters out of the house. They visited the sins of the fathers upon the children - with a vengeance. I think we should throw over those harsh rules of the past. They are not rules of law. They are only guides to the construction of documents. They are quite out of date'.

This case is a clear example of Lord Denning's anxiety to do justice in spite of the law. To construe the word 'descendant' as a term of art would import prima facie legitimate children and thus would exclude a three year old girl from sharing the benefits of the assurance scheme simply because she is illegitimate. This result was repugnant to the Master of the Rolls and he therefore sought to do justice by rejecting the construction of the word 'descendant' as a term of art on the basis that that word should be given its ordinary meaning socially acceptable in the third quarter of the twentieth century. Few would disagree with the fairness of the result thus achieved, but the means by which Lord Denning reaches this result and the assumptions upon which it is based are, as Diplock L.J. pointed out, open to question:[53]

'Documents which are intended to give rise to legally enforceable rights and duties contemplate enforcement by due process of law which involves their being interpreted by courts composed of judges, each one of whom has his personal idiosyncracies of sentiment and upbringing, not to speak of age. Such documents would fail in their object if the rights and duties which could be enforced depended upon the personal idiosyncracies of the individual judge or judges upon whom the task of construing them chanced to fall. It is to avoid this that lawyers, whose profession it is to draft and to construe such documents, have been compelled to evolve an English language, of which the constituent words and phrases are more precise in their meaning than they are in the language of Shakespeare or of any of the passengers on the Clapham omnibus this morning. These words and phrases to which a more precise meaning is so ascribed are called by lawyers 'terms of art' but are in popular parlance known as 'legal jargon'. We lawyers must not allow this denigratory description to obscure the social justification for the use of 'terms of art' in legal documents. It is essential to the rule of law'.

Miscellaneous critical perspectives

These concerns have ranged far and wide from areas of considerable political controversy to particularly obscure fields. They apply to 'middle range' situations from family law,[54] the law of landlord and tenant,[55] the law relating to building and civil engineering contracts[56] and the law relating to the rights of mortgagees to repossession.[57] Not only has the scope of criticism been wide-ranging, but their tone has been highly critical of the scholarly attributes of the work of the Master of the Rolls. H.W.R. Wade observed that the statement of the law on judicial review by Lord Denning in Coleen[58] 'would not earn an examination candidate very high marks ...'[59] However, it is in the area of the law relating to labour relations that Lord Denning has received the most regular and extensive criticism.

In this field, not only has Lord Denning sought to reduce the power of 'the great trade unions'[60] and extend the ambit of judicial control over admission and expulsion decisions made by trade unions,[61] he has also sought to impose very considerable restraints upon the Advisory, Conciliation and Arbitration Service in the exercise of its discretion when carrying out investigations over trade union recognition issues.[62] The essence of Lord Denning's work in this field appears to be based on a strong individualistic notion concerning the role of labour law in our society. In Grunwick Processing Laboratories v ACAS, for example, Lord Denning said of the trade union recognition provisions of the Employment Protection Act 1975, that they make:

> '... great powers available to trade unions. By means of [them] they can bring immense pressure on an employer who does not wish to recognise a trade union and on his workers who do not wish to join a trade union. The union can go to ACAS and get a recommendation for recognition and thence to the [CAC] and get an award. By the award there can be inserted, in every man's contract, terms and conditions to which neither he nor his employers have agreed. Such an interference of individual liberty could hardly be tolerated in a free society unless there were safeguards against abuse. So I would construe the safeguards in favour of the individual and not in favour of the trade union'.[63]

The lengths to which Lord Denning will go to protect the individual have been criticised in a number of quarters. His treatment of the right to work issue in Langston v AUEW[64] has led Fraser Davidson to claim that:

> 'The ... Langstons of this world may be an anathema to trade unions and trade unionists, but for many judges such determined individualism would strike a responsive chord. The man who thinks for himself and stands up against the 'big batallions' for what he believes, may be regarded as an infernal nuisance by union and employer alike, but Lord Denning would probably argue that such a person was only exercising the rights of every free born Englishman ... Any crank may find a kindred spirit in the learned Master of the Rolls'.[65]

Lord Denning's desire to 'let justice be done' has led other labour lawyers to criticise him for the unscholarly nature of his judgments. Roger Rideout, for example, has commented about Lord Denning's decision in ASLEF (No.2)[66] that it is 'unlikely to occupy a prominent place in legal theory, if only because its statements of principle are, at best, half digested and its arguments are characterised by lack of authoritative support'.[67] This opinion about the level of Lord Denning's judgments in labour law cases is supported by the view of Michael Zander that the decision of the Court of Appeal in Duport Steels Ltd. v Sirs[68] 'whatever its political merits [would appear] to be legally and intellectually indefensible'.[69]

One major problem which has flowed from Lord Denning's lack of respect for authority in his judicial work has been the potential confrontation with the legislature. Indeed, Lord Denning's decision on the scope of judicial review in Pearlman has led John Griffiths to suggest that this approach 'threatens to expose the courts to a direct confrontation with Parliament'.[70]

JUDICIAL CRITICISM

The House of Lords v Lord Denning

In 1957, Lord Denning became a Lord of Appeal in Ordinary. Five years later he returned to the Court of Appeal to take up office as Master of the Rolls. In The Discipline of Law, Lord Denning explains why he chose to step down from the Lords to the Court of Appeal in 1962: "'I was too often in a minority. In the Lords it is no good to dissent'. In the Court of Appeal it is some good".[71] In fact, Lord Denning's differences with the Law Lords are not limited to the five years from 1957 to 1962 when he was a member of that judicial Chamber, but stretch back to his appointment as a High Court judge in 1944 and forward to the present time. Indeed, it would be no exaggeration to say that Lord Denning and the House of Lords have been at odds for over thirty years and that sniping in this 'judicial war' has occurred in the law courts,[72] the debating chamber of the House of Lords[73] and the extra-judicial writings of Lord Denning and the Law Lords.[74] Their differences are fundamental and there is no sign that the hostilities are likely to cease. In this part of the essay, I wish to examine the three main areas of disagreement between Lord Denning and the House of Lords - the limits of judicial creativity, statutory interpretation and the handling of precedent and the rule of stare decisis.

Judges as lawmakers

Should judges be lawmakers? Few judges would now disagree with Lord Radcliffe's observation that 'there was never a more sterile controversy than that upon the question whether a judge makes law'.[75] However, if the majority of judges no longer adhere to the declaratory theory of law which so amused Laski,[76] it does not follow that judges view their powers to create laws to be unlimited. Lord Devlin, for example, is firmly of the opinion that judges should not be lawmakers, law reformers or even social reformers. In the preface to The Judge,[77] Lord Devlin argues that the task of the judge is to be a craftsman, they must work with the material which they have and by modification, extension and restriction of principles attempt to make them fit. However, designing new suits and new fashions in Lord Devlin's view are not for the judiciary but the legislature. Lord Denning, on the other hand, passionately believes that judges should create law. As the passage from Liverpool City Council v Irwin[78] cited at the beginning of this essay, demonstrates Lord Denning is unwilling to await the Law Commission and Parliament, but will remedy defects in the law himself. Indeed, the theme of The Discipline of Law is the need for judicial creativity and in The Siskina[79] Lord Denning even goes so far as to taunt those timorous souls who decline to arrogate legislative powers with the words of William Cowper.[80]

Lord Denning's enthusiasm for lawmaking and his apparent belief in his own infallibility,[81] however, are not shared by the Law Lords. And in 1961 Lord Denning's most bitter critic, Lord Simonds, took the opportunity of reminding Lord Denning that law reform was not part of the function of a judge:[82]

> 'For to me heterodoxy, or, as some might say, heresy, is not the more attractive because it is dignified by the name of reform. Nor will I easily be led by an undiscerning zeal for some abstract kind of justice to ignore our first duty, which is to administer justice according to the law, the law which is established for us by Act of Parliament or the binding authority of precedent. The law

is developed by the application of old principles to new circumstances. Therein lies its genius. Its reform by the abrogation of those principles is the task not of the courts of law but of Parliament'.

Arguments in favour of judicial restraint no doubt sound trite, but as they are based on constitutional and democratic principles of the first importance, it is worth rehearsing them here. Firstly, judicial lawmaking poses constitutional problems.[83] The largely unwritten British constitution is based on the idea of a separation of powers. Parliament makes the laws, the judiciary interprets them. The remedying of defects and the filling of gaps in the law are tasks more properly for Parliament than the courts. Judges must give effect to legislation irrespective of the fact that they themselves consider that the consequences of doing so would be inexpedient, unjust or immoral. Failure to adhere to the constitutional limits of the powers of the judiciary will bring the courts into conflict with Parliament, undermine public respect for the rule of law and bring judicial impartiality into question. Secondly, judicial lawmaking at bottom is anti-democratic.[84] Judges form a non-elected elite of powerful decision-makers. Although there is provision for the removal of judges, that power is very rarely used. Judges are largely unaccountable. Even if one does not accept the conclusion made by J.A.G. Griffith in The Politics of the Judiciary[85] that judicial partiality stems from a strikingly homogeneous collection of attitudes, beliefs and principles which the policy-making judges have acquired by their education, training and pursuit of their profession as barristers,[86] there can be little doubt that judges are unrepresentative. Public policy, despite Lord Denning's confident assertion of his belief in his equestrian abilities,[87] remains an unruly horse which the judiciary are unqualified and perhaps singularly unsuited to ride. Recently, the House of Lords have repeatedly had to ask Lord Denning to dismount. The bounds to the scope of judicial law reform are elegantly outlined by Lord Scarman in Lim Poh Choo v Camden and Islington Area Health Authority:[88]

'Lord Denning MR in the Court of Appeal declared that a radical reappraisal of the law is needed. I agree. But I part company with him on ways and means. Lord Denning believes it can be done by the judges, whereas I would suggest to your

Lordships that such reappraisal calls for social, financial, economic and administrative decisions which only the legislature can take ... For so radical a reform can be made neither by judges nor by modification of rules of court. It raises issues of social, economic and financial policy not amenable to judicial reform, which will most certainly prove to be controversial and can be resolved by the legislature only after full consideration of factors which cannot be brought into clear focus, or be weighed and assessed, in the course of the forensic process. The judge, however wise, creative, and imaginative he may be, is 'cabin'd, cribb'd, confin'd, bound in' not, as was Macbeth, to his 'saucy doubts and fears' but by the evidence and arguments of the litigants. It is this limitation, inherent in the forensic process, which sets bounds to the scope of judicial law reform'.

Lord Denning, however, was undeterred and in the case of Duport Steels Ltd. v Sirs, Lord Scarman found it necessary to point out to Lord Denning not only the bounds placed on judicial law reform by the nature of the forensic process, but of the possible consequences of unrestrained judicial lawmaking:[89]

'Legal systems differ in the width of the discretionary powers granted to judges: but in developed societies limits are invariably set, beyond which the judges may not go. Justice in such societies is not left to the unguided, even if experienced, sage sitting under the spreading oak tree.

Within these limits, which cannot be said in a free society possessing elective legislative institutions to be narrow or constrained judges, as the remarkable judicial career of Lord Denning MR himself shows, have a genuine creative role. Great judges are in their different ways judicial activists. But the Constitution's separation of powers, or more accurately functions, must be observed if judicial independence is not to be put at risk. For, if people and Parliament come to think that the judicial power is to be confined by nothing other than the judge's sense of what is right (or, as Selden put it, by the length of the Chancellor's foot), confidence in the judicial system will be replaced by fear of it becoming uncertain and arbitrary in its application'.

Statutory interpretation

'The history of English law and the interpretation of statutes', Lord Hailsham observed during the second reading of The Interpretation of Legislation Bill,[90] 'consisted of a battle between two rival schools of thought. One school looked at what the Act was intended to do while the other looked at what it said'. Lord Denning is a leading member of the former school of thought and has long been an opponent of the literal approach to statutory interpretation. This approach has been criticised as being excessively rigid and has on occasions led to the frustration of the object of the legislation.[91]

However, adherents to the literal approach point to the difficulties inherent in the purposive approach to statutory interpretation.[92] Firstly, when should judges apply the purposive approach in preference to the literal approach to interpretation? Should they take advantage only when the meaning of the statutory words are ambiguous or unclear? Should they take advantage of this approach when in the view of the judge the result of literal interpretation is unjust, inexpedient or immoral? It should be remembered in this context that judges may hold very different views on morality, justice and expediency.

Secondly, what aids should the judge rely on when attempting to discern the purpose of legislation?[93] Should the judges, for example, have regard to Hansard when seeking the purpose of a statutory enactment or the meaning of a word in a statute? In the case of _Davis_ v _Johnson_[94] the House of Lords held that Hansard should not be referred to by judges as an aid to the construction of statutes. Lord Denning, however, illustrated in the case of _R._ v _Local Commissioner for Administration for the North and East Area of England, ex parte Bradford Metropolitan City Council_[95] that he is prepared to flout the spirit and the letter of clear and binding precedent by referring to textbooks which contain extracts from Hansard.

Thirdly, the purposive approach requires judges to make policy decisions in the widest sense of that word. For example, in the case of section 13(1) of the Trades Union and Labour Relations Act 1974, as amended, the House of Lords recognised that the legislative purpose was to exclude trade disputes from judicial review,[96] whereas the approach of the Court of Appeal to the construction of this formula appears to be based on the assumption that Parliament could not have intended to give trade unionists wide discretion to exercise their own judgment as to the steps to be taken in contemplation of furtherance of a trade dispute. And lastly, legislation often represents a compromise between a number of interest groups struggling for statutory recognition of their interests.[97] The result is that the purpose of the legislation becomes blurred and sometimes an Act has a number of purposes. If this is the case, the task of identifying the purpose or ranking the number of purposes which the legislation is designed to promote, even with the aid of Hansard, may be a matter of some difficulty. Indeed, it may be the case that each purpose should receive equal ranking or that purposes are mutually contradictory.[98] The judge is then faced with the task of determining what the purpose of the legislation should be. A task, as Lord Scarman pointed out in Lim Poh Choo, for which the forensic process is unsuited.

Lord Denning, however, has no such qualms about the purposive approach to statutory interpretation and back in the case of Seaford Court Estates Ltd. v Asher, he suggested not only that judges should interpret legislation according to the mischief which the statute was passed to remedy, but when a defect appears in an Act, should look to the purpose of the legislation and remedy the defect:[99]

> 'Whenever a statute comes up for consideration it must be remembered that it is not within human powers to foresee the manifold sets of facts which may arise, and, even if it were, it is not possible to provide for them in terms free from all ambiguity ... A judge must not alter the material of which it is woven, but he can and should iron out the creases'.

Encouraged by the fact that the majority of the House of Lords in upholding the decision of the Court of Appeal in Seaford Court Estates had not expressly disapproved of his arguments[100] Lord Denning returned to the attack against the 'strict constructionalists'. And in Magor and St.

Mellons Rural District Council v Newport Corporation advocated that judges should go further than merely 'ironing out the creases' but should, where a lacuna appears in an Act, look to the purpose of the legislation and supply the omission:[101]

> '... I have no patience with an ultra-legalistic interpretation which would deprive (the appellants) of their rights altogether. I would repeat what I said in Seaford Court Estates Ltd. v Asher. We do not sit here to pull the language of Parliament and of Ministers to pieces and make nonsense of it. That is an easy thing to do, and it is a thing to which lawyers are too often prone. We sit here to find out the intention of Parliament and of Ministers and carry it out, and we do this better by filling in the gaps and making sense of the enactment than by opening it up to destructive analysis'.

This view did not find favour with Lord Simonds. When this case came before the House of Lords, Lord Simonds indicated his concurrence with the opinion of Lord Morton of Henryton on the merits of the case in very few words and devoted the remaining part of his speech to correcting the misconceptions which he believed Lord Denning's views on statutory interpretation might induce:[102]

> 'The duty of the courts is to interpret the words that the legislature has used; those words may be ambiguous, but, even if they are, the power and duty of the court to travel outside them on a voyage of discovery are strictly limited ... [Denning L.J. considers that] the court, having discovered the intention of Parliament and of Ministers too, must proceed to fill in the gaps. What the legislature has not written, the court must write. This proposition, which restates in a new form the view expressed by the Lord Justice in the earlier case of Seaford Court Estates Ltd. v Asher (to which the Lord Justice himself refers), cannot be supported. It appears to me to be a naked usurpation of the legislative function under the thin disguise of interpretation. And it is the less justifiable when it is guesswork with what material the legislature would, if it had discovered the gap,

had filled it in. If a gap is disclosed, the remedy lies in an amending Act'.

Lord Simonds' victory did not prove to be final. For Lord Denning returned to the attack against the literal approach to statutory interpretation some years later. Although from the case of London Transport Executive v Betts[103] it appeared that Lord Denning had accepted that judges cannot fill in gaps in legislation. In Eddis v Chichester Constable, Lord Denning shows that he is not easily shaken from his objective by reaffirming his belief, in spite of Lord Simonds' warning that this amounted to 'a naked usurpation of the legislative function', that judges should fill in the gaps:[104]

> 'I know that this means that we in this court are filling in a gap left by the legislature - a course which was frowned on some years ago. But I would rather the courts fill in a gap than wait for Parliament to do it. Goodness knows when they would get down to it. I would apply the principle which I stated in Seaford Court Estates Ltd. v Asher, a judge should ask himself this question: If the makers of the Act had themselves come across this ruck in the texture of it, how would they have straightened it out?'

Lord Denning has, in recent years, been able to derive support for his views on statutory interpretation from three main sources. Firstly, there is the judgment of Lord Diplock in the case of Kammins Ballrooms Co. Ltd. v Zenith Investments (Torquay) Ltd.[105] in which Lord Diplock outlines a new approach to statutory interpretation which he describes as the 'purposive approach'. The requirements of this approach according to Lord Diplock was that the judge must impute 'to Parliament an intention not to impose a prohibition inconsistent with the objects which the statute was designed to achieve, though the draftsman has omitted to incorporate in express words any reference to that intention'.[106] The essence of the purposive approach, according to Lord Diplock, is for the judge to answer a series of questions: What is the subject-matter of the Act (or part of the Act) being interpreted? What object in relation to that subject-matter Parliament intended to achieve by the Act? And lastly, what part in the achievement of that object the section under construction was intended to play? The particular section will then be interpreted according to the object which the court deems the legislation is intended to serve. This operates even if Parliament has failed to incorporate the intention which the judge believes that the section possesses.

Lord Diplock in the recent case of Carter v Bradbeer[107] has also observed that over the last thirty years, the House of Lords has increasingly moved away from the purely literal approach to statutory interpretation towards the purposive approach.

The second major source of support for Lord Denning's advocation of this approach has been the Renton Committee on the preparation of legislation.[108] In his evidence to that Committee, Lord Denning placed the blame for lengthy, obscure and largely unintelligible legislation squarely upon the shoulders of the 'strict constructionalists'.[109] The approval of that Committee for the purposive approach to statutory interpretation therefore was a major boost to his campaign against the literal approach.[110] Indeed, in the case of Nothman v Barnet London Borough Council he makes the claim that the literal approach has been superseded by the purposive approach:[111]

> 'The literal method is now completely out of date. It has been replaced by the approach which Lord Diplock described as the 'purposive approach' ... In all cases now in the interpretation of statutes we adopt such a construction as will 'promote the general legislative purpose' underlying the provision. It is no longer necessary for the judges to wring their hands and say: 'There is nothing we can do about it'. Whenever the strict interpretation of statute gives rise to an absurd or unjust situation, the judges can and should use their good sense to remedy it - by reading in, if necessary - so as to do what Parliament would have done, had they had the situation in mind'.

The third source of support Lord Denning claims for the purposive approach stems from the implications of the accession of the United Kingdom to the European Economic Community. For the purposive approach to statutory interpretation is more in line with the practice of courts in the European mainland where the tradition of drafting statutes has been to set down general principles only and to leave it to the courts to complete the details.

Palm Tree Justice and The Lord Chancellor's Foot

Membership of the Community, Lord Denning argued in the case of H.P. Bulmer Ltd. v J. Bollinger S.A., necessitates that the English courts should, when interpreting Community law, apply the same principles of statutory interpretation as are applied by the European Court and the courts of the other Member States:[112]

> 'The Treaty is quite unlike any of the enactments to which we have become accustomed ... It lays down general principles. It expresses its aims and purposes. All in sentences of moderate length and commendable style. But it lacks precision. It uses words and phrases without defining what they mean. An English lawyer would look for an interpretation clause, but he would look in vain. There is none. All the way through the Treaty there are gaps and lacunae. These have to be filled in by the judges, or by Regulations and Directives. It is the European way'.

The logic of Lord Denning's argument is false. There is, as Lord Denning points out, a considerable difference between UK statutes and the Treaty of Rome and while it may be necessary for judges, when interpreting Community law, to 'fill in the gaps' it does not follow that the same approach should be adopted towards the detailed enactments passed by the United Kingdom Parliament. However, there is some force in that argument that the literal approach is being gradually eroded and replaced by the purposive approach to statutory interpretation. Yet, the difficulties inherent in this approach (outlined at the beginning of this section) remain to be resolved. Whether these difficulties prove to be insuperable or not, the dangers of allowing judges wide discretion in this field are all too apparent. For as the decisions of the Court of Appeal on trade union immunity demonstrate, it is a very small step from allowing judges to seek the purpose of and to fill in gaps in legislation to judges inventing 'fancied ambiguities as an excuse for failing to give effect to (a statute's) plain meaning because they themselves consider that the consequences of doing so would be inexpedient, or even unjust or immoral'.[113] The House of Lords, if not the Master of the Rolls, appears to be aware of the depth of the Constitutional waters and the Law Lords now appear to be swimming briskly back towards the shore of literal interpretation.

From precedent to precedent

The doctrine of precedent is based on the idea of distributive justice. For it is axiomatic that if justice is not to vary with the length of the Lord Chancellor's foot that like cases should be treated alike. Otherwise the administration of justice would become uncertain and arbitrary and public respect for the rule of law and the legal system would be diminished. In English law, it is therefore essential that lower courts follow the decisions of the courts above them in the court hierarchy. Thus, the High Court is bound to apply the decisions of the Court of Appeal and the Court of Appeal is bound to apply the decisions of the House of Lords. This point was made very forcefully to Lord Denning by Lord Hailsham in Broome v Cassell and Co. Ltd:[114] [1972] 1 All E.R. 801

> 'The fact is, and I hope it will never be necessary to say so again, that, in the hierarchical system of courts which exists in this country, it is necessary for each lower tier, including the Court of Appeal, to accept loyally the decisions of the higher tiers'.

However, the advantages of consistency, predictability and certainty which are said to justify the strongly coercive nature of the English doctrine of precedent hold little attraction for the Master of the Rolls. For Lord Denning regards these advantages as overrated, if not unattainable and in any event, as clearly outweighed by the requirements of justice. In W. & J.B. Eastwood Ltd. v Herrod, Lord Denning argued that the endless task of distinguishing the indistinguishable and reconciling the irreconciliable merely makes confusion worse confounded and it is preferable where the court is satisfied that a prior precedent is wrong, to make a clean cut.[115] This view is, of course, perfectly consistent with Lord Denning's belief that the path to justice must be kept clear of obstructions which would impede it.[116] Indeed, in his Romanes Lecture in 1959, Lord Denning points to the fact that the doctrine of precedent is not of great antiquity and like any other practice of the courts can be changed or abandoned.[117] Given Lord Denning's teleological method of legal reasoning and his desire to mould and shape the principles of law laid down by the judges in the nineteenth century to the social necessities and social opinion of the twentieth century, it is inevitable that he should be opposed to the doctrine of precedent. And during his term of office as Master of the Rolls, Lord Denning has devised a stratagem to undermine that doctrine.

Before discussing the three-part stratagem of the Master of the Rolls to mitigate the effect of applying precedents which he regards to be erroneous or unjust, it is important to point out that within the formal limits of the rules of precedent there exists considerable discretion whereby a judge can distinguish precedent which he believes to be mistaken.[118] The process may appear to be one of Procrustean conceptualism but, as the judgment of Lord Reid in Conway v Rimmer[119] illustrates, seemingly authoritative precedents can be distinguished on a number of grounds. For example, the judge must first decide what the *ratio decidendi* of the previous case is and then consider whether the material facts in that case are sufficiently similar to the facts in the case under consideration for that *ratio* to be regarded to be in point. The judge can then distinguish these cases by arguing that either the fact situations in each case are not sufficiently similar for the *ratio* to be regarded as in point or that the proposition of law relied upon by one of the parties in the case was not part of the *ratio decidendi* of the previous case, but was made *obiter* and therefore is not binding on the court.

Other methods of distinguishing precedent are to argue that the rule laid down was wider than necessary for the decision, that the decision is obscure, that the decision is in conflict with other authorities or legal principles, that the reasoning of the judge was deficient in some respect, or that the judge primarily had one fact situation in mind when he made his judgment and his reasoning therefore cannot by analogy be applied to the fact situation in the present case. The list is not exhaustive. While Lord Denning is quite capable of distinguishing precedent within these formal limitations,[120] and is aware that this doctrine 'is the foundation of our system of case-law',[121] he believes that its application narrows the basis of freedom and stultifies the development of law. The strategem developed by the Master of the Rolls for avoiding precedent is designed to overcome these defects and to allow justice to prevail.

The first part of Lord Denning's stratagem is an extremely flexible, if not cavalier, handling of precedent. Authorities are cited for propositions which they do not support,[122] inconvenient precedents are glossed over or pronounced as outdated, inequitable or unjust,[123] legal principles are put forward for which there is no authoritative support,[124] speeches of Law Lords are misconstrued or quoted out of context,[125] and support for value decisions are sought from history, poetry and literature.[126]

The best known example of this part of Lord Denning's strategem undoubtedly is the creation of the doctrine of promissory estoppel in the High Trees case.[127] In that case, armed with a number of cases which he had unearthed during his labours as a pupil at No 4 Brick Court and as an editor of Smith's Leading Cases, Lord Denning sought to clear away the obstacle of Jorden v Money.[128] A case in which Lord Cranworth had declared that 'the doctrine (of estoppel) does not apply to a case where the representation is not a presentation of a fact but a statement of something which the party intends or does not intend to do'.[129] Faced with a clear and binding precedent, Lord Denning attempted to remedy the injustice which he believed could result from the requirement that consideration is necessary to the validity of every promise not under seal by arguing that the decision of the House of Lords could be distinguished on the basis that subsequent developments had made it outdated and inequitable.[130]

> 'With regard to estoppel, the representation made in relation to reducing the rent, was not a representation of an existing fact. It was a representation, in effect, as to the future, namely, that payment of the rent would not be enforced at the full rate but only at the reduced rate. Such a representation would not give rise to an estoppel, because, as was said in Jorden v Money, a representation as to the future must be embodied as a contract or be nothing'.

However, Lord Denning pointed out that Jorden had been distinguished over the past fifty years. Moreover, on close examination of the authorities which Lord Denning cites for distinguishing Jorden v Money and for 'extending' the doctrine of estoppel to representations as to future conduct, we discover that Lord Denning's argument lacks substance.

Palm Tree Justice and The Lord Chancellor's Foot

Neither the case of Hughes v Metropolitan Railway Co.,[131] from which Lord Denning extracted 'the broad rule of justice' upon which he based promissory estoppel, nor Birmingham and District Land Co. v London and North Western Railway Co.[132] support the proposition which Lord Denning puts forward. Both Hughes and Birmingham District Land Co. in spite of what Lord Denning states in The Discipline of Law,[133] concern relief against forfeiture and nothing else. The recommendations of Law Revision Committee on Consideration, referred to by the Master of the Rolls, although interesting in their own right, hardly afford authority for distinguishing a decision of the House of Lords. And the case of Salisbury (Marquess) v Gilmore[134] was one in which Lord Denning, then as a King's Counsel, unsuccessfully argued before the Court of Appeal for the adoption of the Law Revision Committee's recommendations. As Lord Denning himself notes in The Discipline of Law,[135] 'An appeal might have ruined everything' had these limitations been fully exposed.

The second part of Lord Denning's strat gem involves the invocation of the latin maxims per incuriam and cessante ratione legis cessat ipsa lex. By the incantation of these words, Lord Denning has sought to deny the House of Lords the last word on points of law which he does not agree with. A dramatic example of the application of the per incuriam rule by Lord Denning occurred in 1971. In Broome v Cassell and Co.[136] Lord Denning refused to follow the decision of the House of Lords in Rookes v Barnard[137] concerning the restriction of the award of exemplary damages. The decision of the House of Lords in Rookes v Barnard, Lord Denning argued, was 'hopelessly illogical and inconsistent' and he concluded that ' if every there was a decision of the House of Lords given per incuriam, this was it'. The reaction of the House of Lords to the advice given by the Court of Appeal to inferior courts that the decision of the House of Lords in Rookes v Barnard should be ignored was one of anger. Lord Hailsham, for example, had some harsh words to say about the Court of Appeal's application of the per incuriam rule:[138]

> '[I]t is necessary to say something of the direction to judges of first instance to ignore Rookes v Barnard as 'unworkable'. As will be seen when I come to examine Rookes v Barnard in the latter part of this opinion, I am driven to the conclusion that when the Court of Appeal described the decision of Rookes v Barnard as decided 'per

> incuriam' or 'unworkable' they really only meant that they did not agree with it. But, in my view, even if this were not so, it is not open to the Court of Appeal to give gratuitous advice to judges of first instance to ignore decisions of the House of Lords in this way and, if it were open to the Court of Appeal to do so, it would be highly undesirable'.

Not even this rebuke could deter the Master of the Rolls. And in Schorsh Meier GmbH v Hennin[139] Lord Denning refused to follow the rule laid down by the House of Lords in Re United Railways of the Havana and Regla Warehouses Ltd.[140] that an English court could only give judgment in sterling. On this occasion applying the maxim *cessante ratione legis cessat ipsa lex*, Lord Denning declared this rule to be obsolete as Article 106 of the Treaty of Rome entitled a creditor in a Member State, in this case Germany, to receive payment for goods supplied to a person in another Member State in the currency of the creditor's Member State if that was the currency of the contract under which the goods had been supplied. In granting judgment in Deutschmarks, Lord Denning argued that the rule in the Havana case could be disregarded because the reasons, mainly the stability of sterling, for the rule no longer existed. Again, this is an example of Lord Denning attempting to do justice *in spite* of the law. For if the Court of Appeal had upheld the rule in the Havana case in Schorsch Meier the German creditor would have lost one third of the debt because of a particularly unfavourable exchange rate.

A short time later the Court of Appeal was faced with a similar situation to that faced in Schorsch Meier. The only differences between that case and Miliangos v George Frank (Textiles) Ltd.[141] was that in the latter case the creditor was a Swiss firm, and therefore the transaction did not come within the ambit of Article 106, and that judgment was sought in Swiss Francs. The Court of Appeal followed its decision in Schorsch Meier, however, on appeal to the House of Lords the Law Lords, while upholding the decision of the Court of Appeal, and therefore over-ruling their own decision in the Havana case, emphatically rejected the view that the Court of Appeal could review decisions of the House of Lords:[142]

> 'It is not for any inferior court - be it a county court or a division of the Court of Appeal presided over by Lord Denning MR - to review decisions of this House'.

The final part of the stratagem has been described by Lord Diplock as 'a one-man crusade to free the Court of Appeal from the shackles of stare decisis'.[143] Basically, what Lord Denning is attempting to achieve in this part of his stratagem is an extension of the privilege enjoyed by the House of Lords under the 1966 Practice Statement to enable the Court of Appeal to depart from its previous decisions when it appears right to do so. In 1966, the House of Lords had attempted to mitigate the harshness of their decision in London Street Tramways Co. v London County Council[144] that the House of Lords is absolutely bound by its own decisions by way of a Practice Statement.[145] Lord Gardiner's Practice Statement provided that while the Law Lords regard the use of precedent to be an indispensible foundation upon which to decide what the law is and its application in individual cases and that precedent provides certainty, predictability and consistency, they also recognise that too rigid adherence to precedent may lead to injustice and restrict the development of law. The Law Lords, the Statement continues, 'propose therefore to modify their present practice and, while treating former decisions of this House as normally binding, to depart from a previous decision when it appears right to do so'. Prior to his return to the Court of Appeal, Lord Denning had vigorously argued that the House of Lords is a great deal more than a court of law or a court of appeal, but acting for the Queen as the fountain of justice in this country should not only correct the errors of inferior courts, but while laying down and adhering to the fundamental principles of law, to govern the people, should also overrule its own precedents if they are found to be at variance with the requirements of justice.[146] In The Discipline of Law, Lord Denning writes that he understood the limitation of the Practice Statement to the House of Lords meant 'We are only considering the doctrine of precedent in the Lords. We are not considering its use elsewhere'.[147] This understanding of the Practice Statement, if not his persistence in attempting to uphold it in the face of clear repudiations of that interpretation of the meaning of the Practice Statement by the House of Lords, is consistent with Lord Denning's attempts to erode the authority of Young v Bristol Aeroplane Co. Ltd.[148]

While the rule that the House of Lords is absolutely bound by its own decisions was established in London Street Tramways in 1898 it was not until 1944 that the question whether the Court of Appeal is absolutely bound by its prior decisions was finally decided.

In Young v Bristol Aeroplane Co. Ltd. the full Court of Appeal decided that in the interests of certainty and uniformity the Court of Appeal would be absolutely bound by its prior decisions. However, Lord Greene MR outlined three exceptions to this general rule:

(1) The Court is entitled and bound to decide which of two conflicting decisions of its own it will follow.
(2) The Court is bound to refuse to follow a decision of its own which, though not expressly overruled, cannot, in its opinion, stand with a decision of the House of Lords.
(3) The Court of Appeal is not bound to follow a decision of its own if it is satisfied that the decision was given per incuriam.

Notwithstanding these three exceptions to stare decisis, Lord Denning has expressed intense dissatisfaction with the rule in Young v Bristol Aeroplane Co. Ltd.

In Conway v Rimmer,[149] Boys v Chaplin,[150] W. & J.B. Eastwood v Herrod,[151] Gallie v Lee,[152] Hanning v Maitland (No 2),[153] Barrington v Lee,[154] Farrell v Alexander,[155] and Davis v Johnson,[156] he has unsuccessfully argued that the effect of the 1966 Practice Statement has been to free the Court of Appeal from the fetters of this rule. Although, Lord Denning's argument that the rule is a self-imposed limitation and as a practice of the court can be departed from appears to be supportable,[157] neither his method of reform nor his view that the rule is merely a practice of the court has found favour with the Law Lords. In Davis v Johnson, for example, Lord Denning put forward the general principle that, 'while this court (the Court of Appeal) should regard itself as normally bound by a previous decision of the court, nevertheless, it should be at liberty to depart from it if it is convinced that the previous decision was wrong'.[158] On appeal to the House of Lords, however, Lord Salmon pointed out that as this rule of practice was laid down by the full Court of Appeal in Young's case, it could only be altered by a pronouncement of the whole court.[159] Lord Diplock, on behalf of the House of Lords, reaffirmed, 'expressly, unequivocably and unanimously that the rule laid down in the Bristol Aeroplane case ... as to stare decisis, is still binding on the Court of Appeal'.[160]

CONCLUSION

Lord Denning is the most powerful judge in the English legal system. As President of the central appeal court in that system, he exercises wide and largely unaccountable powers of decision-making. However, unlike other major decision-makers in British society, the actions and perspective of the Master of the Rolls have never been systematically examined. He is a judge of great character and great personality who enjoys high public esteem. This, in part, may explain the paucity of critical studies of his contribution to the development of law. For, as Ian Willock has argued,[161] there exists a taboo against public reference to the British judiciary in any terms other than those of unqualified admiration.

The contributors to this collection of essays in arguing for an overall reappraisal of Lord Denning's contribution to the development of law have therefore eschewed a polemical approach in favour of an approach which we hope satisfies the criteria of fairness outlined by Lord Denning in R. v Commissioner of Police of the Metropolis.[162]

In this essay, I have attempted to highlight the issues which the other contributors will explore in greater detail. Firstly, I have tried to demonstrate that we do not stand alone against Lord Denning's method. Other legal academics with widely differing interests and political view-points, share our fears and doubts about the correctness of Lord Denning's method of judicial decision-making and his views on law reform. The House of Lords too are unhappy with Lord Denning on a number of counts. His fervour for lawmaking, his cavalier treatment of precedent and his apparent infidelity to that House have all provoked stern reactions from the Law Lords.

Secondly, I have attempted to point to the limitations and dangers of this practice. The idea of a judge who dispenses justice in preference to law and regards himself as free to 'iron out the creases' in legislation sounds fine as a piece of rhetoric, but in practice it represents a challenge to the supremacy of Parliament. The requirements of justice are notoriously subjective and any individual's opinion on justice, if not the law, can claim to be as valid as that of the Master of the Rolls.[163] Indeed, as David Pannick observes in the New Law Journal,[163] if Lord Denning is deciding cases by reference to criteria other than legal criteria, it is far from clear why judges should not be elected to apply their sense of justice. For, if judicial decision-making was merely a matter of applying justice, legal learning would be irrelevant and political appointees would be better qualified for the task than the judiciary. At least, unlike Lord Denning, they would have a mandate from the public to apply their conception of the requirements of justice.

Lastly, at the root of my fears about Lord Denning's method is a fundamental disagreement with the premises upon which this practice is based. Whether or not the great trade unions are too powerful,[164] and whether or not England has been invaded by new friends who seek a refuge in our welfare system,[165] are matters of political opinion and as such should not be the basis of judicial decision-making. Without denying the political function of the judiciary or the interdependence of judges and the state, my view and that of the other contributors to this collection of essays, is well summed up by the words of John Griffith:[166]

> '(T)he law is not and cannot be a substitute for politics'.

PAUL WATCHMAN

NOTES

(1) Although formally number three in the judicial ranking after the Lord Chancellor and the Lord Chief Justice, the Master of the Rolls as President of the central appeal court in the legal system exercises substantial powers. Admittedly, the Lord Chancellor is in a position to exercise wide powers of judicial patronage, but the tendency to make 'political' appointments to the bench has markedly declined. [See R.V. Heuston, Lives of

the Lord Chancellors, 1885-1940 (1964, Oxford U.P., London)]. In other ways the Lord Chancellor is at a substantial disadvantage to the Master of the Rolls. Most importantly, the Lord Chancellor is a political appointment and he must retire from office with the defeat of his government. On the other hand, the Master of the Rolls holds office at Her Majesty's pleasure and can only be removed in a limited number of circumstances. Lord Denning was appointed before the age for retirement for judges was fixed at 75 and shows no signs that he is thinking of bringing his reign as Master of the Rolls to an end.

(2) A privilege which Lord Denning has not been slow to exploit. Consider, for example, Lord Denning's account of the 'chance' occurrence that led to him hearing the Gouriet appeal: "On Friday evening, 14 January 1977, I was just about to leave the Courts to walk over Waterloo Bridge. It was 5.30. My train was at 6.10. I looked into the clerk's room to say I was going. My clerk told me 'There is an urgent application to be made tomorrow morning. But there is no need for you to come up for it. There are two Lord Justices in London who can take it'. I asked what it was about. He told me in a sentence: 'The judge in chambers has just refused an injunction against the Post Office Union. The losers want an appeal'. I said: 'I think I ought to come up and sit on it myself'". The Discipline of Law, Butterworths, London, 1979, p.137.

(3) Person to Person, BBC 1, 12 July 1979. See also Lord Scarman's speech in Tiverton Estates Ltd. v Wearwell Ltd. [1975] Ch. 146, 172-3 on the pivotal position of the Court of Appeal in the English legal system. Young, H., 'England's Most Revolutionary Judge', The Sunday Times, 17 June 1973, p.33.

(4) R. Stevens, Law and Politics: The House of Lords as a Judicial Body 1800-1976, Weidenfeld & Nicolson, London, 1979, p.489.

(5) Person to Person, supra.

(6) See 'From Precedent to Precedent', pp.26-33.

(7) See 'Judges as Lawmakers', pp.17-20.

(8) Liverpool City Council v Irwin [1976] 1 QB 319, p.332.

(9) A.T. Denning, 'The Way of an Iconoclast', 5 Journal of the Society of Public Teachers of Law, 1959, p.77.

(10) J. Mortimer, 'A St George of the Law courts, sub nom Denning v House of Lord, ex parte Butterworths', The Sunday Times, 2 March 1980, p.43.

(11) Central London Property Trust Ltd. v High Trees House Ltd. [1947] KB 130; Plasticmoda Societa per Azioni v Davidsons (Manchester) Ltd. (1952) 1 Lloyd's Reports, 527; David C Builders Ltd. v Rees [1966] 2 QB 617; Panchaud Freres SA v Et General Grain Co. (1970) 1 Lloyd's Reports, 53; W.J. Alan & Co. v El Naser Exports [1972] 2 QB 189; Evenden v Guildford Football Club [1975] 1 QB 917; Crabb v Arun D.C. [1976] 1 Ch. 179; Smith and Snipes Hall Farm Ltd. v River Douglas Catchment Board [1949] 2 KB 500.

(12) Drive Yourself Hire Co. (London) Ltd. v Strutt [1954] 1 QB 250; Midland Silicones Ltd. v Scruttons Ltd. [1962] AC 446; Beswick v Beswick [1966] Ch. 538.

(13) British Movietonews Ltd. v London & District Cinemas [1951] 1 KB 190; [1952] AC 166.

(14) Karsales (Harrow) Ltd. v Wallis [1956] 1 WLR 936; Bridge v Campbell Discount Co. [1962] AC 600; UGS Finance Ltd. v National Mortgage Bank of Greece [1964] 1 Lloyd's Reports, 446; Harbutt's 'Plasticine' Ltd. v Wayne Tank & Pump Co. Ltd. [1970] 1 QB 447; Farnworth Finance Facilities v Attryde [1970] 1 WLR 1053; Thornton v Shoe Lane Parking Ltd. [1971] 2 QB 163; Photo Production Ltd. v Securicor Transport Ltd. [1978] 3 All ER 146.

(15) Candler v Crane, Christmas & Co. [1951] 2 KB 164; Dorset Yacht Co. v Home Office [1969] 2 QB 412; Ministry of Housing v Sharp [1970] 2 QB 273; Dutton v Bognor Regis UDC [1972] 1 QB 373; Spartan Steel & Alloys Ltd. v Martin & Co. Ltd. [1973] 1 QB 27; Esso Petroleum Co. Ltd. v Marden [1976] 1 QB 801; Sparham-Souter v Town & Country Developments (Essex) [1976] QB 858.

(16) Merricks v Nott-Bower [1965] 1 QB 57; in Re Grosvenor Hotel, London (No 2) [1965] 1 WLR 261; Conway v Rimmer [1967] 1 WLR 1031.

(17) Robertson v Minister of Pensions [1949] 1 KB 227; Wells v Minister of Housing and Local Government [1967] 1 WLR 1000; Lever (Finance) Ltd. v Westminster (City) London Borough Council [1971] 1 QB 222.

(18) R. v Gaming Board of Great Britain, ex parte Benaim [1970] 2 QB 417; Re Pergamon Press Ltd. [1971] Ch. 338; Breen v AEU [1971] 2 QB 175; R. v Liverpool Corporation, ex parte Liverpool Taxi Fleet Operators' Association [1972] 2 QB 299; Clarke v Martlew [1973] QB 58; Causton v Mann Egerton (Johnstone) Ltd. [1974] 1 WLR 162; R. v Race Relations Board, ex parte Selvarajan [1975] 1 WLR 686; R. v Secretary of State

for the Home Department, ex parte Hosenball [1977] 1 WLR 766.

(19) Padfield v Minister of Agriculture, Fisheries and Food [1968] AC 997; Coleen Properties Ltd. v Minister of Housing and Local Government [1971] 1 WLR 433; Secretary of State for Employment v ASLEF (No 2) [1972] 2 QB 455; Congreve v Home Office [1976] QB 629; Secretary of State for Education and Science v Tameside Metropolitan Borough Council [1977] AC 1014; Laker Airways Ltd. v Department of Trade [1977] QB 643; Pearlman v Keepers and Governors of Harrow School [1978] 3 WLR 736.

(20) Conway v Rimmer, supra; Boys v Chaplin [1968] 1 All ER 283; W. & J.B. Eastwood v Herrod [1968] 2 QB 923; Gallie v Lee [1969] 2 Ch. 17; Hanning v Maitland (No 2) [1970] 1 QB 580; Barrington v Lee [1971] 3 All ER 1231; Farrell v Alexander [1976] 1 All ER 129; Davis v Johnson [1978] 1 All ER 841.

(21) Beloff, M., 'Reforming Judge', New Society, 7 February 1980, p.300.

(22) Rahimtoola v Nizam of Hyderabad [1958] AC 379 - State Immunity Act 1978; H v H (1947) 63 T.L.R. 645; Bendall v McWhirter [1952] 2 QB 466; National Provincial Bank v Hastings Car Mart Ltd. [1964] Ch. 665; Matrimonial Homes Act 1967; BBC v Hearn [1977] 1 WLR 1004; Associated Newspapers Group v Wade [1979] 1 WLR 697; Express Newspapers v McShane [1979] 1 WLR 390; Duport Steels Ltd. v Sirs [1980] 1 WLR 142 - the Employment Bill 1980 contains provisions in line with Lord Denning's views.

(23) Clive M. Schmitthoff, 'Lord Denning and the Contemporary Scene: A Homage to Lord Denning on the Occasion of his 80th Birthday on 23 January 1979', Journal of Business Law, p.97.

(24) The Times, 5 January 1977.

(25) R. Stevens, Law and Politics: The House of Lords as a Judicial Body 1800-1976, supra at p.499; also Lords Diplock and Scarman in Duport Steels Ltd. v Sirs, supra at p.157 and p.169 and Lord Simonds in Magor and St. Mellon's RDC v Newport Corporation [1952] AC 189, p.191.

(26) Clive M. Schmitthoff, 'Lord Denning and the Contemporary Scene', supra, p.98.

(27) See 'Merits before Law', 1980, 235 Estate's Gazette, 577: '(I)n the rushed atmosphere of the Court of Appeal 'merits' counts for a good deal and the law takes second place'.

(28) Suisse Atlantique Societe d'Armement Maritime SA v NV Rotterdamsche Kolen Centrale [1967] AC 361.
(29) [1970] 1 QB 447.
(30) J.A. Weir, 'NEC Tamen Consumebatur - Frustration and Limitation Clauses', Cambridge Law Journal, 1970, 189, p.191.
(31) Photo Production Ltd. v Securicor Transport Ltd. [1980] 1 All ER 556.
(32) Ibid, p.560.
(33) Ibid, p.561.
(34) The Case of James Sommersett (1772) 20 State Trials 1 (per Lord Mansfield, p.82) but note the comments of Anthony Lester and Geoffrey Bindman in Race and Law, Penguin, London, 1972, pp.30-4.
(35) A.T. Denning, Freedom Under the Law, Stevens, London, 1949.
(36) Ibid, p.4.
(37) Schmidt v Secretary of State for Home Affairs [1969] 2 Ch. 149.
(38) Ibid, p.169.
(39) R. v Immigration Officer, ex parte Thakrar [1974] QB 684, p.702.
(40) M. Akehurst, 'Uganda Asians and The Thakrar Case', 38 Modern Law Review, 1975, 72, pp.74-5.
(41) Lord Denning, The Due Process of Law, supra, p.158. But see R. v Governor of Brixton Prison, ex parte Enahoro [1963] 2 All ER 477 and R. v Governor of Brixton Prison, ex parte Soblen [1963] 2 QB 643 which dramatically illustrate the limitations of the writ of habeas corpus and the extreme reluctance of the courts to overcome those limitations in the case of political fugitives and the article 'Dr. Soblen and the Alien Law of the UK', by Cedric H.R. Thornberry, 12 International and Comparative Law Quarterly (1963) 414 (especially at pp.456-465) which is highly critical of Lord Denning's reasoning on Soblen's fourth argument that the deportation order was being used to give a cloak of legality to a starkly illegitimate act - the extradition of a political fugitive.
(42) R. v Governor of Pentonville Prison, ex parte Azam [1974] AC 18.
(43) Ibid, p.33.
(44) J.A. Wade, 'Sophistry and Small Boats', 37 The Modern Law Review, 1974 , 192.
(45) R. v Secretary of State for the Home Department, ex parte Choudhary [1978] 1 WLR 1177, p.1180.
(46) David Lloyd Jones, 'The Role of Habeas Corpus in

Immigration Cases', 95 Law Quarterly Review, 1979, 171, p.173.

(47) Lawton L.J. in McPhail v Persons Unknown [1973] 3 WLR 71, p.78.

(48) Re Jebb [1966] Ch. 666.

(49) Ibid, p.672.

(50) J.H.C. Morris, 'Palm Tree Justice in the Court of Appeal', 82 Law Quarterly Review, 1966, 196, p.202.

(51) Sydall v Castings Ltd. [1967] 1 QB 302.

(52) Ibid, p.311.

(53) Ibid, pp.313-4.

(54) R.E. Megarry, 'The Deserted Wife's Right to Occupy the Matrimonial Home', 68 Law Quarterly Review, 1952, 372.

(55) A.D. Hargreaves, 'Licensed Possessors', 69 Law Quarterly Review, 1953, 466; R.E. Megarry, 'The Rent Acts and the Invention of New Doctrines', 67 Law Quarterly Review, 1951, 505.

(56) I.N. Duncan Wallace, 'Set Back to Set-Off', 89 Law Quarterly Review, 1973, 36.

(57) R.A. Pearce, 'Keeping a Mortgagee Out of Possession', 38 Cambridge Law Journal, 1979, 257.

(58) Coleen Properties Ltd. v Minister of Housing and Local Government [1971] 1 WLR 433.

(59) H.W.R. Wade, 'Evidence and Ultra Vires', 87 Law Quarterly Review, 1971, 318.

(60) Lord Denning, 'The Freedom of the Individual Today', 45 Medico-Legal Journal 49, 1977, pp.52-3 and see infra, The Labours of Lord Denning.

(61) See Lord Denning, The Discipline of Law, Part IV, 1, 'Abuse of Group Powers; see his judgments in Bonsor v Musician's Union [1954] Ch. 479; Faramus v Film Artistes Association [1963] 2 QB 527; Edwards v SOGAT [1971] Ch. 354; Breen v AUEW [1971] 2 QB 175.

(62) Grunwick Processing Laboratories Ltd. v ACAS [1978] AC 655, p.658; United Kingdom Association of Professional Engineers v ACAS [1979] ICR 303; Engineers' and Managers' Association v ACAS [1979] ICR 637. R.C. Simpson has suggested that the individualist approach favoured by Lord Denning would reduce the role of ACAS '... in the recognition procedure ...to that of a glorified balloting agency'. R.C. Simpson, 'Judicial Control of ACAS', 8 ILJ, 1979, 69, p.83.

(63) [1978] AC 655, pp.661-2. Lord Denning's views seem to be predicated on the belief that individual employees when there is no recognised trade union, bargain with their employers as equals, in arranging their terms and conditions of employment. The

fundamental weakness of this belief is exposed by the judgment of Lord Diplock in the Grunwick case when he says that, '... individual bargaining of this kind as distinct from collective bargaining is seldom practical for individual employees in industrial undertakings of any considerable size' at p.691.

(64) [1974] ICR 180.

(65) F.P. Davidson, 'Employment Bill III', SCOLAG, No.42, 1980, 37.

(66) Secretary of State for Employment v ASLEF (No 2) [1972] ICR 19.

(67) R.W. Rideout, 'When is a Rule Not a Rule?', 1973, 36 MLR, 73.

(68) [1980] 1 WLR 142.

(69) Michael Zander, The Guardian, 28 January 1980, p.13.

(70) J. Griffiths, 'Judicial Review for Jurisdictional Error', 38 Cambridge Law Journal, 1979, 11, p.14.

(71) Lord Denning, The Discipline of Law, supra, p.287.

(72) For example, British Movietonews Ltd. v London and District Cinemas [1952] AC 166; Magor and St. Mellons Rural District Council v Newport Corporation [1952] AC 189; Scruttons Ltd. v Midland Silicones Ltd. [1962] AC 446; Broome v Cassell and Co. Ltd. [1972] AC 1027; Davis v Johnson [1978] 2 WLR 553; Lim Poh Choo v Camden and Islington Area Health Authority [1979] 2 All ER 910; Duport Steels Ltd. v Sirs [1980] 1 WLR 142; Photo Production Ltd. v Securicor Transport Ltd. [1980] 1 All ER 558; Nothman v Barnet Council [1978] 1 WLR 220; The Siskina [1977] 2 Lloyd's Reports 230; R. v Local Commissioner for Administration for the North and East Area of England, ex parte Bradford Metropolitan City Council [1979] 2 All ER 881.

(73) For example, see 248 Parl. Deb. H.L. (5th ser.), col. 1332, et seq (25 April 1963) cited by R. Stevens, Law and Politics: The House of Lords as a Judicial Body 1800-1976, supra, p.497.

(74) A.T. Denning, 'From Precedent to Precedent', London, 1959; Lord Denning, The Discipline of Law and The Due Process of Law, Devlin, P.'Judges as Law-makers', 39 Modern Law Review, 1976, 1.

(75) 110 Solicitor's Journal, 1966, 733.

(76) Laski to Holmes, 8 March 1922. 'My fight was the old one against regarding a judge as an automatic slot machine into whom you put a statute and from whom you get a construction in which there is no articulate major premise'.

(77) P. Devlin, The Judge, Oxford, 1979, p.vii.

(78) [1976] 1 QB 319, p.332.

(79) [1977] 2 Lloyd's Reports 230, p.231.

(80) 'Why should the judges wait for the Rules Committee? The judges have an inherent jurisdiction to lay down the practice and procedure of the courts; and we can invoke it now to restrain the removal of these insurance moneys. To the timorous souls I would say in the words of William Cowper: 'Ye fearful saints, fresh courage take; the clouds ye so much dread; are big with mercy, and shall break; in blessing on your head'. Instead of 'saints' read 'judges'. Instead of 'mercy' read 'justice'. And you will find a good way to law reform'.

(81) R. v Sheffield Crown Court, ex parte Brownlow, The Times, 4 March 1980.

(82) Midlands Silicones Ltd. v Scruttons Ltd. [1962] AC 446, pp.467-8.

(83) For example, see the speech of Lord Diplock and Lord Scarman in Duport Steels Ltd. v Sirs [1980] 1 WLR 142, which provide a summary of the separation of powers in the United Kingdom and a salutory warning of the dangers of judicial law-making.

(84) See, for example, J.A.G. Griffith, The Politics of the Judiciary, London , 1977, pp.15-31; R. Miliband, The State in Capitalist Society, London, 1973, pp.124-130.

(85) J.A.G. Griffith, The Politics of the Judiciary, Fontana, London, 1977.

(86) Ibid, at p.193.

(87) Enderby Town Football Club v Football Association [1971] Ch. 591, pp.606-7.

(88) [1979] 2 All ER 910, p.914.

(89) Duport Steels Ltd. v Sirs, supra, pp.168-9.

(90) House of Lords, Wednesday, 13 February 1980, reported in The Times, 15 February 1980.

(91) Whiteley v Chappell (1868) 4 QB 147; Fisher v Bell [1961] 1 QB 394; R. v Munks [1964] 1 QB 304; London and North Eastern Rail Co. v Berriman [1946] AC 278; Bourne v Norwich Crematorium Ltd. [1967] 2 All ER 576.

(92) See, for example, the article by Kenneth Miller, 'The Purposive Approach in Labour Law', 1979, Scots Law Times 213, which examines the limitations of this approach to statutory interpretation in relation to sex discrimination and equality of opportunity.

(93) Sir Rupert Cross, Statutory Interpretation, London, 1976, pp.156-164; The Interpretation of Statutes, Law Commission 21, Scottish Law Commission 11; The Preparation of Legislation, Cmnd 6953, 1975.

(94) Davis v Johnson [1978] 2 WLR 182.
(95) R. v Local Commissioner for Administration for the North and East Area of England, ex parte Bradford Metropolitan City Council [1979] 2 All ER 881.
(96) See, for example, the speech of Lord Scarman in NWL Ltd. v Woods [1979] 1 WLR 1294, p.1312.
(97) J. Hall, 'Theft, Law and Society', in W. Chambliss (ed.) Crime and the Legal Process, New York, 1969; W. Chambliss, 'A Sociological Analysis of the Law of Vagrancy', Social Problems, 12 (summer) 1964, 66; W.G. Carson, 'Symbolic and Instrumental Dimensions of Early Factory Legislation', in R. Hood (ed.) Crime, Criminology and Public Policy, London, 1974; N. Gunningham, Pollution, Social Interest and the Law, London, 1974; J.J. McManus, 'The Emergence and Non-Emergence of Legislation', British Journal of Law and Society, vol. 5, No 2 (winter) 1978, 185; P. Watchman, 'The Origin of the 1915 Rent Act', Law and State No. 5, 20; E.P. Thompson, Whigs and Hunters, Hamondsworth, 1975; P. McHugh, Prostitution and Victorian Social Reform, London, 1980.
(98) K. Miller, 'The Purposive Approach to Labour Law', supra, p.217.
(99) [1949] 2 QB 481, p.488.
(100) [1950] AC 508, Lord MacDermott (diss).
(101) [1950] 2 All ER 1226, p.1236.
(102) [1952] AC 189, p.191.
(103) London Transport v Betts [1959] AC 231.
(104) [1969] 2 Ch. 345, p.358.
(105) [1971] AC 850,81. See also the speech of Lord Diplock in R. v National Insurance Commissioners [1972] AC 914, p.1005.
(106) Ibid, p.881.
(107) [1975] 3 All ER. 158, p.161.
(108) 'The Preparation of Legislation', Cmnd 6953, 1975.
(109) Ibid, para. 19.1.
(110) Ibid, para. 19.2.
(111) [1978] 1 WLR 220, p.228.
(112) [1974] Ch. 401, p.425.
(113) Lord Diplock in Duport Steels Ltd. v Sirs, supra, p.157.
(114) [1972] AC 1027, p.1054.
(115) [1968] 2 QB 923, p.934.
(116) Lord Denning, The Discipline of Law, supra, p.314.
(117) A.T. Denning, From Precedent to Precedent, London, 1959.
(118) See, Sir Rupert Cross, Precedent in English Law, Oxford, 1977, Ch.3 and 4.
(119) Conway v Rimmer [1968] AC 910, p.950.

(120) See the speeches of Lord Denning in London Transport Executive v Betts [1959] AC 213, and Fawcett Properties Ltd. v Buckingham County Council [1961] AC 636.
(121) Lord Denning, The Discipline of Law, supra, p.314.
(122) See, for example, British Movietonews Ltd. v London and District Cinemas Ltd. [1951] 1 QB 190.
(123) See, for example, Errington v Errington [1952] 1 QB 290.
(124) For example, Promissory estoppel - Central London Property Trust Ltd. v High Trees House Ltd. [1947] KB 130; jus quaesitum tertio - Midlands Silicones Ltd. v Scruttons Ltd. [1962] AC 446; equitable right of relief - Bridge v Campbell Discount Co. [1962] AC 600; extension of the principle of estoppel to statements by Crown officers - Robertson v Minister of Pensions [1949] 1 KB 227.
(125) See, for example, Harbutt's 'Plasticine' Ltd. v Wayne Tank and Pump Co. Ltd. [1970] 1 QB 447.
(126) See, for example, Gouriet v Union of Post Office Workers [1977] 2 WLR 310 - Thomas Fuller: 'Be you ever so high , the law is above you'. Langston v Amalgamated Union of Engineering Workers [1974] 1 WLR 185 - Longfellow: 'Something attempted, something done, has earned a night's repose'. Hubbard v Pitt [1975] 3 WLR 201 - Peterloo.
(127) Central London Property Trust Ltd. v High Trees House Ltd. [1947] K.B. 130.
(128) (1854) 5 H.L. Cases 185.
(129) Ibid.
(130) Central London Property Trust Ltd. v High Trees House Ltd, supra, p.134.
(131) (1877) 2 App. Cas. 439.
(132) (1888) 40 Ch. D. 268.
(133) Lord Denning, The Discipline of Law, supra, p.201.
(134) [1942] 2 QB 38.
(135) Supra, p.205.
(136) [1971] 2 QB 354.
(137) [1964] AC 1129.
(138) Broome v Cassell & Co. [1972] AC 1027, p.1054.
(139) [1975] QB 416.
(140) [1961] AC 1007.
(141) [1975] 1 QB 487.
(142) [1976] AC 433, p.496.
(143) Davis v Johnson [1978] 2 WLR 553, p.559.
(144) [1898] AC 375.
(145) 26 July 1966, reported [1966] 1 WLR 1234.
(146) Lord Denning, From Precedent to Precedent, supra.
(147) Supra, p.297.
(148) [1944] KB 718.

(149) [1967] 1 WLR 1031.
(150) [1968] 2 QB 1.
(151) [1968] 2 QB 923.
(152) [1969] 2 Ch. 17.
(153) [1970] 1 QB 580.
(154) [1971] 3 All ER 1231.
(155) [1976] 2 All ER 721.
(156) [1978] 2 WLR 182.
(157) C.F.F. Richett, 'Precedent in the Court of Appeal', 43 Modern Law Review, 1980, 136.
(158) [1978] 2 WLR 182, p.193.
(159) [1978] 2 WLR 553, per Lord Salmon, p.577.
(160) Ibid, p.562.
(161) 'The Judiciary', Scots Law Times, 1972, 217.
(162) [1968] 2 QB 150, p.154: 'We (the judges) do not fear criticism, nor do we resent it. For there is something far more important at stake. It is no less than freedom of speech itself. It is the right of every man, in Parliament or out of it to make fair comment, on matters of public interest. Those who comment can deal faithfully with all that is done in a court of justice. They can say that we are mistaken, and our decisions erroneous, whether they are subject to appeal or not. All we would ask is that those who criticise us will remember that, from the nature of our office, we cannot reply to their criticisms. We cannot enter into public controversy. Still less into political controversy. We must rely on our conduct to be its own vindication'.
(163) 'Election of the Judiciary', 128 New Law Journal, 1979, 1064.
(164) Lord Denning, Person to Person, supra.
(165) Lord Denning, The Due Process of Law, supra, p.155.
(166) J.A.G. Griffith, 'The Political Constitution', 42 Modern Law Review, 1979, 14, p.16.

Problems of Judicial Study

RELATIVE AUTONOMY AND THE COURTS

The fact that the judiciary are able to pursue policy lines independently of legislative backing seems to suggest that their role in the State is relatively autonomous. That is to say, whilst on the one hand being strongly supportive of the central values and institutions of the political economy, this commitment sits alongside a degree of free space within which to operate against the dominant State interests. This formal and informal autonomy is encapsulated in the notion of judicial independence. Not only are the judiciary largely left on their own in their decision-making so that their relationship to the State is indirect, but judicial ideology explicitly rejects the notion of subservience to anything other than 'the law'. This has been buttressed both by legal commentators and politicians in the past and more recently. There seems to be little doubt that the judiciary 'believe' in their independence. The tension with the most visible formal institution of the State, the Executive, is a product of this particular orientation. Genuine conflict between judiciary and the aims of governments stem, then, from their autonomous position. The level of unpredictability, though, is restricted both by the socialisation of the judiciary pool and the areas of work ascribed to them. This is not to suggest that this relatively harmonious mode of government is constant or sacrosanct. In certain very obvious areas like industrial struggles, the ideology of independence is not widely adhered to within the Labour movement. Any informal institutional arrangement like this is in danger of straying beyond the discreet bounds which are unacknowledged, but capable of practical inference. The judiciary are vulnerable in a representative democracy where whilst they can generally be counted on by the dominant forces within the social formation, this is a possible area of sacrifice. They _do_ share similar backgrounds. The open textured nature of the rules which the judiciary work with, whether in statutory or common law form, mean that their support cannot be certain. Just as economic and political systems do not have clear goals in relation to each eventuality and development, so too, within the relatively marginal areas of disputed legal rights and obligations the most 'desirable' decision for the present or future may not be clear. There is a curious ambivalence in a secular world with no obvious value consensus towards a new breed of possible Prince-philosophers. This has meant that the notion of entrusting difficult matters 'beyond' politics to a Bill of Rights with judicial review has produced a renaissance recently of judicial eulogies with Lord Denning the new people's champion. It is important to see how this revival of judicial fortunes has occurred and why critical accounts have failed to confront this issue effectively.

CRITICAL PERCEPTIONS AND ALTERNATIVE REALITY

Hitherto most critical accounts of the role and function of the judiciary today have failed to confront the images and myths of the impartial independent judiciary. Both by their class position and more particularly by their class function, the policy-making judiciary of the middle and higher echelons have been seen as part of the ruling class.[1]

The judiciary have not been regarded as a fruitful field for assessing the operation of society. In fact, they provide a valuable microcosm of the operation of the subtleties and complexities of capitalism. Critical discussion of the legal system tends to proceed from the formulation of Marx and Engels that this was 'but the will of your class made into a law for all, a will whose essential character and direction are determined by the economical conditions of the existence of your (bourgeois) class'.[2] This approach requires much fuller specification particularly in relation to the judiciary otherwise judges become mere class ciphers.

Alternatively, other radical views of the judicial role have tended to concentrate on the social background of the judiciary and infer from this a class bias:

> 'No one can be a judge who hasn't been a barrister. And no one can be a barrister without some form of 'independent means' and an initiation into a curious, spooky world of 'dinners', inns of court and cranky

> 'uniforms. Eighty-six per cent of judges were educated at public school'.[3]

Not only is the elitist background proof of their class sympathy, but the way that they operate is evidence of their class function, 'The law that flows from these gentlemen is a law for the rich'.[4] All of which is plain to see for anyone observing the behaviour of the judiciary, 'The class priorities of these gentlemen are ... obvious from their statements in court and their sentences'.[5]

So the judges are self-evident warriors of the ruling class in the class war so far as it is fought out in struggles in the courts, whether it be in attacks on labour, attacks on dissemination of radical politics, the defence of the rights of property or the defence of the current State. There are a whole series of judicial policy decisions in the fields of labour relations, and property rights and radical politics which are cited to establish the partiality of the judiciary towards preservation of the capitalist State. Thus, Miliband can talk of:

> 'The general bias which the courts, in their concern to protect 'society' (i.e. unequal class societies) have consistently displayed in favour of privilege, property and capital. Thus the unending struggle against the courts' attempt to curb and erode the unions' ability to defend their members' interests; and there moreover, the judicial arm has not been simply content to second the curbing endeavours of government and legislatures; the courts have often taken the initiative and sought, through the exercise of judicial creativeness in the interpretation of statutes, to reduce or annul trade union and working class rights which even quite conservative governments and legislatures had, under pressure, come to endorse and promulgate ... More generally the courts have always conceived it as one of their many duties to 'society' to protect the rights of property against such attempts as the State has been compelled to make to reduce their scope'.[6]

MEN OF THE PEOPLE

This is not the image of the judiciary which is generally portrayed, however. Rather, we have the judge as the guardian of the rights of the individual. The 'little man' is now protected from the great bureaucracies of our day - the local Planning and Licensing Authorities; the Department of Trade; the Department of Education; the Department of Health and Social Security. In a number of symbolic peripheral areas of the law indeed the 'little man's' right is vindicated through the courts. The areas are very special. The total impact on the major social economic and political arrangements is very limited but the symbolic effect of these governmental reverses is tremendous.

The purported consensus on the apolitical function of the judges is buttressed by a series of decisions in favour of the little man. A conspiracy is hardly tenable since the judiciary are unable to instigate political decisions in the first place giving rise to legal actions.[7] Rather, we have a series of minor matters 'marketed' in such a way that the emergent image is of the judiciary as the protector of liberty and guarantor of human integrity in Britain today. Hence, the judiciary have built up their credibility as both independent, impartial adjudicators as well as socially responsive reformers keeping the law 'up to date' with changing social modes.

The judicious selectivity for these outbursts of individual concern can be gauged from brief examination of some of the major areas where the much maligned Executive is given free reign where the interests of the individuals involved in certain kinds of disputes do not fit into the judicial notion of what constitutes desirable rights. Over this same period of time, where the courts are expressing a confidence in such notions as popular democratic control and restraints on apparently unaccountable power groupings, it is possible to draw very different conclusions from a series of much less publicised decisions in less glamorous fields. Lord Denning's work is itself a valuable illustration of precisely this contrast.

It is not so much that the decisions in themselves were in any particular way supportive of capitalist interest or ruling class strategy, but rather that the juxtaposition of the individual and his protector, the judiciary, present a highly distorted picture of the majority of judicial conduct in the crucial areas of social decision-making - in the workplace; where property is at stake; where the political order is under attack or where any institutions of the State are threatened.

With decisions like Congreve[8] and Tameside[9] it is easy to see how one could possibly portray the judiciary as the protectors of the individual in fact of central bureaucracy. In an area where parental wishes may differ from 'official' policy there was clearly scope for conflict resoluble by the judiciary.

This broadly, then, is the picture of the judge which is juxtaposed against the standard critical view of the judge. Here is the individualist using his skills and power to hinder the progress of the powerful when they fail to go by the rules, all the while keeping the criteria of judgment in touch with contemporary community standards of public and private conduct.

CONTROL OF THE JUDICIAL ROLE

The role of the judiciary has not been an unvaried constant one. Elements of democratic control have been injected into the State with universal adult suffrage, the removal of much of the effective blocking power of the hereditary House of Lords, the introduction of Life Peerages and the expansion of the jobs undertaken by public authorities to cover health care, housing, income support programmes, direction of industry and commerce. Paradoxically, this has not led to a more accountable controlled judiciary. The reverse in fact, with proposals afoot for the extension of judicial supervision of such democratic institutions as exist within the British State.

The significance of the judiciary is by no means constant. We can see in the past two decades in Britain a fall in the stock of the judiciary followed by a partial recovery and then further setback and finally a renaissance in the later seventies. What I have in mind is the reaction of the political parties to the judiciary over this period as reflected in the work farmed out to them in legislation and the direct attacks mounted on judicial work. As Gavin Drewry points out, the existence of bitter pointed attacks on the judiciary was more prevalent in the nineteenth century than has been the case for most of the twentieth century.[10] The process, though, is not one of straightforward progress towards the rehabilitation of the judiciary in the eyes of the political and social critics. Even the more severe critics of the judiciary have always been careful to stress that it is specific individuals and specific issues with which they are dissatisfied rather than the structural relationship between politicians and the judiciary. This cosy, though occasionally uneasy, relationship between politicians in the mainstream Parliamentary parties has meant that within none of these parties has the judiciary or their composition ever been an issue in itself. The labour distrust of the judiciary in certain fields based on the experiences of the judiciary in the nineteenth century in trade unions conflicts and struggles and such legislation as the Workmen's Compensation Acts had its reflection in the adoption in a number of instances of the 'tribunal' solution and the 'Ministerial discretion' solution. The planning innovations of the Labour Government in the 1947 Acts, relied on giving the Minister the final ultimate discretion in what were perceived to be essentially political decisions rather than legal ones. The very notion of this split though is one which has pervaded the most consistent critics of the judiciary, the representatives of organised labour. Rather than accept a view that 'Law is Politics', there has been a line of radical argument over the years to the effect that there are two kinds of legislation and law. One consists of straight technical law and the other involves political law. A number of contentious political disputes have thrown up the argument that some legislation is motivated by sectional interest and in a different category from that which is normally produced by Parliament. The most bitter examples of this in the recent past centred around the legislation of the Conservative administration in the early seventies. We find arguments used in the media as well as in the law courts that the refusal of Labour Councillors to implement the rent rises required under the Housing Finance Act 1972 were somehow in a different category from other sorts of rule disobedience and should not attract standard criminal penalties.[11]

The judiciary are not perceived as playing a constant role by those with whom they interact. By association with certain policies as well as by their actual specific decisions, the judiciary's 'image' can be tarnished or enhanced in the eyes of those examining their own relationship to the legal process.[12] This identification of issues as being inappropriate for the judiciary and the courts has characterised the housing legislation in all fields since the Great War. The motives of the various interested parties have been somewhat different. The early rejection of Fair Rent Courts both before and during the Great War had its explanation in the desire to deny a platform for propaganda to those wishing to stress the inequalities and housing deficiencies. By the time we had reached the second half of the century the sorts of reasons for rejecting a specific judicial input into the fair rent process as well as a technical formulation of the 'fair rent' method, lay in a faith in professional expertise.

Thus very different considerations have been brought to bear on the form of legislative activity in relation to matters being directed towards the courts or elsewhere.

DEPENDING ON INDEPENDENCE

The role though that judges are asked to play within the State is more than neutral refereeing. They are asked to make political choices in the courts; they are invited to sit on and frequently chair Committees and Commissions; they are within sight of a new and more dynamic role within our constitutional framework. As Lord Denning put it so eloquently on the Profumo Enquiry:

> 'There are occasions when the only suitable person in whom the public will have confidence is a judge ... The only person who could be regarded as impartial and independent would be a judge'.[13]

These features of their work and self-presentation allow a mask of neutrality to be successfully assumed so that they not only effectively play a legitimating role in their court work, but are also called on specifically to provide overt impartiality in other areas of politico-social conflicts. But there is, of course, an obvious circularity in this kind of account of the judicial function and impact. It is no good the State simply taking the puppets who claim to operate the legal system fairly and impartially and attempt by sleight of hand to strengthen their legitimating factor by giving them clear political roles to play. This in itself would not go to explain why it is that the notions of independence and impartiality are ever born in the first place.

The notions of independence and impartiality could be described as key judicial characteristics. These are qualities which no one else could really hope or expect to aspire to. Others have loyalties to religious affiliations, commerce or labour, or even to politics and the political order. Again as Lord Denning expressed it, 'Take the Profumo case which had political ramifications in it. You couldn't appoint a Civil Servant or an industrialist'.[14]

Thus the impartiality comes from the special knack judges are claimed to have of avoiding any kind of affiliation to party or interest groups. Even assuming some interest were dear to the heart of a judge, the impartiality school suggest that he is able to put these to the back of his mind for the purposes of the judicial work, despite the doubts expressed by Lord Justice Scrutton as to the ease with which class affiliation can be discarded.

The point really though is not that judges are partial. They do not find against organised labour out of dislike or antipathy towards <u>workers</u> or <u>trade unionists</u>, but out of antipathy towards their goals and methods. The question of impartiality is quite irrelevant to any claim that judges are political animals making political decisions favouring a particular socio-economic philosophy and practice. In the words of a distinguished former judge, Lord Devlin, 'Judges are inevitably part of the establishment and the establishment's ideas are those which are operating in our minds'.[15]

A number of factors though obscure this reality. There are the strenuous denials of most of the judiciary to any concern with politics in their work, like Sir John Donaldson of the ill-fated National Industrial Relations Court:

Problems of Judicial Study

> 'My attitude towards political life is much the same as that of a monk towards sex, nostalgic memories of youthful indiscretion, a frank acknowledgement of its attractions and an unshakeable conviction that I could do better than those currently engaged in it'.[16]

There is the notion of independence. Judges, so political and legal commentators tell us, are independent. Ralph Miliband poses the pertinent question: 'Independent of what?'[17] This generally means independent of the whims of the government of the day which appoints them. There is a generally established 'convention' that judges may not be sacked simply for failing to deliver the goods in terms of satisfactory decisions to the liking of the government. This is the crucial area where the judiciary manage to achieve their transmogrification from political to apolitical. Even though appointed and paid for by the government of the day, like the Civil Service, the judiciary transcend politics.

The evidence for this independent, apolitical, technocratic judiciary is the way in which they confront power and its manifestations in the modern State. Again, to draw on the thoughts of Lord Denning:

> 'In our modern times Ministers have greater powers than they ever did in the old days. The question is 'What have the courts done in order to protect the citizen from the abuse of that power?' ... We've developed a machinery whereby the courts can see as far as we can that the individual is treated fairly by governments, by government departments, by education authorities and the like. That is one of the big developments of our time'.[18]

It is in this role that the judges have been particularly active over the past thirty years or so. They have moved away from the lethargy with which they initially met the expanding functions and scope of Ministers and Departments. For long, the British judiciary was criticised for its failure to adjust to the changing configurations of power within the political,business and economic sphere.

All that has now changed. The citizen now finds the judiciary interposed between himself and the State (i.e.

the Executive Government whether at local or national level). The judges now consider themselves to have evolved ways whereby they can continue their role as protector of the individual from traditional arbitrary State power.

Thus we can see, perhaps, how it is possible for this particular group to be put forward as independent and impartial administrators of the law. How it is that when an issue arises of a particularly delicate political nature that these men can form the major contributors to such enquiries. The number of judicially chaired enquiries is legion in this field. The Parker Committee on interrogation of terrorists (1971/72), the Diplock Committee on dealing with terrorists (1972), the Red Lion Square Affair (1974/75) under Lord Scarman, are typical examples of such sensitive areas being entrusted to the senior judiciary.

It is significant that of all the post-War enquiries which have been set up to examine a wide range of matters from the problems of one-parent families to miners' pay whenever there was the least hint of controversiality then these Committees were chaired by a judge. One eminent judge explained why:

> 'Something arises and an enquiry is demanded and the politicians think they ought to quieten public disquiet the method is to get a judge'.[19]

As his colleague on the Bench, Lord Denning, explained, there were:

> '... occasions when the only suitable person in whom the public will have confidence is a judge'.[20]

Certainly from the evidence of all enquiries in the post-War era it seems evident that Governments of whatever political hue have had confidence in the legitimating function of a judge in any sensitive enquiry. Of some 350 major post-War Commissions and Committees appointed by Government, 118 were chaired by a judge - by far the most prominent occupation of Chairman. Judges are above politics it seems.

Talking of the value of having a judge presiding over an enquiry like Red Lion Square in dispelling rumours and myths and generally demystifying events, Lord Scarman suggested:

> 'It is perhaps only a judge that can do this because he is trusted to be independent, to be impartial and to be thorough in his investigation'.[21]

Now when one juxtaposes these two areas of extra-judicial work - service on politically significant enquiries and the proposed judicial scrutiny of a Bill of Rights, there is an obvious contradiction between highly political crucial decision-making of the judiciary and this independent impartial aspect of judicial life.

Traditionally, in Britain this has been answered by the 'hats' or 'split personality' theory of politico/legal figures. So it was in relation to the Angry Brigade trial that Sir Peter Rawlinson replied to charges that the pursuit of the Stoke Newington Eight was on direct Cabinet orders which he received as a member of Heath's Cabinet. He was pursuing the Angry Brigade not as an act of political repression but as simply a piece of normal law enforcement wearing his legal 'hat' as Attorney General rather than his political Cabinet 'hat'. There is some substance to the success of this as an obfuscatory ploy.

By some strange process Quintin Hogg was able to bedeck himself in ermine and a fresh title and emerge on to the legal stage as Lord Hailsham, Lord Chancellor. In his new depoliticised role he was able to 'pass legislation' in the House of Lords (judicial side) which was highly controversial in relation to controlling peaceful demonstrations and sit-ins with far less bother than the Tory Government (of which he was currently a Cabinet member)had with their Industrial Relations Act 1971. His particular innovation was the expansion of conspiracy through the application of venerated judicial techniques. There was so little complaint about this that one might infer that the 'hats' theory has some subscribers. Politicians who become judges cease to be political in their work.

Although minor ripples may be caused within legal circles and there may be some discreet correspondence in the 'trades' this kind of judicial politics is permissible because of the divorce between politics and law which is fostered by our Constitution of checks and balances. On this model, in theory, the Executive is restrained by the judiciary who are in turn subject to control by the Legislature. By these lights the judiciary cannot go too far in their judicial law-making or the Executive/ Legislature will simply invalidate their decisions. This is done every year in connection with the job which the judges make of interpreting the Finance Acts. More notably, perhaps, we have the infamous Burmah Oil case where despite threats of legislative overturning, the House of Lords (judicial branch) awarded damages to the oil company against the British Government. This in turn was followed by the War Damage Act 1965, the effect of which was to annul the House of Lords decision by making the award retrospectively void.[22]

Despite these tensions between the various arms of the State, this only serves to foster notions of the independence and impartiality of the judiciary. After all, if the judiciary show that they are not craven lackeys of the Government, then this is proof positive that they are in fact administering not just political judgments and decisions, but something altogether more special - the law.

UP TO DATE AND OFF THE TRACK

Crucial, though, to an expanded role and set of duties for the judiciary is the notion, not only of fair adjudication, but of adjudication in accordance with 'up to date' standards applied by the judge as the official 'everyman'. This is based onabstract notions of 'fair' and 'reasonable' postulated within a timeless generalised social reality where politics and economics have no apparent meaning to the judiciary. This is the rhetoric of freedom - freedom of property, freedom to exercise one's economic power. Here the key concept is the changing law in the changing society. An unspecified moral consensus is implied in the first place - the realm of public interest, and public morals. This, in some strange way, changes and alters from time to time. The judges, to ensure their current and future employment and possibly an expansion of same, must be locked into this process so that they perceive it when it is happening and can respond to it. Even better if the judges, without being outrageously modern, can help foster the birth of new changes. 'Society' may not yet fully accept the new role of the mistress but the judge does. Much of the criticism of the past era from radicals as well as liberals has been the way in which their social background and professional isolation prevents judges having access to common consciousness that makes up public morals or social attitudes and opinions.

The argument is relatively simple as we noted. Over eighty per cent of High Court judges, the policy-making judiciary, went to public schools and Oxbridge. Parental class position was largely upper middle class. This allied with their restricted social lives in Circuit, and their limited contact with the public, produces a rarefied being unsocialised in the ways of the majority of his fellows. As indicated, some judges have recognised some of the difficulties of cross-cultural adjudication. Others, today, strenuously deny it.

> Lord Denning: 'To say that judges are remote from ordinary life is a complete misconception'.
> Lord Scarman: 'Most of us use the tubes and walk the streets and talk to ordinary citizens and ordinary citizens probably take a fairly lordly view of us when they meet us in the grocer's shop. And that's absolutely right is it not?'
> Lord Denning: 'Some judges are imagined to be the sort of people who say 'Who is Mick Jagger?' as if only judges know nothing of ordinary life. But that's completely wrong nowadays. Well, Leslie, you and me, any of us I think, have been brought up amongst ordinary people, live amongst ordinary people and are just as much ordinary people as anybody else'.[23]

What is false here, though, is the nature of the debate. It only makes sense to talk of how 'out of touch' or 'in touch' the judiciary are if there exists a clear consensual reality with which they measure their own perceptions.

Problems of Judicial Study

Notions of judicial independence and impartiality only have an existence within a shared world of goals and values, within a shared belief in the economic and social order. Where such a consensus does not exist, the judiciary cannot bridge the gap. One of the fundamental errors one can make is to assume that the judiciary bridges this by the exercise of political self-restraint or conspicuous impartiality. Merely by widening the social backgrounds area of the judiciary only provides a less homogeneous social group attempting to operate on a non-existent base, namely the shared purpose society. It is to deal with the limitations of polemical radical approaches to the judiciary that these essays choose to deal in depth with the more arcane, less spectacular work of Lord Denning.

PETER ROBSON

NOTES

(1) Jack Cohen, 'Some Thoughts on the Working Class Today', October 1973. 'Marxism Today' - reprinted along with three other class articles under the overall title _Class Structure_.
(2) Karl Marx & Frederick Engels, _The Manifesto of the Communist Party_, Penguin, London, 1963, p.83.
(3) Paul Foot, 'Why you should be a socialist', _SWP Publications_, 1977, p.26.
(4) _Ibid_, p.27.
(5) _Ibid_.
(6) Ralph Miliband, '_The State in Capitalist Society_', Quartet, London, 1973, pp.128,129.
(7) Alan Paterson, 'Judges: A Political Elite', 1 _British Journal of Law and Society_, 1974, 118, p.127. Alan Paterson suggests that the selection of Law Lords known to favour an extension of conspiracy before the _Kamara_ case was due more to 'tactless insensitivity than any ulterior motive'. Similarly, in the squatting cases noted below, the presence of the influential Lord Denning is a constant factor in all the major squatting cases' developments. It should be noted that Denning as Master of the Rolls decides who shall hear the Court of Appeal cases.
(8) _Congreve_ v _Home Office_ [1976] QB 629.
(9) _Secretary of State for Education and Science_ v _Tameside Metropolitan Borough Council_ [1976] 3 WLR 641.

(10) Gavin Drewry, Law, Justice and Politics, Longman, London, 1975, p.68.
(11) Asher v Secretary of State for the Environment [1974] Ch. 208.
(12) Thus in one specific area we can find an ad hominem attack on the stance of one indiscreet judge in a minor case involving a speech by a racist politician attacking the Asian community in Britain drawing great support in the media and the Parliamentary Labour Party with motions of censure as occurred with Judge McKinnon and the Kingsley Read case in January 1978 whilst no criticism of any kind seems to have been made in the press or in the political parties over the policies of the House of Lords in their interpretation of the Race Relations Act 1968. In global terms the House of Lords' decision was far more extensive in practical effect than the Kingsley Read decision. See press for January 1978 from 7 January.
(13) 'Judges, The Courts and Society', BBC Radio 3 broadcast, 3 March 1977, featuring Lord Denning and Lord Scarman.
(14) Ibid.
(15) 'The Judges', Thames Television, 12 October 1971.
(16) 'The Times', 24 November 1972, addressing a High Court Journalists' Dinner.
(17) Miliband, ibid, p.124.
(18) 'Judges, The Courts and Society', supra.
(19) Ibid, per Lord Scarman.
(20) Ibid.
(21) Ibid.
(22) Burmah Oil Co. v Lord Advocate [1965] AC 75.
(23) 'Judges, The Courts and Society', supra.

Media, Politics and the Judiciary

WRITE ON ... THE JUDGES?

In a political democracy the position of important unelected decision-makers drawn from a socially exclusive professional elite might reasonably be expected to be under pressure. At least one might expect such a position to have a clear rationale. This is not the case at the end of the 1970s in Britain. The judiciary are most definitely not a political issue. This is in itself significant and an important contribution appears to come from the continued existence on the practical and theoretical planes of the Great Judge.

Traditionally, the Great Judge was regarded as unproblematic partly through the limited extent of political democracy and through the fiction that judges were merely declaring what the law was rather than developing and changing social policy in their work.[1] Even where this position came to be regarded as a mere convenient cloak for judicial innovation, it was a situation which was regarded as unproblematic.[2]

Old style reverence for the common law and its discoverers, the judges, might be expected to have disappeared in the cost benefit based decade of the seventies. The reverse has been the case with an increase in the mystificatory aspects of the judicial role and that very special product, the Great Judge.

In the first decade of the century to benefit from the expansion in higher education in Britain, we find two distinct examples of an acceptance of the notion of the Great Judge. The approaches seem initially diametrically opposed, but in fact share the same frame of reference for the judicial task. Judges provided problems for Brian Abel-Smith and Robert Stevens[3] because they shrank back from altering some of the old rules of the common law in the spirit of the welfare state. Their complaints centred around issues like the decline of the legal profession and particularly the decline of the activist judge keeping law 'up to date' with modern social needs. Louis Jaffe for his part[4] urged the judiciary in Britain to abandon their pusillanimous approach and revive the bold judge.

The reason why Lord Denning needs to be examined is that his work has indeed encompassed what Sir William Holdsworth referred to as developing principles[5] and fits in clearly with Louis Jaffe's definition of the Great Judge, 'The great judge was great because when the occasion cried out for new law he dared to make it ...'[6]

As the other essays in this collection testify, Lord Denning has been an innovator where he chose and the criteria involved in this enterprise appear to be essentially tied in with his own idiosyncracies. Since Lord Denning is, from time to time, overturned on appeal or operates as a minority in his own Court, his true danger may come from his ability to satisfy Jaffe's other criterion of a great judge:

> 'The great judge was great because he could dare to do these things and yet convince his public that he spoke with an authority greater than his own ...'[7]

The media have taken up this aspect of Lord Denning and seized on his fine-sounding perorations on liberty and justice as an indication of the possibilities of the judiciary protecting fundamental freedoms. It is this longterm impact of being fooled by the Lord Denning rhetoric as mediated through press and radio that makes a full assessment of his less well-known work necessary. The media have ensured that his 'populist' work will receive ample coverage even to the extent of reporting <u>his</u> judgment as the Court's decision when he was in a dissenting minority.[8]

ACADEMIC APPROACHES - THE ABSENCE OF CHALLENGE

The debates within academic legal philosophy in the past decade appear to have continued to centre around the question of the structure of the legal order.[9] So whilst issues and debates abound in the area of whether the legal system comprises rules or principles and whilst judicial activity formed a significant part of the arguments of the debaters, this work was conducted at a largely abstracted level, seeking empirical support only very occasionally. The question of how judges should exercise their discretion in dealing with rules or which of a group of competing principles to adopt was left largely untouched.

There appears to have been no parallel to the voluminous studies in the United States in the behavioural train.[10] Apart from lack of commitment to behaviouralism this would appear to reflect the relative inaccessibility of the judiciary in Britain. Except for a small number of former MPs,[11] the direct political, social and economic orientations of the judiciary are unavailable. The possibility of setting up correlations on the lines of Glendon Schubert[12] or Stuart Nagel[13] poses severe practical problems. The publicly available data on most judges fails to reveal little than their social origins and their educational background.[14] In order to elicit further information the co-operation of the judiciary is necessary. Wilson found that the reluctance of the judiciary to express themselves on their attitudes and pre-conceptions was a major block to effective research.[15]

What data and analysis there has been, has been highly simplistic. Deprived of all but the most rudimentary information on the judiciary, comments from outside academic legal circles have tended to restrict themselves to pointing out the high pre-ponderance of public school and Oxbridge in the path to the upper reaches of the Bench.[16] Rather more revealing work has been carried out in Scotland where the party political badge carries more weight in reaching the bench.[17] The studies have tended to leave these background factors to speak for themselves or acknowledge that the impact on decision-making needs to be separately assessed.[18]

In the actual field of analysis of the specific work of the judiciary, this has tended to be conducted within one of two explanatory modes. The simplest and most frequent has been the measuring of judicial performance against legislative intention. This has produced interesting work in a variety of sensitive areas of social legislation like race relations, housing and social security.[19]

The alternative approach lines up judicial decisions which are anti-labour, or civil liberties and in favour of private property and offers the available data on the educational and family background of the decision-makers and suggests this provides some sort of adequate class analysis of the judicial role. *Prima facie* it fails to offer any explanation of how 'progressive' decisions can be explained if the judiciary are mere janissaries for the bourgeoisie. More recently, John Griffith has attempted to fill out this picture by indicating that there is a compatibility between authoritarianism in issues involving the state and an anti-government stance where private property is concerned.[20] Judges can both support the state in some activities and resist it in others without any internal contradiction. Griffith's resort to some kind of apolitical 'professional ideology' explanation does not seem entirely to square with his own data,[21] although his work is innovatory in attempting to document judicial practice on a wide basis over time and subjects.

In the wider field of sociological studies in law, one emergent feature has been the flight from the judiciary as an object of study. In view of the state of theory in the sociology of law this is perhaps not surprising.[22] The judiciary are clearly not the central motor force in the organisation of the state. However, it would be distorting if the judiciary disappeared totally from the frame altogether in view of their roles as purveyors of the authority of the law and a morality above crude political motives. The early sociology of law in Britain has concentrated on the emergence of legislation and the operation of more visible and accessible enforcement agencies in the state.[23] Precisely where the policy-making judiciary fit in has yet to be dealt with although a number of historical descriptive studies do suggest a rather more active political role than the judges themselves have owned to.[24] Beyond this work, though, the judiciary remain the invisible power.

POLITICIANS AND THE JUDGES - ODD BREEZES

Surprisingly perhaps in view of the subordinate constitutional position of the judiciary, Parliament has in the recent democratic period eschewed criticism of the judiciary. This has been described by the most extensive study on the mechanics of the judiciary,[25] as only being deemed appropriate in very serious cases of misconduct.

On occasion, a couple of highly unpopular decisions have led to direct criticism in the form of motions of censure from MPs in the past decade.[26] However, this has only occurred in situations where the court has stepped well out of line with its remarks as in the case of Judge McKinnon and the 'wogs' remark of the racist John Kingsley Read. Here McKinnon J. praised Read for having the courage of his convictions and wished him well. Free speech here involved commenting on the death of an Asian youth 'one down a million to go'. The remarks of McKinnon J. and the response of the MPs is clearly an exceptional situation aided by the very heavy publicity accorded to the trial in the media.[27]

Similar sorts of considerations applied to the other motion of censure put forward in connection with Sir John Donaldson[28] and his decision in Con-Mech (Engineers) Ltd. v AUEW in 1973. Here, again, the issue was very 'high profile' in the media and the repeal of the Industrial Relations Act 1971 figured as a central plank in Labour Party policy. What, then, we have are exceptional situations where members of Parliament have broken with tradition and dared to criticise Her Majesty's judges. It is by no means a standard practice.

When in an apparently very mild address to the Post Office workers[29] in 1977, Michael Foot made the bland observation that trade unions owed little to the judiciary by way of thanks for securing them freedom from oppression, there was an 'outcry' filling the media for several days in which Foot was likened to Adolf Hitler by a former Attorney General.[30] Both Lord Hailsham and Lord Denning himself attacked the whole principle of judicial criticism:

> 'The repeated attacks on our judiciary are becoming too serious to ignore. Does it not make it all the worse when he [Foot]

> 'said he was not talking about any particular judge or decision because that can only be construed as an attack on the judiciary as a whole?'[31]

As a rule, little can be expected from this quarter by way of a sustained monitoring of the work of the judiciary and the reaction to those few criticisms that have been voiced indicate that it is in the 'national interest' that the judges should be treated as sacred objects of reverence like the Royal Family. Criticising either seems to suggest an implicit attack on the Constitution and the freedoms of Magna Carta.

> "It is of the first importance that the judges should be upright and independent, and known to be so and that the public should have confidence in them. Yet in these times we have seen an attack made in high quarters on their good sense and fairmindedness. We have seen them portrayed as limiting freedom instead of preserving it. Excuses have been made for this assertion, but there has been no withdrawal. No apology has been offered for it. To those who make that assertion, I would say: 'If they undermine the confidence of the people in the judges, they strike at the very root of law and order'".[32]

The possibility that the assertions are founded in reality and the exposure of prejudices and bias of the judiciary might be socially beneficial was apparently beyond comprehension.

MEDIA PRESENTATION - DISPLAYING THE GOODS

The concentration on Lord Denning specifically is a relatively recent phenomenon in common with the institution as a whole. In the sixties the dominant theme of articles on the judges was descriptive[33] and more attention was paid to the possibility of alternative channels of law reform like the Law Commission. They were contrasted with the judges and earned the epithet of the 'legal dambusters'.[34] Apart from this interest in law reform in a general modernising sense, the figure who reappears throughout this period is Lord Devlin whose views on public morality had been put into effect in the Ladies' Directory case,[35] and who took the opportunity to discuss the morality/law relationship in 1964.[36] His line at this time earned a rebuke from Alan Ryan in connection with the enforcement of morals by such a group as judges.[37] However, Lord Devlin's early retirement in 1964 removed him from the debate about appropriate judicial approaches and concentrated his contributions on the technical deficiencies of the court system.[38]

This anodyne analysis of the problems of the legal system in terms of delays and speeding up trials in court with electronic apparatus, whilst it does not trench directly upon the issue of the judicial role is significant in that it implicitly endorses other aspects of the process and regards them as unproblematic.[39]

SELLING THE PRODUCT

However, what has occurred in the latter part of the seventies has been not simply an absence of criticism, but a positive move in the media to 'sell' the judiciary. The unique selling proposition has been Lord Denning. Lord Denning fits the traditional conception of the Great Judge. He himself perceives his role as the protection of the fount of English liberty Runnymede, taking as his touchstone the invocation of Rudyard Kipling:

'And still, when mob or monarch lays,
Too rude a hand on English ways,
A whisper wakes, the shudder plays,
Across the reeds at Runnymede'.[40]

Despite the glowing tributes to Lord Denning by such colleagues as Lord Scarman that the last twenty five years had been characterised by Legal Aid, Law Reform and Lord Denning,[41] professional views of Lord Denning have not always been so generous. From the beginning of his career his cavalier and unorthodox approach have caused concern to those in sympathy with his policy objectives in some fields by reason of his desire to emulate his hero, Lord Mansfield,[42] and invent or drastically reformulate doctrines.

This occasional manifestation of professional scepticism has informed some of the comments on Lord Denning which have become a feature of the media in the seventies. However, coverage of Lord Denning has tended to be laudatory going on adulatory. Two extensive pieces on Lord Denning in the 'Sunday Times' in 1973 set the stage Although in these, Hugo Young indicated that Lord Denning's radicalism was strictly limited to certain fields like matrimonial property, the title of the first article set the overall tone - 'England's most Revolutionary Judge'.[43] Lord Denning is described as a 'great reforming judge' and the interesting area of his social, political and economic conservatism are left unexplored. The hints from Hugo Young that Lord Denning was crucially concerned to protect Authority, defend Morality and uphold Order, receives only a mention. The same sort of overall glowing picture emerges from a description of the work of Lord Denning in the 'Spectator' in 1975.[44]

FROM APPRECIATION TO ADULATION

The last couple of years have witnessed an apparent flight from even the 'balance' of 1973 in the portrayal of Lord Denning. What has prompted this outpouring of eulogies to Lord Denning and his colleagues has been the _Tameside_[45] and _Laker Airways_[46] cases. These have been packaged, given the lead of Lord Denning himself,[47] as pieces of executive oppression of the 'little man'. Hugo Young cast aside any lingering doubts as to Lord Denning's overall goals when he wrote of 'the great Lord Denning' standing out as a 'brilliant exception' to the normal run of the mill judges who failed to act as the 'guardians of the people'.[48] 'The Economist' took the same line suggesting Lord Denning's 'efforts to extend judicial review are very welcome',[49] and applauding _Laker_ and _Tameside_ and the emergence of a more active judiciary.[50] 'The Economist' continued its reverence for Lord Denning although they were moved to wonder whether where a judge with 'lesser wisdom' was involved they would be quite so confident about judicial activism. They banished any doubts about the democratic propriety of Lord Denning's action suggesting that 'it is the job of great judges to be adventurous'.[51] The ultimate accolade was paid by 'The Economist' three months later when a cartoon showed him as Superman and the article pointed to his great work in ensuring excessive union power was curbed and that parents were able to send their children to school as well as the rights of the wife in the matrimonial home rather than the homeless or mistresses.[52] He was urged to 'Carry on Denning'[53] which apparently entailed using the 'common sense view' to 'do justice rather than administer the law'.

'EVERYONE OUT OF STEP BUT JOHN ...'

The only jarring note in this process of Lord Denning appreciation appears to come from the pages of the 'New Statesman' and particularly the pen of John Griffith. In a series of articles leading up his Politics of the Judiciary book in 1977, Professor Griffith has commented through the late sixties and seventies on the political nature of apparently technical decisions in such arcane fields as administrative law.[54] Most of these pieces have been written in response to specific judicial decisions, although Griffith has collected his data together to formulate an account of the judicial role in the Politics of the Judiciary. Griffith responded then negatively to the extension of conspiracy,[55] the contortions of the House of Lords to limit the effect of the race relations legislation[56] and the likely impact of a Bill of Rights on fundamental freedoms[57] as advocated by Lord Scarman in his 1974 Hamlyn Lectures. Drawing these various threads together, Griffith provided a 'taster' for his book in February 1977 where he perceived threads running through judicial activity including the protection of private property, and an unwillingness to support trade union activity and racial discrimination legislation as well as support for 'Establishment', economic, social and moral attitudes.[58]

Griffith's work has been subject to a variety of 'technical' comments[59] and can be criticised for its selectivity of case material and its failure to delineate any time frames within which changes might be discernible. Essentially, though, the point made by Griffith and later echoed controversially by Michael Foot, was that organised labour would do well to look elsewhere than the courts for rights to protect their position at work and in the home. The problem, though, with attempting to characterise a whole body of distinct levels and stages of decision-makers within a single definition as 'anti-working class' or 'racist' or 'sexist' is always likely to be doomed by the complexity of classification of issues as well as possibly judicial diversity. The essence of the politics of the judiciary requires a perception by the political actor, the judge, that the issue in question is 'political'. Where labour relations are concerned this is no problem. The response of the judiciary can be gauged. As we can see elsewhere in this collection, Lord Denning's record on trade union matters is not one to inspire confidence in organised labour. In less visible areas of social life, his work has been less predictable. The classic area is the matrimonial home. Here he has pioneered certain rights for wives[60] whilst limiting those of some mistresses[61] and supporting those of others.[62] Drawing a general hypothesis from this work is less than straightforward and the tendency has been to simplify this complex issue.

CONCLUSION

What the media have tended to do both in the mainstream and in the pages of the 'New Statesman' has been to select those aspects which appeal to them about Lord Denning and present this as if it were the total. This is a question of judgment. Here we have attempted to answer the claim that Lord Denning is the 'uncommon spokesman for the common man'.[63] Lord Denning has largely been free from direct criticism on the left other than two brief invitations to retire from Jeremy Smith,[64] and the Haldane Society.[65] Much more typical has been the approach of 'The Economist', 'The Observer', 'The Sunday Times' and the portrait in the 'Illustrated London News' by Joan Bakewell which dealt in uncritical fashion with the legend of the liberal Lord Denning without touching on any challenge to this image. The only concern appears to emanate from Lord Denning himself who notes that 'there is a falling off in respect for law and order, for judges and everyone. I think it's disturbing'.[66] This perception combined with 'the popular enthusiasm for Denning' noted by Christine Verity may well have its source in the doubt which has been raised as to whether Lord Denning has 'sufficient intellectual equipment' to carry through the task he sets himself of 'modernising the law'.[67] The only doubts appear to be whether he is actually a great judge - not the concept or its implications. Leadership is to be respected it seems wherever it stems from and whatever authority it lays claim to. Its relationship to democratic accountability is left unexplained and faith in judicial charisma is likely to obscure this vital issue.

PETER ROBSON

NOTES

(1) *Cassell & Co.* v *Broome* (1972) AC 1027, *per* Viscount Dilhorne, p.1107.

(2) John Austin, *The Province of Jurisprudence Determined*, Weidenfeld & Nicolson, London, 1955, p.191; John Salmond, *Jurisprudence*, Stevens & Haynes, Lon 1902, p.178 ff; E.C. Clark, *Practical Jurisprudence*, Cambridge, 1882, pp.244 ff.

(3) *Lawyers and the Courts*, Heinemann, London, 1967, pp.125, 302 ff.

(4) Louis Jaffe, *English and American Judges as Lawmakers*, Clarendon, Oxford, 1969.

(5) *Some Makers of English Law*, Cambridge 1938, p.291.

(6) Jaffe, *supra*.

(7) *Ibid*.

(8) *Gouriet* v *UPW* [1977] QB 729 and newspapers of 28 January 1977.

(9) The work of Raz, Dworkin, MacCormick and other 'Oxford' legal philosophers comes to mind.

(10) B. Schwartz, *The Supreme Court*, Ronald, New York, 1957; R. Berger, *Government by Judiciary*, Harvard, Cambridge, Mass., 1977; and the extensive work of Glendon Schubert from *Judicial Decision-Making*, Free Press of Glencoe, New York 1963 through to *Political Attitudes and Ideologies* Sage, London 1977

(11) Lords Wheatley, Johnson and King-Murray in the Court of Session and Lord Chancellors like Lord Hailsham and Lord Elwyn-Jones, for example

(12) *The Judicial Mind*, North Western, *Evanston,* 1965.

(13) 'Judicial Backgrounds and Criminal Cases', *Journal of Criminal Law, Criminology and Police Science*, 1962.

(14) *Who's Who*, for example, the 'Justice' study and that by Blom-Cooper and Drewry (see note 16).

(15) R.J. Wilson, Judicial Decision-Making, Ph.D. Thesis, University of London LSE, 1970.
(16) G. Drewry, Law, Justice and Politics, Longman, London, 1975; The Judiciary Report of a Justice Sub-Committee, London, Stevens, 1972; L. Blom-Cooper & G. Drewry, Final Appeal, Clarendon, Oxford, 1972.
(17) Ian Willock, 'Scottish Judges Scrutinised', Juridical Review, 1969, p.193.
(18) Ibid, p.205.
(19) W.I. Jennings, 'Courts and Administrative Law - The Experience of English Housing Legislation', 49 Harvard Law Review, 1936, p.426; J.I. Reynolds, 'Statutory Covenants of Fitness and Repair - Social Legislation and the Judges', 37 MLR, 1974, p.377; C. Smith, 'Judicial Attitudes to Social Security', 2 BJLS, 1975, p.217; J.K. Bentil, 'Interpreting the Race Relations Act' , Public Law, 19 , p.157.
(20) John Griffith, The Politics of the Judiciary, Fontana, London, 1977.
(21) Ibid, pp.202 ff.
(22) Colin Campbell & Paul Wiles, 'The Study of Law and Society in Britain', Law and Society Review, 1976, p.547.
(23) Neil Gunningham, Pollution, Social Interest and the Law, Martin Robertson, London, 1974; W.G. Carson, 'Some Sociological Aspects of Strict Liability and the Enforcement of Factory Legislation', 33 MLR, 1970, p.396; Pat Carlen, Magistrates Justice, Martin Robertson, London, 1976.
(24) R.F.V. Heuston, Lives of the Lord Chancellors, Clarendon, Oxford, 1964; Alan Paterson, 'Judges, A Political Elite?', 1 BJLS, 1974, p.118.
(25) Shimon Shetreet, Judges on Trial, North-Holland, Amsterdam, 1976.
(26) Ibid, Chapter VIII.
(27) Press for January 1978, from 7 January onwards.
(28) 'The Times', 27 November 1973.
(29) 'The Times', 16 May 1977.
(30) 'The Times', 19 May 1977, per Lord Shawcross.
(31) 'The Times', 17 May 1977. per Lord Hailsham.
(32) 'The Times', 29 June 1977.per Lord Denning
(33) Sybille Bedford, 'View from the Bench', Observer, 15 May 1966; Christine Verity, 'The Judge', Sunday Times, 26 May 1968.
(34) 'The Legal Dambusters', Guardian, 26 May 1966.
(35) Shaw v DPP [1962] AC 220.

(36) 'Judges as Lawmakers', Listener, 20 August 1964.
(37) Alan Ryan, 'Judges Stick to Your Bench', New Society, 25, March 1965.
(38) 'Who is at fault when injustice occurs?', Listener, 12 December 1968, although his more recent contribution, 'Judges and Lawmakers', 39 MLR, 1976, 1, does take up some issues raised by John Griffith, infra.
(39) 'Man Alive Report', BBC 2, March 1976 featuring Lord Devlin; 'The Practice of Judging', Listener, 29 March 1979.
(40) 'Runnymede - Fount of English Liberty', The Times, 9 June 1965.
(41) 'Judges, the Courts and Society', featuring Lord Denning and Lord Scarman, BBC Radio 3, 3 March 1977.
(42) A. Hargreaves, 'Licensed Possessors', 69 LQR, 1953, p.466.
(43) 'The Sunday Times', 17 June 1973.
(44) David Wyn Williams, 'The Power, Not the Glory', Spectator, 1 February 1975. One needs to take the panegyric on Lord Denning from Auberon Waugh with a pinch of salt in view of the subsequent treatment of Lord Denning in Waugh's major outlet 'Private Eye' as a figure of juridical fun to rank along with Ronald Dworkin - 'One just man', Spectator, 5 March 1977.
(45) Secretary of State for Education and Science v Tameside Metropolitan Borough Council [1976] 3 W.L.R. 641.
(46) Laker Airways Ltd. v Department of Trade [1977] QB 643.
(47) 'The Freedom of the Individual Today', 45 Medico-Legal Journal, 1977, p.49.
(48) 'The Judges Begin to Fight Back', Sunday Times, 1 August 1976.
(49) 'Westminster Law, Judges' Law', Economist, 31 July 1976.
(50) 'The Lords Taketh Away', Economist, 7 August 1976.
(51) 'Too Many Candles for a Cake', Economist, 27 January 1979.
(52) See elsewhere in this collection.
(53) 'Carry on Denning', Economist, 7 April 1979.
(54) 'Judges in Politics - England', Government and Opposition, 3, Autumn 1968, p.485.
(55) 'Conspiracy and the Judges', New Statesman, 17 December 1971.
(56) 'Judges, Race and Law', New Statesman, 22 November 1974.

Media, Politics and The Judiciary

(57) 'Judges and a Bill of Rights', New Statesman, 10 January 1975.
(58) 'The Politics of the Judiciary', New Statesman, 4 February 1977.
(59) Kenneth Minogue, 'The Biases of the Bench', Times Literary Supplement, 6 January 1978; Review in Law Teacher, January 1978, p.58.
(60) National Provincial Bank v Hastings Car Mart [1964] Ch. 665.
(61) Tanner v Tanner [1975] 1 WLR 1346.
(62) Davis v Johnson [1978] 2 WLR 182; and Eves v Eves [1975] 1 WLR 1338.
(63) John Silverlight, 'The Judge on the Clapham Omnibus', Observer, 21 January 1979.
(64) 'Lord Denning by himself', New Statesman, 19 January 1979.
(65) 'The Guardian', 23 January 1979.
(66) 'Lord Denning, A Profile', Illustrated London News, March 1978.
(67) 'Denning's Justice', Spectator, 27 January 1979.

PART II
The Law and Lord Denning

Lord Denning and Morality

Following the revolt and successful overthrow of the Grand Duke in Brecht's The Caucasian Chalk Circle, Azdak, a Village Scrivener, is made a judge by the Ironshirts. Two years later, confronted by the Grand Duke's imminent return to power, Azdak hastily considers how he has used his power and contemplates his future:

> '... The people's quarters are already aflame. Go and get me the big book I always sit on [Shauwa brings the big book from the judge's chair. Azdak opens it.] This is the Statute Book and I've always used it, as you can testify. Now I'd better look in this book and see what they can do to me. I've let the down-and-outs get away with murder, and I'll have to pay for it. I helped poverty onto its skinny legs, so they'll hang me for drunkeness. I peeped into the rich man's pocket, which is bad taste ...'[2]

Azdak had only managed to sit on the Statute Book for two years. As 'England's Most Revolutionary Judge',[3] however, Lord Denning has frequently chosen to sit on precedent ever since he was appointed a High Court judge in 1944. The fact that he has often rightly been seen as an innovating and substantial force on the development of the law though, should not obscure those facets of his personality and beliefs that have led him into less constructive and enlightened pronouncements. Azdak only faced the hangman's noose; the principles that Lord Denning has espoused face the dangers of reification, of being accepted as a valid means of law-making.

Unfortunately, his style of law-making is such that there is no coherent pattern of legal thought behind it. That is not to say that it is aleatory or capricious, but only that he expresses his own views, his own morality, his own ideology, unrestrained by the constraints that precedents impose, and thereby often offering an idiosyncratic interpretation of the law. Such a system has had beneficial results, blatant as they have sometimes been, for as Stevens observed:

'Distasteful as it is ...'
Lord Denning on Sexual Morality

> '... if one were to criticise Denning's courageous assaults on the citadels of substantive formalism generally, it would be in terms of a lack of sophistication. This observation should in no way cloud his remarkable contribution to the debates about law and justice over this extended period, but as one moves away from the 'pure' common law areas, the inherent weaknesses of the Denning style of law-making become more obvious... indeed, in Denning's makeup ran a strong streak of nineteenth-century morality that sometimes emerged in criminal cases and, for him, rapidly became entwined in rather emotional aspects of personal morals. This same tendency affected his outlook in some aspects of family law'.[4]

Certainly, he has sometimes been prepared to put forward progressive views in this area of the law, such as when he argued for the deserted spouse's right to a share in the matrimonial home,[5] and similarly a mistress's,[6] but equally he has also been prepared to allow his own view of morality to intervene in his judgment.

The purpose of this essay is to look at only one aspect of this latter tendency, namely his attitude towards sex in Her Majesty's courts. It may be asked, however, both why his attitude towards sex should be considered important and how, even if it is relevant, it helps us to come to any better understanding of Lord Denning himself. Although it has only occupied a small part of Lord Denning's time and concern, it does illustrate the approach that he often takes to the cases before him. He seems to decide what is the correct, in his terms, approach to take to a case and then seeks for the law, or in the absence of it, the logic, to justify such a position.

Such a method often involves convoluted reasoning in order to justify the position that he has taken, and this is clearly borne out by Lord Denning's attitude to sex. For it is clear that public manifestations of sex are, for him, distasteful and alarming; but he is not simply a Whitehouse in ermine; he also happens to be the Master of the Rolls. As such he has a power and an influence far beyond that of ordinary prejudices, as well as the opportunity to express and clarify them. Certainly, when given such an opportunity, Lord Denning is not slow to speak out and establish his own position, even if it is a position, for many, 'not suited to the social necessities and social opinion of the twentieth century'.[7] He has his own attitude to sex; is prepared to express it and, at times, to impose it. It is therefore relevant to look at this attitude in order, first of all, to see how a particular prejudice is utilised by Lord Denning and, secondly, to use it to illustrate the defects of Lord Denning's method, insofaras there is an imminent danger of a tendentious judgment coming from it.

In 1954, Lord Denning sat with Evershed M.R. and Hodson L.J. in a divorce case, Bravery v Bravery.[8] The couple had married in 1934 and a son had been born in 1936. 'About eighteen months later, in 1938', to use Lord Denning's words, 'a shocking thing took place. The husband underwent an operation to have himself sterilised ...'[9] Eventually, in 1951, the wife left her husband and later sought a divorce on the grounds of cruelty. She alleged that her husband had had dirty habits, an excessive interest in Indian philosophy, art and music, had been mean in keeping her short of money and been cruel in having himself sterilised without her consent. The other allegations were rejected and it came down to the question of the sterilisation, of whether, as Mrs Bravery alleged, it had been done without her knowledge and consent, and consequently amounted to cruelty because of the damage that had been done to her health, her maternal instincts and her marriage. In defending the action, Mr Bravery maintained that after the birth of their child his wife had decided that she did not want any more children and, as she disliked using contraceptives, he had, with her consent, arranged to have himself sterilised. Evershed M.R. and Hodson L.J. found that the wife had consented, but Lord Denning had been able to perceive that what was at issue was far more than a simple divorce. Nefarious and licentious instincts must have been at work. It therefore obviously followed that the husband must have had an unconscious desire to deny his wife further children by having himself sterilised, as well as seeking irresponsible sexual gratification from the results of the operation. Denning went on to say of sterilisation:

'Distasteful as it is ...'
Lord Denning on Sexual Morality

> 'When it is done with the man's consent for a just cause, it is quite lawful, as, for instance, when it is done to prevent the transmission of a hereditary disease: but when it is done without just cause or excuse, it is unlawful, even though the man consents to it. Take a case where a sterilisation operation is done so as to enable a man to have the pleasure of sexual intercourse without shouldering the responsibilities attaching to it. The operation then is plainly injurious to his wife and, to any woman whom he may marry, to say nothing of the way it opens to licentiousness; and, unlike contraceptives, it allows no room for a change of mind on either side'.[10]

Evershed M.R. and Hodson L.J. had to dissociate themselves from Lord Denning's contention that a sterilisation operation without a just cause amounted to a criminal assault, but undaunted, he was later to repeat his argument in the House of Lords:

> 'Take sterilisation. There was a case a little while ago where a hospital porter arranged with a doctor at the hospital that he should, by a slight operation, sterilise him, so that he could have all the gratification of sexual intercourse without any of the responsibilities. I thought, and still think, that it was a criminal offence between consenting adults - if you please, in private'.[11]

And did Mr Bravery enjoy the rampant licentiousness that had been bestowed on him by the operation? In delivering his judgment, Lord Denning had gone over the husband's evidence. The husband was asked:

> 'How do you say things went on from 1942? A - Things became very difficult. Q - In what way? A - My wife could not bear me near her. If I tried to embrace her, she became frivolent (sic) to begin with, and then she refused, and I had to give up'.
>
> 'I must say that that is just what I should expect. I cannot think of anything more disruptive of a marriage than for a party to

sterilise himself in this way'.[12]

Hardly lascivious behaviour, but then Lord Denning had to be able to justify the position that he had taken. He had tried to describe the voluntary sterilistation as criminal and found his fellow judges dissociating themselves from him. Indeed, the analogies that he had tried to use to support this contention, of an old English prize-fighting case[13] and the caning of a seventeen-year old girl, with her consent, for the defendant's pleasure,[14] were rejected by his colleagues. Evershed M.R. and Hodson L.J. had declared:

> 'In our view, these observations are wholly inapplicable to operations for sterilisation as such, and we are not prepared to hold in the present case that such operations must be regarded as injurious to the public interest'.[15]

Did the sterilisation amount to cruelty then? In Lord Denning's view it did, either on the basis of the sexual proclivities that it may have unleashed or the repellant nature of the operation itself, but in either case it was for Lord Denning injurious to the marriage. In Lord Denning's view:

> 'Those cases under the criminal law have a bearing on the problem now before the court, because the divorce law, like the criminal law, has to have regard to the public interest, and consent should not be an absolute bar in all cases. If a husband undergoes an operation for sterilisation without just cause or excuse, he strikes at the very root of the marriage relationship. The divorce courts should not countenance such an operation any more than the criminal courts. It is severe cruelty ...'[16]

But then Lord Denning was not simply considering a divorce case. The sanctity of marriage, family life and the dangers of promiscuity were, for him, all apparent in the case before him. He therefore had to find that there had been severe cruelty, paradoxical though it may appear that in arguing that the divorce should be allowed he was in effect arguing for the sanctity of marriage. Given that objective he then had to attempt to bolster his position by nebulous arguments, because he had nothing else by which he could justify his position. The achievement of his objective was more important than the means by which it was gained.

He has decided opinions about the importance of religion and its relevancy on family life, because it is on this that he considers social stability depends. He once declared:

> 'The family is the primary social unit. The well being of the whole community requires that children should, so far as possible, be brought up by their own parents as members of one family ... The institution of marriage is the legal foundation of this family life ... The only real remedy is the growth of a strong public opinion condemning divorce, and I would add, condemning infidelity. It should not be regarded, as it now is, as the private concern of the parties with which no one else has anything to do. It is the concern of everyone who has the welfare of the country at heart'.[17]

Later, though, he was to lend his support for a more flexible divorce law, and to praise the beneficial effects of the Divorce Reform Act 1969.[18] In the same speech, however, to the Nottingham branch of the Marriage Guidance Council, of which he was national president, he still felt compelled to warn of the dangers of unchastity, which could lead to promiscuity and thereby threaten family life. 'It is a time for all good folk to take a stand', he declared, 'else the permissive society will soon become the decadent society'.[19]

Lord Denning made another stand in *Ward* v *Bradford Corporation*,[20] which concerned a woman student teacher who had been expelled from a teacher training college. She, along with four other women students, had been found one night to have had a man in their rooms in the hall of residence, which was in contravention of the rules of the college. It was suggested to her that it might be prudent if she were to find alternative accommodation, which she duly did. The story was reported in some newspapers,however, along with some statements made by Miss Ward. Under the rules of the college it was the responsibility of the Principal to decide whether or not to refer a case to the disciplinary committee, and she decided in this instance not to refer any of the cases involving students who had been found with men in their rooms. That decision though, incurred the displeasure of the governing body of the college, and so they decided to change the rules in order to allow them to refer cases to the disciplinary committee themselves. They also decided to make the new rules retrospective, and were thus able to haul the recalcitrant women students before the disciplinary committee, where the other students were reprimanded, although some were required to leave the hall of residence, but Miss Ward found herself expelled and the decision ratified by the governing body. Not unnaturally, she was not too happy with this and applied to the courts for a remedy.

She argued that the governing body had been wrong in changing the rules and applying them retrospectively anyway, but they had then gone on to aggravate their error by the conduct of the disciplinary committee. The committee was composed of three members from the governing body, three from the staff and three from the students. This meant that the three members of the disciplinary committee from the governing body had in effect been instrumental in referring Miss Ward's case to the committee, had then heard the case and finally approved their own decision when the governing body accepted the committee's recommendation. An assistant education officer from the local authority had also sat, and participated, in the disciplinary committee, even although the director of education of the local authority, or his representative, was only entitled to attend meetings of the governing body of the college. Consequently, Miss Ward had had her career virtually ruined and been denied natural justice in the manner of her dismissal, but when it came before Lord Denning he remained unimpressed by such arguments, and declared:

> 'Instead of going into lodgings she had this man with her, night after night, in the hall of residence where such a thing was absolutely forbidden. That is a fine example to set to

> others'. And she a girl training to be a teacher'. I expect the governors and the staff all thought that she was quite an unsuitable person for it. She would never make a teacher. No parent would knowingly entrust their child to her care'.[21]

The decision, though, prompted Griffith to observe:

> 'In Ward's case, it is difficult to resist the impression that Lord Denning was more affected by moral conduct of which he disapproved ... than by the applicability of the rules of natural justice'.[22]

Apart from sterilised husbands, recalcitrant women students and the permissive society in general, other areas that have attracted Lord Denning's moral ire have been pornography, artificial insemination and homosexuality. In R. v Commissioner of Police of the Metropolis, ex parte Blackburn[23] he considered the effects of pornography:[24]

> 'Mr. Blackburn condemned it in a telling phrase. Pornography, he said, is powerful propaganda for promiscuity. So it is for perversions. To those who come under its influence, it is altogether bad. We have been shown examples of it. The court below declined to look at them. We felt it our duty to do so, distasteful as it is. They are disgusting in the extreme. Prominent are the pictures. As examples of the art of coloured photography, they would earn the highest praise. As examples of the sordid side of life, they are deplorable'.[25]

The same tone was applied to homosexuals in a House of Lords Report on Homosexual Offences and Prostitution:[26]

> 'It is said that adultery and fornication are not criminal offences, so why should homosexuality be? The law answers natural sin is different from unnatural vice. Natural sin is, of course, deplorable, but unnatural vice is worse; because, as the law says, it strikes at the integrity of the human race -

really?

> and indeed there is a whole category of offences which come within that very circle'.[27]

Finally, when considering artificial insemination of married women in the House of Lords,[28] Lord Denning felt compelled to say:

> "So much for the legal considerations. Just one word on its social significance. It seems to me that if this practice became widespread it would strike at the stability and security of family life; it would strike at the roots of our civilisation. I would say to the doctors 'Where by your science are you leading us? Seek to relieve suffering by all means, but do not do it by secrecy and deception'. 'For what is a man profited if he shall gain the whole world and lose his own soul?'"[29]

The same phraseology recurs in all the above quotes; moral turpitude, the dangers of promiscuity, the integrity of the human race and the stability of family life. These are sincere concerns of Lord Denning, but too often he appears to be a Don Quixote tilting at the windmills of immorality, armed only with moral denunciations. He can on occasion overcome these prejudices, however, as occurred in the case of Attorney General, ex rel McWhirter v Independent Broadcasting Authority.[30] A film had been made on the life of Andy Warhol and was due to be screened on television, but it was preceded by a newspaper warning that it was a 'TV shocker'. The 'News of the World',[31] for example, who had seen the film, warned:

> 'This TV shocker is the worst ever. A programme which goes further than anything I have ever seen on TV is to be screened on Tuesday night. Millions of viewers will find its frankness offensive'.

Ross McWhirter, one of the twin brothers who had produced the Guinness Book of Records, had not seen the film but applied to the courts for an injunction against it being shown on the basis of the newspaper reports and the fact that there had been a contravention of section 3(1) of the Television Act 1964. The section stipulated that the

Independent Broadcasting Authority had to satisfy themselves, so far as was possible, that the programmes broadcast by the Authority did not, amongst other things, offend against good taste or decency or be offensive to public feeling. On the basis of the newspaper reports an injunction was granted, but the court later went on to view the film and decided that it could be shown. Lord Denning said:

> 'To test these submissions we ourselves saw the film. I hesitate to express my own views upon it, but it is part of the evidence before us and I feel I should do so. I can understand that some people would think it entertaining, but I must speak as I find. Viewing it as a whole, the film struck me as dreary and dull. It shows the sort of people - the perverts and homosexuals - who surround Mr Warhol and whom he portrays in his work. But, taken as a whole, it is not offensive. Viewing it piece by piece, there are some incidents which seemed to me to be inserted in an attempt to liven up the dullness - an attempt which did not succeed, at least so far as I am concerned ... I should have thought that these individual incidents could be regarded as indecent and likely to be offensive to many. But my views do not matter, unless they go to show that the Independent Broadcasting Authority misdirected themselves or came to a conclusion to which they could not reasonably come. I am certainly not prepared to say that'.[32]

Even when expressing an opinion against his own inclinations, Lord Denning had been able to make his own views on morality plain, but he had been able to overcome his own prejudices. That he has these prejudices is clear enough from his judicial opinions, Parliamentary debates and writings, and the danger with Lord Denning's style of law-making is that it can too often leave his prejudices unrestrained. He can quite sincerely believe that he is countering a social evil, but once he has perceived the particular evil, there is an inherent danger that Lord Denning may allow his desire to combat the 'evil' override his consideration of the case in point. This is not, of course, confined to cases of sexual morality,[33] but to his style of law-making in general. Cases involving morality are merely one illustration of this tendency, but they do show how he can find himself in a false position regarding morality and having to then attempt to retrieve the position by tendentious and tortuous argument. It can then be seen, as Halifax observed, that:

> 'There is more learning now required to explain a law made, than went to the making it'.[34]

RAY GEARY

NOTES

(1) R. v Commissioner of Police of the Metropolis ex parte Blackburn [1973] 1 QB 248. Denning was commenting on having to look at some pornography as he felt it was his duty to do so.
(2) Bertholt Brecht, The Caucasian Chalk Circle, Penguin, London, 1966, p.193.
(3) Hugo Young, 'England's Most Revolutionary Judge', Sunday Times, 17 June 1973.
(4) Robert Stevens, Law and Politics, Weidenfeld & Nicolson, London, 1979, p.499.
(5) National Provincial Bank Ltd v Hastings Car Mart [1964] Ch. 665.
(6) Eves v Eves [1975] 1 WLR 1338 (CA).
(7) Lord Denning, The Discipline of Law, Butterworths, 1979, p.v: It is ironical Lord Denning should have said, 'My theme is that the principles of law laid down by the judges in the nineteenth century - however suited to social conditions of that time - are not suited to the social necessities and social opinion of the twentieth century. They should be moulded and shaped to meet the needs and opinion of today'. Lord Denning, though, would argue that his interpretation of current morality is shared by the majority of people, at least right thinking people.
(8) [1954] 1 WLR 1169.
(9) Ibid.
(10) Ibid.
(11) 206 Parl. Deb. H.L. (5th Ser.) Col. 807.
(12) [1954] 1 WLR p.1178
(13) R. v Coney (1882) 8 QBD 534.

(14) R. v Donovan [1934] 2 KB 498.
(15) [1954] 1 WLR p.1176
(16) Ibid.
(17) Lord Denning, The Changing Law, Stevens, London, 1953, p.121.
(18) The Times, 1 October 1971.
(19) Ibid.
(20) Ward v Bradford Corporation 70 LGR 27
(21) Ibid.
(22) J.A.G. Griffith, The Politics of the Judiciary, Fontana, 1977, p.166.
(23) [1973] 1 QB 241.
(24) The mutual appreciation of Mr Blackburn and Lord Denning for one another was to continue. They were to meet again in R. v Police Commissioner, ex parte Blackburn, reported in The Times, 7 March 1980. Again it concerned an appeal by Mr Blackburn against the refusal of a Divisional Court to grant him an order of mandamus compelling the Commissioner of Police to enforce the law against the publication and sale of obscene material. The appeal was dismissed but, as The Times reported, "Mr Blackburn while addressing the court on costs and leave to appeal, referred to Lord Denning as the 'greatest living Englishman', Lord Denning retorted, 'Tell that to the House of Lords'".
(25) [1973] 1 QB 248.
(26) 206 Parl. Deb. H.L. (5th Ser.) Col. 806-11.
(27) Ibid, Col. 807.
(28) Ibid, Col. 943-7.
(29) Ibid.
(30) [1973] QB 629.
(31) 14 January 1973.
(32) [1973] QB 652.
(33) Lord Scarman, for example, has criticised Lord Denning's assumption that reforms can be implemented by the judiciary, utilising the existing judiciary mahcinery, without recourse to the legislature in Lim Poh Choo v Camden and Islington Area Health Authority [1979] QB 196. The case concerned the quantum of damages in an action for damages against a health authority for the admitted negligence of their servants or agents in the provision of medical treatment to the plaintiff, but Lord Scarman's stricture can be appropriately applied to Lord Denning's method of law-making as a whole. In

regard to Lord Denning's suggestions as to how damages should be awarded, Lord Scarman said at p. 914, 'For so radical a reform can be made neither by judges nor by modification of rules of court. It raises issues of social, economic and financial policy not amenable to judicial reform, which will almost certainly prove to be controversial and can be resolved by the legislature only after full consideration of factors which cannot be brought into clear focus, or be weighed and assessed, in the course of the forensic process. The judge, however wise, creative, and imaginative he may be, is 'cabin'd, cripp'd, confin'd, bound in' not, as was Macbeth, to his 'saucy doubts and fears' [Macbeth, III, iv, 24] but by the evidence and arguments of the litigants. It is this limitation, inherent in the forensic process, which sets bounds to the scope of judicial law reform'.

(34) Halifax - Complete Works, J.P. Kenyon (ed.), Penguin, London, 1969, p.208.

Spies, Subverters and Saboteurs

Lord Denning has played a major role in the development of the law relating to the disclosure of information, particularly in relation to disclosure by Ministers and the issue of 'national security', and has been a front-runner in the development of what he terms 'Public Interest Privilege'.[1]

The basis for this development was Duncan v Cammell Laird and Company Limited,[2] in the course of which Viscount Simon stated that '... an objection validly taken to production on the ground that this would be injurious to the public interest, is conclusive ...'[3]

LORD DENNING, GUARDIAN OF JUSTICE

The legal position, then, was that the Minister had virtually unfettered discretion in withholding documents, and that the only body that could change this doctrine was the House of Lords. Challenges to this position did, of course, appear and amongst the challengers was Lord Denning. In a 1965 case he produced the following:

> 'The objection of a Minister, even though taken in proper form, should not be conclusive. If the court should be of opinion that the objection is not taken in good faith, or that there are no reasonable grounds for thinking that production of the documents would be injurious to the public interest, the court can override the objection and order production. It can, if it thinks fit, call for the documents and inspect them itself so as to see whether there are reasonable grounds for withholding them: ensuring, of course, that they are not disclosed to anyone else. It is rare indeed for the court to override the Minister's objection, but it has the ultimate power, in the interests of justice to do so. After all, it is the judges who are the guardians of justice in this land: and if they are to fulfil their

> trust, they must be able to call upon the Minister to put forward his reasons so as to see if they outweigh the interests of justice'.[4]

Two years later, he again followed this line, this time in Conway v Rimmer,[5] the case in which the House of Lords amended its decision in Duncan, and broadly adopted Lord Denning's point of view.

His view, as stated here, seems liberal enough, concerned to limit the powers of the executive, and intent, above all else, on the achievement of justice. One would expect that in all cases, even those involving 'state security', the sort of probing and weighing up hinted at, would be the normal procedure. There are a number of reasons why it would appear to be applicable even to cases involving claims of national security. If the courts are to be the guardians of justice, should they not be so in all cases, if we admit of exceptions to this then the courts must in some cases permit, and even promote, injustice and surely then they cannot be described as the guardians of justice. Secondly, Ministers have been found by the courts to have been in error in claiming Crown Privilege for documents, as indeed in Conway v Rimmer, and there is little reason to suppose that they cannot be mistaken in relation to national security. Finally, it cannot be seriously argued that the judiciary are too untrustworthy to inspect documents relating to national security. Lord Denning was a fit and proper person to hold an inquiry into matters related to national security in 1963 and nothing, presumably, happened in the supervening period to make him no longer so.

From this, therefore, it would seem that the logic behind Lord Denning's remarks would have led to the beginning of judicial scrutiny of Ministerial claims of national security. It seemed even more likely in the light of one of Lord Denning's later statements, in relation to the control of administrative discretion:

> 'The great problem before the courts in the twentieth century has been: In an age of increasing power, how is the law to cope with the abuse or misuse of it? ... In these pages now I hope to show how the challenge has been met. I will take one

by one the law as it stood thirty years ago: and the law as it stands today. It is a fascinating story. I will show that previous decisions have been departed from; that long-accepted propositions have been overthrown; that 'ouster' clauses have themselves been ousted; and that literal interpretation has gone by the board. All in support of the rule of law. All done so as to curb the abuse of power by the executive authorities'.[6]

DISCLOSING INFORMATION

However, the story, fascinating though it may be, does not end happily and in the same case from which the earlier quotation was taken, in Re Grosvenor Hotel, London No.2, Lord Denning did for himself what Marx did for Hegel. Commenting on the Duncan case, he said:

"The First Lord of the Admiralty said on oath that their disclosure would be injurious to the public interest. Every court in the land refused to order their production. And quite rightly. The national security was at stake. Suffice it for the decision to say, as the House did say: 'Those who are responsible for the national security must be the sole judges of what the national security requires'".[7]

More recently, Lord Denning has repeated the same line in R. v Secretary of State for Home Affairs ex parte Hosenball.[8] This case involved a deportation order on an American journalist. He was heard by the special panel of three advisers provided for by the Immigration Act 1971. However, at no point was he furnished with any particulars of the case against him, and he appealed to have the deportation order set aside basing himself largely on the claim that this means of proceeding was contrary to natural justice. When the case reached the Court of Appeal, Lord Denning was one of the judges sitting. He provided again the assertion that the ultimate power of decision as to the withholding of information lay with the judiciary, and again he backed down on the issue whether the courts could examine a Minister's claim of 'national security'. The point of view was perhaps best expressed by Lord Widgery in the Divisional Court:

> 'We do not know what the basis of his objection was in any sort of detail, and we are bound, having no alternative, to accept what he says when, through his representatives, he swears that he has formed the opinion that no matter can safely be disclosed beyond those already included'.[9]

Lord Denning then stands firmly on the side of the preservation of the secrecy surrounding the state and government, but to be fair to him, this is not the only area affected by his concern about the disclosure of information. In D. v NSPCC,[10] a mother sought to have the name of an informant who had alleged that she was mistreating her child revealed. Although the Court of Appeal upheld her claim, Lord Denning, and later the House of Lords, were of the opinion that the name should be kept secret. The rationale behind Lord Denning's view is as follows:

> 'When information has been imparted in confidence, and particularly where there is a pledge to keep it confidential, the courts should respect that confidence. They should in no way compel a breach of it, save where the public interest clearly demands it, and then only to the extent that the public interest requires'.[11]

This seems very much to be a case of secrecy for the sake of it, and it leads on to a discussion of the basis for Lord Denning's beliefs that certain kinds of information should be kept confidential.

In D. v NSPCC, the basis appears to be that if the names of informants are revealed, then people will be put off providing information, the public interest in the prosecution of person maltreating children depends on the provision of this information and outweighs the public interest in its disclosure. In answer to this line of reasoning, Lord Scarman made the following remarks in the Court of Appeal:

> '... it has to be accepted that some may be deterred from giving information to the NSPCC if Crown Privilege cannot be claimed. This is a loss which could be damaging to the public interest. But the damage has to be considered in a wider context even than the welfare of children. What sort of society is the law to reflect?
>
> If it be an open society, then men must be prepared to face the consequences of giving information to bodies such as the NSPCC protected, as they will be, by the promise of the NSPCC not to disclose their sources of information save when compelled by law in subsequent legal proceedings to do so, and by the defence of qualified privilege available to them in the event of a defamation suit. If it be a society in which as a general rule informers may invoke the public interest to protect their anonymity, the law may be found to encourage a Star Chamber world wholly alien to the English tradition'.[12]

Lord Scarman correctly identifies the major problem with Lord Denning's public interest privilege, anonymity can be a cloak for frivolous and even malicious accusations, and the object of one of these would, in Lord Denning's world, be denied proper recourse. The position holds other dangers. If it was to be faithfully followed it would effectively prevent individuals from discovering information held on them, and from correcting errors in that information. Lord Denning's position here also seems to be inconsistent with that in Hosenball, where he seems to suggest that only in cases where the state is itself endangered should the public interest in justice above all else take second place.

GUARDIAN OF THE STATE

In the Hosenball case we again find references to the possible drying up of a source of information. Hosenball had requested further information regarding, for example, the information he had which was alleged to be prejudicial to the safety of servants of the Crown. Commenting on this, Lord Denning says:

> '... it is apparent that if the Secretary of State complied with that request, it would be quite possible for a clever person, who was in the know, to track down the source from which the Home Secretary got the information. That _might_ put the source of the information himself in peril. Even if not in peril, that source of information _might_ dry up'.[13] (My emphasis).

This line of reasoning is clearly vulnerable to the criticisms by Lord Scarman quoted above. In the first place, both the danger and the drying up are completely hypothetical. No good reason is provided which would make us suspect that anything of the kind might happen. Further, in what might be termed 'ordinary' criminal cases, the identity of an informant is often revealed, particularly recently in the case of the 'supergrasses', this is despite the fact that the problems of peril and drying up would seem to be much more tangible in such cases than in the _Hosenball_ case. It is not even clear whether the information was provided by an outside informer, or whether it was generated exclusively by the security services.

At least four further assumptions are needed to justify this line of argument:

(1) That Hosenball was a participant in some sort of organisation which would have both the will and the ability to harm the informant in some way;

(2) That the information was true. Unless this was the case, there was of course no justification for the Home Secretary's attempt to secure Hosenball's deportation, yet Lord Denning's formulation rules out any possibility of ascertaining the truth of the information, since it is to be revealed to no one, and simply assumes its truth;

(3) That the security services are unable to provide adequate protection for the informant;

(4) That the drying up of the informant would have serious consequences - in other words, that the informant has something else of importance to tell the security services.

All these assumptions would have to be true, yet there is no way in which they can be checked, and we are forced back on to trusting the integrity of the Home Secretary. This appears to be Lord Denning's second justification for his position:

> 'There is a conflict here between the interests of national security on the one hand and the freedom of the individual on the other. The balance between these two is not for a court of law. It is for the Home Secretary'.[14]

This displays a touching faith in the Home Secretary, not completely justified even on the basis of reported cases, several ministers have been ordered to produce documents against their wishes. But, according to Lord Denning, 'they have never interfered with the liberty or the freedom of movement of any individual except where it is absolutely necessary for the safety of the state'.[15] A highly dubious statement for a number of reasons. The record of successive governments on secrecy and security has not been good as far as those on the left have been concerned. There is good reason to doubt the sincerity and impartiality of Home Secretaries. Simply looking at prosecutions in the area of official secrets demonstrates this. It is usually groups and individuals who can be broadly placed on the left who are prosecuted - the Committee of 100, Peace News, The Leveller - not the mainstream press and journalists who publish official secrets with almost monotonous regularity and get away with it.

In the second place, Lord Denning, if he has been observing his own rules, cannot possibly know that this is the case. He cannot possibly have had access to the evidence presented to the Home Secretary to be able to see for himself that this is the case. The statement seems to be drawn from the vague haze which appears to surround Lord Denning and to constitute his reality (of which more later) and as with many other of the statements in his <u>Hosenball</u> judgment, has absolutely, and in this case can have, no warrant in fact.

We can also ask questions about the difference that publication of the material allegedly possessed by Hosenball would make to the safety of the state, the answer must be, in this case, none. It is highly unlikely, first of all, that the information would be of such importance as to pose a serious threat to the state. Secondly, it is probable that the information was already known to what might be euphemistically termed 'foreign powers', deportation and secrecy would have little practical effect if this was the case. It is possible indeed, that some of theinformation was publicly available, either in this country, or overseas where official secrets legislation is less restrictive. Finally, deportation solves no problems, if the material was intended for publication there would be nothing to prevent an aspiring author from publishing elsewhere once expelled from the UK.

For these reasons then, I think we can dispense with Lord Denning's second reason - but this reason goes deeper than the above considerations. There seems first of all to be a tension in Lord Denning's own thought. On the one hand, the judges are 'guardians of justice', on the other the balance between national security and the freedom of the individual is not for a court of law. It would seem that if the judges are indeed what Lord Denning claims them to be, then they must function as independent assessors on questions such as this and not, as seems to be the case at the moment, as instruments of the executive authority. We can also glimpse again at Lord Denning's apparent purpose in this field to keep as much as secret as possible (though we should note that public interest privilege does not, for Lord Denning, extend to journalists[16]). In D. v NSPCC he clearly says that confidence should only be breached to the extent that public interest requires - this seems to put the onus of proof on those seeking discovery and openness, and so to favour secrecy. It also raises the interesting question of how the decision as to what the public interest requires is to be made in the absence of the information for which privilege is claimed. How can we be sure that something should not be revealed if we do not know what it is? The assumption seems to be that a claim of national security is conclusive of a paramount public interest in withholding of information. The question of public interest will be taken up again later, but one further point can be made. Photographs of the Post Office Tower are in contravention of the Official Secrets Acts and so, presumably, represent a threat to national security. An alien could, therefore, presumably be deported for intending to publish such a photograph, and the details of his crime could be withheld on the grounds of national security. This perhaps illustrates the elasticity of the concept of national security, and so the difficulties of making a decision as to release or otherwise of documents purely on the basis of a claim of national security.

Now we come to what is Lord Denning's final justification in the Hosenball case - this theme appears several times:

> '... Mr. Hosenball is one of a group of people who are trying to obtain information of a very sensitive character about our security arrangements. Their intention is to publish it ... in a way which will imperil the lives of the men in our secret service'.[17]

> '... times of peace hold their dangers too. Spies, subverters and saboteurs may be mingling amongst us, putting on a most innocent exterior. They may be endangering the lives of men in our secret service, as Mr. Hosenball is said to do.
> ... The rules of natural justice have to be modified in regard to foreigners here who prove themselves unwelcome and ought to be deported'.[18]

The spectre of a plot to endanger those penetrating foreign espionage networks owes more to thrillers of the more garish variety, than to the modern world where secret service agents are a relic of the pre-technological age and of strictly limited use. Exactly how Hosenball was going to imperil the lives of men in the security services and bring about the downfall of the state is unclear. It is worth noting that the danger, as well as the spies, subverters, etc, are purely hypothetical, adding even further to the insubstantiality of Lord Denning's reasoning in support of his position. Allied to this position is the following, presumably a justification for national security establishing a paramount public interest claim:

> 'It is a case in which national security is involved, and our history shows that, when the state itself is endangered, our cherished freedoms may have to take second place'.[19]

Let us ignore the fact that Lord Denning confuses two distinct situations, cases involving national security and cases in which the state itself is endangered, instead let us consider how this relates to the Hosenball case and to the concept of public interest. As I have said previously, the Hosenball case was not one in which the state itself was endangered. The most Lord Denning could imagine was that the informant might be in peril and that the lives of some of the men in the security service might be put at risk, although presumably it is put at risk at least from Lord Denning's point of view by the very nature of their employment. This, therefore, was by no stretch of the imagination one of the cases in which natural justice would have to take second place, if it was it would be naive to assume that the only action taken would be deportation.

In The Due Process of Law, Lord Denning devotes a chapter to justification of the Hosenball case. However this adds little we do not already know. Lord Denning states:

> 'We did not compel disclosure of it [the information sought by Hosenball] - and for it we have been criticised in many quarters. So I would like to explain it'.[20]

Our hopes are raised, only to be dashed, the 'explanation' consists of edited hightlights of Lord Denning's judgment in the case.

However, the first two paragraphs are interesting for the light they shed on Lord Denning's perception of reality:

> 'There is some information which is so secret that it cannot be disclosed - except to a very few. This country, like all others, has its own intelligence service ... Their lives may be endangered if there is the slightest hint of what they are doing. In one case (of which the public know nothing) many of our agents disappeared ... The information is known to the security service but to no one outside.

It is information of this kind which was hinted at - no more than hinted at - in the case of Mark Hosenball ...'[21]

Once again the decision is justified on the basis of information of which Lord Denning cannot possibly have knowledge. Once again, he is operating on a view of the secret service which bears little relation to reality. Perhaps most interesting here is Lord Denning's admission that there was only a mere hint that the information sought by Hosenball was of a type protected by a claim of national security. This admission only compounds his offence, and raises more forcefully the need for an explanation as to why the judges did not take steps to check the Home Secretary's claims, and examine the truth behind the hints.

Lord Denning's formulation of the public interest component is very narrow, restricted to this area. He does not attempt to set it in the perspective, as Lord Scarman suggests, of society as a whole. Thus, questions such as the public interest in having more information about the operations of the security services, or in having more information about what the government, which is supposed to represent us, is doing, are completely avoided by Lord Denning. The public interest in more open government is denied, even in cases where release of the information could do no harm, because it was already known elsewhere and because it does not pose any real threat to the state. It would indeed be difficult to find a case where the publication of information could pose a real danger to the state, even the acquisition of the atomic bomb secrets by the USSR did not bring about the fall of western civilisation. One is almost forced to the conclusion that the danger to the state is the publication of materials which it wishes to keep secret. In this way its total control is breached, and its virility as a state endangered.

All that is left to say is that none of Lord Denning's rationalisations provide a secure foundation for his position on this question. The only sound position is that these documents are not to be revealed because they are not to be revealed. That is all that can safely be said. Lord Denning is only, by his insistence on the types of rationalisation outlined above, placing himself firmly on the side of, and in support of, one of the world's most secretive state apparatuses.

TOM GUTHRIE

NOTES

(1) Lord Denning, The Discipline of Law, Butterworths, London, 1979, p.304.
(2) [1942] AC 624.
(3) Ibid, p.642.
(4) In re Grosvenor Hotel, London (No.2) [1965] 1 Ch. 1210, pp.1245, 1246.
(5) [1967] 1 WLR 1031.
(6) The Discipline of Law, pp.61, 62.
(7) Supra, p.1244.
(8) [1977] 1 WLR 766.
(9) Ibid, p.774.
(10) [1978] AC 171.
(11) Ibid, p.190.
(12) Ibid, pp.199, 200.
(13) Supra, p.783.
(14) Ibid.
(15) Ibid.
(16) Attorney-General v Mulholland [1963] 2 QB 477.
(17) Supra, p.777.
(18) Ibid, p.778.
(19) Ibid.
(20) The Due Process of Law, Butterworths, London, 1980, p.85.
(21) Ibid.

Negligence — a Dagger at the Doctor's back?

Most professional groups have a self-regulating function, i.e. they deal internally with breaches of professional codes. Such breaches are generally dealt with as cases of 'serious professional misconduct'. Nonetheless, it is imperative that professions are accountable to the public. This public accountability is achieved by the jurisdiction of the courts (usually civil) over allegations of professional negligence.

In addition to its internal disciplinary structure, the medical profession has a further channel for filtering cases of allegations of negligence, which comes into operation before the civil courts become involved. This additional filter takes the form of Defence Unions, which all doctors are encouraged to join (and almost all do), and which will consider all allegations of negligence and decide whether to attempt an out of court settlement or to defend the case. These Unions were founded at the end of the last century[1] and have proved to be '... a big contributory factor in reducing litigation and legal costs.[2]

The intervention of the Defence Unions has generally been welcomed by the medical profession, but it has paradoxically had the effect that the cases which reach the courts and are therefore subject to public scrutiny, tend to be those which are more contentious. The Pearson Commission[3] noted that the number of successful claims in negligence against the medical profession was much lower than in all other negligence cases. Some payment is made in approximately 30-40 per cent of medical cases as compared to approximately 86 per cent of all personal injury cases. The Commission felt that the apparent difficulty of gathering the relevant evidence in these cases might explain the lower success rate. It is, however, possible that other factors influence the decisions of courts in these situations.

It is left to the courts to set standards of care which are required of professionals for legal purposes. The courts must, therefore, assess what is reasonable skill and care in professional practice, and have, of course, shaped the concept of reasonableness which is used to test the behaviour of the general public. As Lord MacMillan pointed out in the case of Glasgow Corporation v Muir:[4]

> 'The reasonable man is presumed to be free both from over-apprehension and from over-confidence, but there is a sense in which the standard of care of the reasonable man involves in its application a subjective element. It is still left to the judge to decide what, in the circumstances of the particular case, the reasonable man would have had in contemplation, and what, accordingly, the party sought to be made liable ought to have foreseen. Here there is room for diversity of view ...'[5]

It can be seen then that the attitude of individual judges may be influential in decisions about professional standards. However, there is of course a considerable measure of agreement as to the basic legal requirements for establishing negligence. Essentially, in taking decisions of this sort, judges are applying basic legal rules to a given set of facts. These rules have been laid down on many occasions and reflect an agreement within the judiciary. Thus, Viscount Simon laid down three broad rules for the establishment of negligence:[6]

(1) that the defendant failed to exercise due care
(2) that he owed the injured man the duty to exercise due care
(3) that his failure to do so was the cause of the injury.

As Lord Wright has pointed out:

> '... mere sequence of cause and effect is not enough in law to constitute a cause of action in negligence, which is a complex concept, involving a duty as between the parties to take care, as well as a breach of that duty and resulting damage'.[7]

Lord MacMillan adds the caveat that, 'legal liability is limited to those consequences of our acts which a reasonable man of ordinary intelligence and experience so acting would have in contemplation'.[8] Thus to Viscount Simon's three tests it is appropriate to add the test of reasonable foreseeability.

It is, of course, in the interpretation of these tests, in view of the facts of particular cases, that there is room for disagreement and there is scope for the legal process to influence the standards set. Lord Denning is the judge who has had perhaps the greatest single influence in cases relating to medical negligence, and indeed he devotes some time to discussing these cases in The Discipline of Law.[9] Not only has he been involved in many leading cases, but his judgments are regularly referred to, as for example in Bolam v Friern Hospital Management Committee,[10] where McNair J. referred to Lord Denning's judgment in the case of Roe v Minister of Health[11] as 'very wise words'.[12] This judgment was again referred to in the recent case of Whitehouse v Jordan and Another.[13]

When assessing whether or not professionals have been negligent, it might be expected that the tests applied would be the same type of tests as those used for the rest of the community. The Pearson Commission[14] declined to place the doctor in a different position from the rest of the community, and therefore did not introduce 'no fault' liability in medical negligence cases. However, given that judges may influence the development of attitudes and standards, the assumption that professionals are treated as the rest of the community is not one which can be made without further analysis. As Lord Denning has been so influential in medical negligence cases, an examination of some of the more important decisions in which he has been involved will help to demonstrate whether or not the doctor is placed in a different position from the public.

One important feature of medical negligence cases which emerges immediately from this examination is the problem facing the courts in assessing and interpreting medical evidence. As Lord Denning himself said,[15] 'The medical people, the engineers, the chemists - all have their jargon which none of the rest of us understands' (emphasis added). Thus immediately, the courts are faced with problems which make it imperative that they depend considerably on the evidence of other professionals as to standards of care, rather than necessarily being in a position to understand medical jargon themselves. As McKinnon L.J. said in considering the appeal case of Mahon v Osborne:[16]

> 'Here again there is the misfortune that the jury were not directed that they must take the standard of care and diligence of a surgeon from those who

> could alone, from their expert knowledge, inform them of it ...'[17]

Aristotle in Politics[18] used the analogy of doctors being judged by their fellow physicians as a demonstration of the value of men being judged by their peers. Nonetheless, it has been suggested by the medical profession itself that this emphasis on the evidence of fellow professionals can lead to problems for the doctor, rather than being in his interests:

> 'In practice, where there has been an error of judgment it is seldom possible to find an expert prepared to go into the witness box and admit that he could have made the same error ...'[19]

Equally, it may be difficult for the lay person to find an expert who is prepared to say that one of his fellow professionals has made an error of judgment. The solution to this problem, in the view of the same author, rests in the hands of the medical profession itself, '... we should not ... be too reticent about admitting our fallibility'.[20]

The dependence on expert evidence of this type does differentiate the medical profession from the reasonable man standard. Whereas courts, in the role as representing the public, feel able to assess foreseeability and behaviour on the basis of what the reasonable man would have done, they have themselves expressed doubts and problems in assessing the technical evidence presented by, for example, doctors. Thus, the courts cannot depend, in these situations, on their own impression of a particular piece of behaviour, but are almost entirely dependent on the testimony of the fellow professionals of those who are alleged to have fallen below a certain standard. In medical cases, this is particularly difficult, since doctors (and therefore courts) recognise the concept of 'clinical judgment'. This concept leaves to the conscience of the doctor questions of morals (according to Lord Denning in the case of Hatcher v Black[21]), and allows the doctor a certain security in his individual decision-making. Thus, the decision of one doctor to lie to a patient about the risks of treatment was assessed by Lord Denning on the basis of the feelings of his fellow professionals as to this type of decision. As Lord Denning said, 'They [his fellow professionals] did not condemn him; nor should we'.[22]

Negligence - A Dagger at the Doctor's Back?

Courts are obliged, in view of the technicalities of medical evidence, to place a great deal of dependence on the integrity of medical practitioners. The concept of 'clinical judgment' places a barrier in front of the person attempting to sue a doctor for negligence. Yet this test is highly dependent on the approval of other doctors, all of whom may feel themselves to be the potential subjects of allegations of negligence and will, therefore, be loathe to criticise a fellow professional. Thus it would appear that the subjective decision of a doctor is likely to be supported, except in extreme circumstances, by his fellow professionals. The test of reasonable behaviour or due care and skill in these circumstances, would seem then to be based entirely on the subjective assessment of a number of doctors who may be inclined to support each other in the face of legal interference in decision-making.

Emphasis is also placed by the courts and Lord Denning in particular, on the risks involved in medical practice. Risk is not, of course, a concept foreign to the assessment of liability. As Lord MacMillan said in the case of Glasgow Corporation v Muir[23] 'Those who engage in operations inherently dangerous must take precautions which are not required of persons engaged in the ordinary routine of daily life'.[24] Lord Denninghas suggested[25] that:

> 'In the case of an accident on the road, there ought not to be any accident if everyone used proper care; and the same applies in the factory; but in a hospital, when a person who is ill goes in for treatment, there is always some risk, no matter what care is used. Every surgical operation involves risk. It would be wrong and, indeed, bad law to say that simply because a misadventure or mishap occurred, the hospital and the doctors are thereby liable'.

In the earlier case of Roe v Minister of Health[26] Lord Denning had further pointed out that:

> 'Medical science has conferred great benefits on mankind, but these benefits are attended by considerable risks ... We cannot take the benefits without taking the risks ... Doctors, like the rest of us, have to learn by experience; and experience often teaches in a hard way'.[27]

Negligence - A Dagger at the Doctor's Back?

The risks involved in medical practice are seen by Lord Denning as being fundamental in deciding on questions of liability. Rather than serving as a means of raising the standards of care required, the risk element would appear to be used as a means of limiting liability.

Professions have a responsibility to the community, and it is clear that they must be permitted to conduct their professional practice without undue interference from the law. Nonetheless, the law has the responsibility of upholding legal standards and has a further responsibility to the community to ensure that where professionals fall below the minimum standards set, then the person injured as a result of this shortfall can be compensated. The interests of the community not surprisingly, then, play a major part in the attitudes of the courts in their assessment of professional behaviour. Lord Denning frequently refers to these interests as a means of explaining his decisions in relation to the doctor, as well as using them as a basis for decision-making. In the case of Roe v Minister of Health he said:

> '... we should be doing a disservice to the community at large if we were to impose liability on hospitals and doctors for everything that happens to go wrong ... We must insist on due care for the patient at every point, but we must not condemn as negligent that which is only misadventure'.[28]

Again in the case of Hatcher v Black[29] he pointed out the risks of holding doctors liable in these circumstances and suggested that to do so would mean that:

> '... a doctor examining a patient, or a surgeon operating at a table, instead of getting on with his work, would be forever looking over his shoulder to see if someone was coming up with a dagger - for an action for negligence against a doctor is for him like unto a dagger'.

The interests of the community then are seen by Lord Denning not as being the facilitation of compensation in the event of damage as a result of medical intervention, but rather as being that medical practice should be interfered with as little as possible. This attitude has clearly influenced his decision-making and was recently restated in the case of Whitehouse v Jordan.[30] In this case, he explained his attitude further by referring to a fear that a change might lead to the same situation as that which exists in the United States where, he claimed:

> '... Medical malpractice cases there are very worrying, especially as they are tried by juries who have sympathy for the patient and none for the doctor, who is insured. The damages are collosal ... Experienced practitioners are known to have refused to treat patients for fear of being accused of negligence ... In the interests of all, we must avoid such consequences in England. We must say, and say firmly, that in a professional man, an error of judgment is not negligent'.[31]

In this case his argument was supported by Lawton L.J., although Donaldson L.J. dissenting, stated that if a doctor failed to exercise the skill which he claimed to have, then he was in breach of his duty of care.

It is interesting, and perhaps indicative of an overly cautious attitude, that the situation in the United States should be held up as an example of what might happen in this country. There are many contributory factors in the American situation which do not, and will not, apply here, for example the fact that medicine is conducted on a private basis - doctors are thus required to carry heavy insurance policies, and the practice of the legal profession in charging contingency fees in personal injury cases. It also contains an implication that courts in the United States decide, not on the basis of legal rules, but on the basis of sympathy. Dr. Leahy Taylor[32] has suggested that even in this country 'The sympathy of the court is a far from negligible factor which the defendant's [doctor's] advisers must weigh with care before deciding to proceed'.[33] It would seem that it is equally the case that the pursuer's advisers must weigh such sympathies with care.

The fear that 'defensive medicine' may become the norm in this country is highly influential in Lord Denning's judgments. Yet one American lawyer has suggested that:

> 'For those who agree with the standard of care, it is seen as a definition of appropriate care. For those who see the standard as unrealistically high, conformity constitutes defensive medicine.

> In short, arguments about defensive medicine inevitably reflect disagreements about the practice of medicine itself'.[34]

As he further suggested, 'The inhibition of ... litigation in many countries may reflect too strong a bias in favour of the authority of the medical profession'.[35] It may indeed be that the interests of the community would be served by demanding higher standards from the medical profession than are required at present.

Quite apart from these additional factors which may influence courts in medical negligence cases, there is the fundamental difficulty of assessing what is 'reasonable' behaviour in the circumstances. In many ways, this is clearly linked to the concept of 'clinical judgment', but it may also go beyond that notion. It has become clear that the standards set may vary according to the subjective approach of the judiciary. Again, Lord Denning has been influential in determining what amounts to the behaviour of the 'reasonable doctor'. In Roe v Mininster of Health[36] and Hatcher v Black,[37] and in many other cases, Lord Denning has made it clear that in the case of the doctor 'You must not, therefore, find him negligent simply because something happens to go wrong ... or if in a matter of opinion he makes an error of judgment'.[38]

In what circumstances, then, can a doctor's behaviour be seen as negligent? In the case of Hucks v Cole and Another[39] Lord Denning said: 'A doctor was not to be held negligent simply because something went wrong. He was not liable for mischance or misadventure, or for an error of judgment ...' Thus we cannot expect a doctor to be held negligent for, e.g. failing to keep up to date with literature in his specialism (Crawford v Board of Governors, Charing Cross Hospital[40]); nor for anything less than a gross error of judgment (Whitehouse v Jordan and Another[41]); and indeed he may be excused, or at least not blamed, where his behaviour is seen as the result of his being overtired (McCormack v Redpath Brown and Co.[42]). Lord Denning did, however, in a dissenting judgment in the case of Chapman v Rix[43] suggest that a doctor would be negligent if he failed to make information available to another doctor regarding the former's treatment of the latter's patient.

The doctor is, according to Lord Denning, '... only liable when he falls below the standard of a reasonably competent practitioner in his field ...'[44] On the face of it this would seem to be the test in general application. However, Lord Denning immediately qualified this statement by stating that the extent to which he fell below this standard was relevant. He must fall below it '... so much so that his conduct might be deserving of censure or inexcusable'.[45] The basic tests which are applied for negligence require only that there was a duty of care, that the duty of care was breached, and that the injury was a result of the breach of that duty. There is no question apparently of the behaviour being 'deserving of censure or inexcusable', although this may also be the case. This adds yet again to the standard of proof which a litigant must attain before successfully suing a doctor. It adds to it primarily because, according to Lord Denning, those who may censure a doctor's behaviour will inevitably be other doctors. Thus, the pursuer must find an expert prepared to identify negligence, and he cannot found his claim on the basis of anything short of a major error in judgment nor on the basis of the fact that the doctor lied about the risks involved in treatment and thereby vitiated informed consent.[46]

It would appear then, that on the basis of Lord Denning's judgments, it will be extraordinarily difficult to establish that a doctor was negligent, and yet surprisingly, the establishing of at least some of the basic criteria for negligence is remarkably simple. The easiest of all is the establishment of the duty of care. As Martin says,[47] 'His [the medical practitioner's] duty is independent of contract and rests upon the fact of a medical practitioner undertaking the care and treatment of a patient ...'[48] Equally, the fact that damage resulted, apparently or obviously, as a result of medical treatment will raise at least a prima facie assumption on the part of the person injured that this was the result of a breach of the duty of care. In certain medical situations, the doctrine of res ipsa loquitur is said to apply, e.g. where there is a failure to remove swabs, etc. from a patient after surgery. Even this, however, is not always the case. In Mahon v Osborne[49] it was held that failure to remove swabs in complicated surgery did not amount to negligence, despite the dissenting judgment of Goddard L.J. who said that, although emphasis must be placed on the evidence of other professionals, nonetheless, 'as it is the task of the surgeon to put swabs in, so it is his task to take them out ...'[50]

The apparent difficulties of establishing medical negligence may arise, because as Dr. Leahy Taylor has pointed out, 'Negligence is a legal, not a medical, concept ...'[51] He further asserted that 'It is no disrespect to Her Majesty's judges to consider that their condemnation should disturb a doctor less than condemnation by his professional brethren'.[52] It might seem, however, that the cases referred to above, lead to the conclusion that the two are likely to be one and the same thing. Lord Denning suggests in The Discipline of Law[53] that the doctor should be held to be negligent only where his professional colleagues would say to him, 'He really did make a mistake there. He ought not to have done it'.[54] This approach of Lord Denning's has helped to shape the attitudes of courts throughout the country to allegations of medical negligence. It may seem that it is small wonder, in the face of these additional criteria, that the success rate in medical negligence cases is so low.

It would, of course, be unreasonable to expect the doctor to display in all circumstances an unusually high standard of skill. Nonetheless, there is always a risk that where professions are given the major responsibility in the setting of their own standards for legal purposes, then the standards may relate rather to the lowest common denominator than to the minimum reasonable standard of care which a patient may expect. In his expressed desire to safeguard the interests of the community, this calculation seems to have been omitted by Lord Denning. It is, no doubt, uncontentious that the community has a legitimate interest in ensuring that the confidence of the medical profession is not destroyed. Equally, it is uncontentious that an element of 'clinical judgment' is essential to the practice of medicine.

However, it is in the interpretation of the weight and credibility to be given to these elements that Lord Denning, perhaps more than other judge , may seem to place the interests of the medical profession in a position superior to that of the legitimate demands of the community that the professions be subject to public scrutiny and accountability. For public accountability to be any more than simply lip service to these demands, it must incorporate justice being seen to be done. This must surely require that special difficulties are not placed in the way of those who wish to challenge professionals' practice.

The motivation and reasons for attributing responsibility are the subject of an illuminating article by Sally Lloyd-Bostock[55] who notes the use made by courts of apparently simple concepts such as 'reasonableness' and 'common sense'.

Such concepts are regularly used by courts in decision-making and are frequently referred to by Lord Denning in his decisions. Nonetheless, it is clear that these notions merely disguise the subjective element in decision-making. In line with the legal doctrine of precedent, however, such appeals to common sense and reasonableness become the basis of subsequent decisions as if they reflected factual assessments. Subsequent decision-makers apparently accept, without question, that the interests of the public are indeed reinforced by protecting the medical profession in courts of law. Equally, they reflect Lord Denning's view that a necessary concomitant of an increase in successful litigation against the medical profession would be the practice of defensive medicine - with the assumption inherent in this that defensive medicine is necessarily bad.

It is, however, insufficient simply to identify an apparent bias towards the medical profession. The existence of such a bias does not help us to discover the reasons lying behind the attitude of the courts and Lord Denning in particular. Some of the reasons have already been considered and can be seen as at best cautious and at worst unpersuasive. It is again in the judgments of Lord Denning that the reason for this apparent bias becomes clear. It is expressed most clearly in the case of <u>Hucks</u> v <u>Cole and Another</u> where Lord Denning said:

> 'A charge of professional negligence against a medical man was serious. It stood on a different footing to a charge of negligence against a driver of a motor car. The consequences were far more serious. It affected his professional status and reputation'.[56]

This is merely a succinct expression of the prevailing attitude which can be readily identified in his other judgments - because the medical man has a status and position to preserve we are invited to maintain that status unless absolutely forced, in extreme circumstances, to criticise or condemn.

This, however, merely expresses a desire on the part of the courts not to hold professionals negligent simply because they make a mistake. Few would disagree with this attitude in general terms. However, it is clear that the attitude of Lord Denning to the medical profession is such that, in his own words, in medical negligence cases, 'The burden of proof was correspondingly greater'.[57] In reaching this conclusion, Lord Denning uses his own subjective opinions relating to the interests of the public, the nature of medical practice and the expectations of the doctor as to his status.[58] Such considerations are not apparently of any necessary value in considering allegations of negligence against the rest of the community.

Equally, such attitudes are untested and reflect the values of a particular judge, whose influence is substantial. It is equally possible to argue that the attitude of Lord Denning and his fellow judges is potentially problematic for the medical profession and for the community. Finding a doctor to have been negligent may do as much for the doctor/patient relationship as would an apparent unwillingness on the part of a court to criticise the medical profession. It is precisely because doctors hold themselves out as having special skills in diagnosis and treatment that the public consult them. If they are not to be held responsible for their decision-making, for explaining to the patient the risks involved in elective treatment, nor for deploying inappropriate techniques, then the public's attitude of restraint in litigation in these cases is likely to undergo change. Already, the Defence Unions are reporting an increase in cases referred to them.[59] The spectre of defensive medicine may be with us in body sooner rather than later if the attitude of the courts is not modified.

SHEILA MCLEAN

NOTES

(1) Medical Defence Union 1885; Medical Protection Society 1892; Medical and Dental Defence Union 1902.
(2) Barnett, 'History, Development and Current Position in the UK', The Influence of Litigation on Medical Practice, (Wood, ed.), Academic Press, London, 1977.
(3) Royal Commission on Civil Liability and Compensation for Personal Injury (Pearson Commission), Cmnd 7054, 1978.
(4) [1943] AC 448.
(5) Ibid, p.457.

(6) Woods v Duncan [1946] AC 401, p.419.
(7) Grant v Australian Knitting Mills Ltd. [1936] AC 85, 101.
(8) Glasgow Corporation v Muir, supra, p.457.
(9) Lord Denning, The Discipline of Law, Butterworths, 1979, Part 6, Ch. 2.
(10) [1957 2 All E.R. 118.
(11) [1954] 2 QB 66.
(12) Bolam v Friern H.M.C., supra, 128.
(13) [1980] 1 All E.R. 650.
(14) Cmnd 7054.
(15) 'The Freedom of the Individual Today', 45 Medico-Legal Journal, 49, p.59.
(16) [1939] 1 All E.R. 535.
(17) Ibid, p.557.
(18) Aristotle, Politics, Book III, Ch. XI, 1282a.
(19) Leahy Taylor, 'Major Current Problems Seen by the Doctor', in The Influence of Litigation on Medical Practice, p.76.
(20) Ibid.
(21) The Times, 29/30 June; 1/2 July 1954.
(22) Ibid.
(23) [1943] AC 448.
(24) Ibid, p.456.
(25) Hatcher v Black, supra.
(26) [1954] 2 QB 66.
(27) Ibid, p.83.
(28) Ibid, p.86-7.
(29) The Times, 29/30 June; 1/2 July 1954.
(30) [1980] 1 All E.R. 650.
(31) Ibid, p.658.
(32) Leahy Taylor, The Doctor and Negligence, Pitman Medical, 1971.
(33) Ibid, p.1.
(34) E.J. Hart, 'Effect of Litigation on the Practice of Medicine in the USA: A Lawyer's View' in The Influence of Litigation on Medical Practice, p.52.
(35) Ibid, p.50.
(36) [1954] 2 QB 66.
(37) The Times, 29/30 June; 1/2 July 1954.
(38) Ibid.
(39) The Times, 9 May 1968.
(40) [1953] TLR 1.
(41) [1980] 1 All E.R. 650.
(42) (1961) The Lancet 736.
(43) (1959) British Medical Journal, 2, 1190.
(44) Hucks v Cole and Another, 'The Times', 9 May 1968.

(45) Ibid.
(46) Hatcher v Black, 'The Times', 29/30 June; 1/2 July 1954.
(47) C.R.A. Martin, Law Relating to Medical Practice, (2nd ed.) Pitman Medical, 1979.
(48) Ibid, p.361.
(49) [1939] 1 All E.R. 535.
(50) Ibid, p.559.
(51) Leahy Taylor, The Doctor and Negligence, supra, p.1.
(52) Ibid.
(53) Lord Denning, The Discipline of Law, Butterworths, 1979.
(54) Ibid, p.237.
(55) Lloyd-Bostock, 'The Ordinary Man and the Psychology of Attributing Causes and Responsibility', 42 MLR, 1979, 143.
(56) The Times, 9 May 1968.
(57) Ibid.
(58) For discussion, see The Influence of Litigation on Medical Practice, particularly, pp.1-6.
(58) Similar sorts of teleological thinking has been applied by Lord Denning in his approach to the broader question of the problems of hospitals facing damages claims. In his most recent work he appears to be reverting to the principles enunciated in Hillyer v St. Bartholomew's Hospital (1909) 2 KB 820 which he had helped to overturn in Gold v Essex County Council (1951) 2 KB 820 (as counsel) and Cassidy v Minister of Health (1951) 2 KB 343 (in the Court of Appeal). This seems to be based on a desire to protect the National Health Service funds which come from the 'pockets of the tax-payers and have to be carefully husbanded' - Lim Poh Choo v Camden and Islington Health Authority [1979] 1 All E.R. 332, 341 - against 'colossal' damages suits - Whitehouse v Jordan [1980] 1 All E.R. 650, 658.

Resisting the Unprivileged

The goal of rules of procedure and evidence and the prerogative writs is the protection of the freedom of the individual. Although in arguments in relation to procedure, evidence of the jurisdiction of these writs often appears to be technical and esoteric we must not lose sight of their significance. If, for instance, the requirement of proof in criminal trials was reduced from the test of 'beyond reasonable doubt' to that applied in civil law 'on the balance of probabilities' it would be a much easier task to obtain convictions. The debate on the provisions of the Criminal Justice (Scotland) Bill provides a good example of the possible impact of 'minor' technical changes in the law.[1]

Given the very real threat to liberty which such minor adjustments to the law represent we should be aware of the dangers of dilution of evidential and procedural requirements. The judiciary have an important role to play as protectors of cherished freedoms from erosion in practice. From the days of his Hamlyn Lectures on Freedom under the Law up until the present day with the issue of jury vetting,[2] Lord Denning has enjoyed a reputation as protector of the weak from abuse by the mighty. Writing in 1949 at the time of the great expansion of universal state welfare provision, Lord Denning noted the problems which the welfare state bureaucracy brought and the indirect threat to freedom posed in this area:[3]

> 'Properly exercised, the new powers of the Executive lead to the Welfare State; but abused they lead to the totalitarian state'.

We are concerned here to examine the experience of Lord Denning in two areas of poverty law concerning social security and homelessness. How zealously has the Master of the Rolls sought to lend his weight to the exposed and weak position of the sections of society whom one can justifiably dub the unprivileged?

CLAIMANTS

> "So fine is the distinction (between an error which entails absence of jurisdiction and an error made within the jurisdiction) that in truth the High Court has a choice before it whether to interfere with an inferior court on a point of law. If it chooses to interfere, it can formulate its decision in the words: 'The court below had not jurisdiction to decide this point wrongly as it did'. If it does not choose to interfere, it can say: 'The court had jurisdiction to decide it wrongly and did so'".[4]

For centuries, the prerogative orders have been available to check the abuse or misuse of executive power. Although the writs of certiorari, prohibition, mandamus and declaration are, as Lord Denning pointed out in his Hamlyn Lectures, no more suited to the winning of freedom in this new age than were the pick and shovel for the winning of coal,[5] they remain important, if outmoded, remedies whereby aggrieved persons can challenge the discretionary decisions of Ministers, public authorities and administrative tribunals. The most important of these remedies is certiorari, which very broadly lies to quash decisions of inferior courts taken in error of law or in excess of their jurisdiction. Yet, as Lord Denning clearly acknowledges in the passage from his judgment in the Pearlman case quoted above, the court's decision to control or not to control the exercise of administrative discretion is one based on their own views as to whether judicial intervention is or is not appropriate in individual cases. It follows, then, that when the Court of Appeal refused to review the way in which Supplementary Benefits Appeal Tribunals discharged their statutory duties under the Supplementary Benefits Act 1966, it did so as a matter of policy and not legal principle.

The first cases to reach the Court of Appeal under the 1966 Act were R. v Preston Supplementary Benefits Appeal Tribunal, ex parte Moore and R. v Sheffield Supplementary Benefits Appeal Tribunal, ex parte Shine.[6] One decision was issued by the Court of Appeal for both cases. In the first case, Moore, a student with a wife and two children, claimed that the tribunal had erred in law in calculating his entitlement to supplementary benefits on the basis of the notional resources which he would have had, had he eked his grant out over a 52 week period, and should have based its calculations on his actual resources. Affirming the Divisional Court's refusal to grant certiorari, the Court of Appeal held that the tribunal's decision to calculate Moore's entitlement to benefit on the basis of his notional resources was not erroneous in point of law. In the second case, Shine argued that the tribunal had erred in law in holding that he was not a householder in terms of the 1966 Act in spite of the fact that he paid one quarter of the rent and contributed to the cost of electricity which prima facie brought him within paragraph 9(b) and Schedule 2 of the Act, whereby a person living alone or householder who contributes or is directly responsible for household necessities or rent is entitled to a higher rate of benefit. In the Court of Appeal, Lord Denning said, 'If this were to be regarded as a strict point of law, there is much to be said for Mr Shine's contention'.[7] However, the Master of the Rolls again refused to grant an order of certiorari, as the error of the tribunal was not, in his view, one that merited interference by the courts. Indeed, Lord Denning went on to say that, 'the High Court should not interfere with the tribunal's decision, even though it may be said to be erroneous in point of law'.[8] Which plainly begs the question: in what circumstances would the Court of Appeal be willing to scrutinise the decisions of Supplementary Benefits Appeal Tribunals?

Lord Denning outlined the circumstances in which the courts should interfere as:

(1) where the decision of a tribunal is unreasonable;
(2) where a tribunal has exceeded its jurisdiction; and
(3) where a tribunal has acted contrary to natural justice.

However, Lord Denning went on to place a number of restrictions on these general guidelines: '... The [courts] should leave the tribunals to interpret the Act in a broad reasonable way'.[9] He explained this approach's rationale at some length:

> '... It is plain that Parliament intended that the Supplementary Benefits Act 1966 should be administered with as little technicality as

> possible. It should not become the happy hunting ground for lawyers. The courts should hesitate long before interfering by certiorari with the decisions of the appeal tribunals ...
> ... The courts should not enter into a meticulous discussion of this or that word in the Act. They should leave the tribunals to interpret the Act in a broad reasonable way, according to the spirit and not to the letter'.
> ... The court should only interfere when the decision of the tribunal is unreasonable in the sense that no tribunal acquainted with the ordinary use of language could reasonably reach that decision ...'[10]

Quite simply, the courts should not interfere with the exercise of discretion by SBATs unless, in Lord Denning's view, they have acted with an almost superhuman disregard for the rules of natural justice, and even then that may not for the Master of the Rolls be sufficient.

The implications of a restrictive policy

The decision not to interfere with the decisions of SBATs was clearly based on policy considerations. There are, to be frank, a number of areas of law which the judiciary regard as unfitted or unsuitable for the courts,[11] and they are not above attempting to discourage litigants from bringing appeals. Plainly, for Lord Denning, social security is one such area. For Lord Denning fears that if the courts choose to control the exercise of discretion by SBATs, '(they) would become engulfed with streams of cases ...'[12]

This approach has been cited with approval on a number of occasions,[13] and the general reluctance of the Master of the Rolls to examine the work of SBATs has provided the framework within which his colleagues have operated review in this area, although this has allowed decisions to be quashed where 'special facts' were involved.[14] The contrast in treatment between those claiming means tested benefits as opposed to insurance based social insurance[15] has helped to contribute to the reform of the statutory position of the former group. New procedures have been introduced to enable an effective appeal mechanism to be established.[16] Whilst this solution may well be regarded as a far more satisfactory solution in the longterm, the judiciary can claim little credit for seeing that for this section of society '[n]othing must be left undone'.[17]

HOMELESS

Strangely absent also from Lord Denning's review of his own work of 'suiting ... principles of law ... to the social necessities and social opinion of the twentieth century'[18] is any discussion of the legal problems produced by increasing homelessness in the post-War era. Yet in a number of crucial decisions Lord Denning helped to limit the effectiveness of the 'family squatting' movement during the last decade, apparently ignoring his own precepts and hinder action by and for the homeless.

Legalism and homelessness

The reaction in the Court of Appeal, and of Lord Denning in particular, must be seen in the light of the goals and strategy of the London based 'family squatting' movement in the late sixties. Family squatters used the forensic medium for highlighting the problems of homelessness.[19] Squatters did not seem to expect to 'win' court cases since their claims to temporary accommodation were against local authorities rather than the property owners. However, they could embarrass local authorities whose policies consisted of closing and smashing up houses which would be affected in the distant future by redevelopment. Initially, there was even an element of success in using the Forcible Entry Act of 1381 to retain possession after squatting. The Act forbade anyone to obtain possession without a court order. In addition, they were able to show that they were not in 'forcible detention' of the premises which was against another old Forcible Entry Act, this time of 1429. This 'legal evading tactic' finally led the councils to go to court against named people. This allowed the squatters to swap around thus avoiding effective carrying out of court orders. The bailiffs would arrive and find a different set of people in the premises from those on their eviction orders from the courts.

Even more successfully, strongarm methods by some bailiffs on behalf of the local authority resulted in a summons from the police under the Forcible Entry Act for the arrest of two bailiffs involved in one attempted eviction in April 1969. Later in the year, the use of court orders against unnamed defendants was ruled illegal and for a brief interlude the squatting movement was 'cock-a-hoop':

> 'We had completely and absolutely twisted up and defeated the council legally'.[20]

The success was shortlived. New rules were approved allowing a swift eviction procedure, available even where it was not possible to find out the names of the squatters involved. One delay tactic was finished.

This defeat led to a move to establish rights for squatters as opposed to obstruct the owner in evicting as long as possible which took place in 1970. Here an attempt was made to defend the position of the squatters from the property owners - the local authority - by putting forward a defence of failure to carry out their duties to provide temporary accommodation:

> 'For persons who are in urgent need thereof ... being need arising in circumstances which could not reasonably have been foreseen or in such other circumstances as the authority may in any particular case determine'.[21]

The Court of Appeal dismissed this[22] suggesting that if the homeless were dissatisfied with the local authority their proper course of action was to complain to the relevant Minister about this alleged breach of statutory obligation.

Alternatively, the squatters put forward the defence of necessity. Echoing St Thomas Aquinas, they claimed they entered the houses as the only course to keep body and soul together. Although there was precedent for such action, this suddenly became a very narrow path for exceptional times only.

Lord Denning admitted that indeed the defence of necessity was part of the common law:

> 'There is authority for saying that in case of great and imminent danger, in order to preserve life, the law will permit of an encroachment on private property ...'[23]

Resisting the Unprivileged

The Master of the Rolls was concerned that this doctrine should be 'carefully circumscribed ... else necessity would open the door to many an excuse'[24] like starving men using this to justify stealing food. The notion of extending the defence to the catastrophe of being without a home, conjured up for Lord Denning visions of a future without law and order.

> 'If homelessness were once admitted as a defence to trespass, no one's house could be safe. Necessity would open a door which no man could shut. It would not only be those in extreme need who would enter. There would be others who would imagine they were in need, or would invent a need, so as to gain entry. Each man would say his need was greater than the next man's. The plea would be an excuse for all sorts of wrong-doing. So the courts must, for the sake of law and order, take a firm stand. They must refuse to admit the plea of necessity to the hungry and the homeless'.[25]

Abandoning legalism

In view of his own anti-legalistic reputation perhaps it might be seen as surprising that the attempts by squatters to test the new 1970 County and High Court rules were looked on unfavourably by Lord Denning in McPhail[26] even where the squatters were only looking for an extension to enable them to obtain fresh accommodation. Lord Denning was not impressed:

> 'What is a squatter? He is one who, without any colour of right, enters on an unoccupied house or land, intending to stay there as long as he can. He may seek to justify or excuse his conduct. He may say that he was homeless and that this house or land was standing empty, doing nothing. But this plea is of no avail in law ... Now I would say this at once about squatters. The owner is not obliged to go to the courts to obtain possession. He is entitled, if he so desires, to take the remedy into his own hands. He can go in himself and turn them out without the aid of the courts of law ... some diffi-

culties were discovered recently ... if squatters did not give their names, or if one squatter followed another in quick succession, no order for possession could be made ... the position was soon put right by new rules of court ... A summons can be issued for possession against squatters even though they cannot be identified by name and even though, as one squatter goes, another comes in ... It is an authority under which anyone who is squatting on the premises can be turned out at once. There is no provision for giving any time'.[27]

The need for strict adherence to even the 1970 rules was rejected by the Court of Appeal in the interests of the smooth running of Warwick University in a 1975 sit-in on the University's price rises affecting students. Lord Denning explained the underlying principle behind this approach:

> 'The occupation of the Senate House by this minority of students is very serious for all the students. The examination programme is going to begin. The papers have still to be printed. The whole of the examination programme will be thrown into confusion by this action if it is allowed to continue. These students, who number from sixty to two hundred, are disrupting the work of the University'.[28]

The inactivity of the University authorities in obtaining only five names out of an estimated occupation of some two hundred was easily accepted by Lord Denning and his colleague, Sir John Pennycuick, 'It is not necessary in these cases to get the names of everyone. The names of the ringleaders are enough'.[29]

Variable principles

This, then, is a clear weighing of competing social goals by Lord Denning using no obviously discernible criteria other than distaste for those involved in the various occupations. To head off homeless squatters, Lord Denning advocated a version of strict legalism with action against the local authority urged, whilst where students were protesting about the running of a university, what was advised was simply to ignore the procedural rules which had been laid down in favour of effective action. The notion of Lord Denning 'bending and shaping' the common law and statutes to some vaguely publicly desirable end, Lord Denning as an everyman in ermine, seems to be flawed in this specific area.

REPACKAGING THE RIGHTS OF THE HOMELESS

> 'The homeless must ... trust that their distress will be relieved by the charitable and the good'.[30]

With this kind of pressure on them, authorities espousing a strongly individualist view of social problems proceeded to operate the 1948 Act in a variety of idiosyncratic ways.[31]

The legislature finally responded to the inadequacies of the provisions for the homeless in the National Assistance Act 1948 with the privately sponsored Housing (Homeless Persons) Act 1977. In its passage through the House of Commons, this measure attracted a number of restrictions and tests designed to protect local authorities against claims from 'scroungers and scrimshrankers' and 'queue-jumpers'.[32] Effective decision-making on the treatment of the homeless was left in the hands of local authorities and the Act contained no appeals mechanisms, although a Code of Guidance does put flesh on the bare bones of the statute. Section 12 of the Act directed that authorities 'shall have regard' to the guidance issued by the Secretary of State. This has taken the form of a Code of Guidance issued in November 1978.

In these circumstances, the homeless faced with unwilling and in some instances obstructive councils, determined to wreck the legislation, have had to seek remedies in the courts. These have included actions for injunctions, damages flowing from failure to carry out statutory obligations, as well as certiorari. The approach of the courts has been less than encouraging to litigating homeless persons, but they have tended to restrict themselves to the issues in point rather than establish wide principles for subsequent cases.[33] In the major case in which he has been involved, Lord Denning has been rather bolder.

Resisting the Unprivileged

In De Falco and Silverstri v Crawley Borough Council[34] Lord Denning rejected the claim of two Italian families for assistance under the Housing (Homeless Persons) Act. The normal obligation on councils to secure accommodation for any homeless person, who is both in priority need and has a local connection with the area in question, can be avoided if the council consider that the applicant has become homeless intentionally. In the De Falco case, there was no problem with either establishing homelessness, priority need, nor local connection. Both families were turned out of their accommodation by relatives, they had children living with them and they had employment in the area. However, the council contended that before moving to Britain the families had failed to arrange permanent accommodation. The approach of Lord Denning in this case was curious. He talked with apparent regret of the impact of EEC regulations on the mobility of labour and suggested that the case was 'another instance of the advancing tide from the Common Market ... (which) gave nationals of Community countries the same rights as indigenous nationals ...'[35]

Lord Denning talked of councils being 'besieged' by the homeless and of the seriousness of this for an 'overcrowded borough'. Here, again, we find the use by Lord Denning of a version of the purposive approach to legislation. The test applied is the impact one. Having discovered that nationals from the EEC appear to have the same rights as 'trueborn Englishmen', Lord Denning chooses to throw over the advice offered in the Department of Environment Code of Guidance as to the test to be applied in determining whether or not an individual is intentionally homeless. The Code suggests that the immediate cause of the homelessness is the relevant issue rather than previous events. The Code specifically states:

> 'It would be inappropriate to treat as intentionally homeless a person who gave up accommodation to move in with relatives and friends who then decided after a few months they could no longer continue to accommodate him'.[36]

This case is on all fours with the Code example with the reason for the De Falco's losing their accommodation being the pregnancy of the host relative's wife. Lord Denning avoided this problem by denying any value to the Code. It was not a binding statute and the Council could depart from it when they thought fit and Lord Denning specified the sorts of times when this was appropriate:

> 'That paragraph (2.18) might be all very well for people coming from Yorkshire, but it should not be applied to people coming from a Common Market country'.[37]

What the basis of this distinction is does not appear on the face of Lord Denning's judgment. Although, Bridge L.J. concurred with the Master of the Rolls, he appeared to be less than enthusiastic in reaching this decision and regarded the arguments of De Falco and Silverstri as having 'considerable force'.

In his eagerness to produce a particular result, Lord Denning appears to have been prepared to override the Code of Guidance on intuitive grounds in order to stem what he called 'an advancing tide' and this line has set the tone for subsequent treatment of the Code and the arguments of obstructive councils.[38]

CONCLUSION

It would appear from our study of the law relating to social security and homelessness that Lord Denning's reputation as a protector of the rights of the weak against the powerful in relation to the homeless and social security claimants, like that in relation to employees' rights[39] is not entirely merited. In these areas of the law, Lord Denning has clearly adopted inconsistent policy decisions. In social security it would seem that he has a fear that if judicial review was granted, the courts would become swamped by claimants and he is unwilling to countenance that. In De Falco, too, it would seem that Lord Denning's decision is based on a fear of Britain becoming swamped by immigrants from the EEC countries. And in relation to squatting rights he seems to have diluted procedural requirements to aid speedy repossession and private violence in the form of forcible ejection. All in all, then, it would seem to us that Lord Denning has been less than vigilant in defence of the limited rights of the unprivileged, and this selectivity of social goals highlights the problems with his 'justice' approach to legal problems.

PETER ROBSON
PAUL WATCHMAN

NOTES

(1) Criminal Justice (Scotland) Bill, SCCL Pamphlet, 1980.
(2) R. v Sheffield Crown Court, ex parte Brownlow, The Times, 4 March 1980.
(3) Freedom under the Law, Stevens, London, 1949, p.126.
(4) Pearlman v Governors of Harrow School [1978] 3 WLR 736, quoted in The Discipline of Law (London, 1979) at p.76 (our emphasis).
(5) Freedom under the Law, ibid.
(6) [1975] 1 WLR 624.
(7) Ibid, p.631.
(8) Ibid.
(9) Ibid.
(10) Ibid.
(11) See, for example, the views of Lord Chief Justice Widgery in Guppys (Bridport) Ltd. v Sandoe (1975) 30 P & CR 69 on rent assessment.
(12) Ex parte Moore, op cit, p.631.
(13) R. v West London Supplementary Benefit Appeal Tribunal, ex parte Clarke [1975] 1 WLR 1396; [1975] 3 All ER 513; R. v Barnsley Supplementary Benefits Appeal Tribunal, ex parte Atkinson [1976] 1 WLR 1052; [1976] 2 All ER 686 - although the Court of Appeal granted certiorari on appeal they still adhered to the general line of non-interference - R. v Barnsley Supplementary Benefits Appeal Tribunal, ex parte Atkinson [1977] 1 WLR 917; R. v Manchester Supplementary Benefits Appeal Tribunal, ex parte Riley [1979] 1 WLR 426.
(14) R. v West London Supplementary Benefits Appeal Tribunal, ex parte Taylor [1975] 1 WLR 1048; [1975] 2 All ER 790; R. v Peterborough Supplementary Benefits Appeal Tribunal, ex parte Supplementary Benefits Commission [1978] 3 All ER 887; R. v West London Supplementary Benefits Appeal Tribunal, ex parte Wyatt [1978] 1 WLR 240.
(15) A. Ogus & E. Barendt, The Law of Social Security, Butterworths, London, 1978, pp.631-5.
(16) S.1 1977/1735 permitting appeals on points of law to the High Court. The Social Security Act 1979, s.6 provides that the Secretary of State may institute an appeal from SBATs to the National Insurance Commissioner.
(17) The Discipline of Law, supra, p.316.
(18) Lord Denning, The Discipline of Law, Butterworths, London, 1979.
(19) Ron Bailey, The Squatters, Penguin, London, 1974. Bailey does mention that there initially are other

communard strands in the squatting movement, and the forensic strategy embraced only those with these shorter term rehousing goals.

(20) Ibid, p.68.
(21) National Assistance Act 1948, Part III, s.21(1)(b).
(22) Southwark London Borough Council v Williams [1971] Ch. 734.
(23) Ibid, p.743.
(24) Ibid.
(25) Ibid, p.744.
(26) McPhail v Persons Unknown [1973] Ch. 447.
(27) Ibid, p.456.
(28) Warwick University v de Graaf [1975] 1 WLR 1126.
(29) Ibid, p.1140.
(30) Southwark London Borough Council v Williams, p.744.
(31) Ron Bailey, The Homeless and the Empty Houses, Penguin, London, 1977.
(32) H.C. Deb. Vol. 926, col. 905 and col. 914.
(33) R. v Beverley Borough Council, ex parte MacPhee (1978) 122 SJ 760; The Times, 27 October 1978; MacKenzie v West Lothian District Council, 1979 Scolag Bulletin 123.
(34) The Times, 13 December 1979; [1980] 1 All ER 913.
(35) The Times, 13 December 1979.
(36) Code of Guidance, HMSO, November 1978, para. 2.18.
(37) [1980] 1 All ER 913, p.921.
(38) Miller v Wandsworth London Borough Council, The Times, 19 March 1980 where Lord Denning's views on the Code of Guidance are cited with approval; Youngs v Thanet District Council, The Times, 21 February 1980 where there was a change of circumstances allowing a fresh application which was not precluded by a previous 'intentionally homeless' finding, on the grounds of willful non-payment of rent. His 'second' homelessness a year later was caused by an eviction order from his 'out of season' lodgings.
(39) R. Stevens, Law and Politics: The House of Lords as a Judicial Body 1800-1976, Weidenfeld & Nicolson, 1979.

The Labours of Lord Denning

INTRODUCTION

Lord Denning, in The Discipline of Law,[1] has left none of us in any doubt about his overriding philosophy in relation to the interpretation of statutes. In The Discipline of Law[2] he quotes with some satisfaction his views about statutory interpretation as they were expressed in Nothman v Barnet London Borough Council.[3] In that case, Lord Denning declared that, '[i]n all cases (author's emphasis) now in the interpretation of statutes we adopt such construction as will 'promote the general legislative purpose' underlying the provision'.[4] In light of this clear and unambiguous statement by Lord Denning concerning the goals he sets himself in interpreting any statute which comes before his court, this essay seeks to examine Lord Denning's actual performance in one particular area of labour law. The area which has been chosen concerns the law as it applies to trade unions who are involved in trade disputes. This is a critical and controversial area of the law where legislative activity has been both regular and extensive. Since the present law does owe its origins entirely to statute, it would seem that this is an aposite area to examine in order to discover whether Lord Denning's treatment of cases in this field accords with the goals he has set himself. Such a study is particularly vital when one considers the importance which Lord Denning, himself, attaches to the issue of trade union immunity in both his judgments and extra-judicial statements. It is the purpose of this essay, therefore, to discover if Lord Denning's rhetoric conforms to his reality.

TRADE UNION IMMUNITY - ITS RATIONALE

The strength of trade unions lies in their ability to act as a countervailing power against the power which the owners of capital clearly possess. The organisation of labour enables those who produce the goods to bargain on equal terms with those who own the means of production. As the late Sir Otto Kahn-Freund has said, '[t]he formation of unions, that is the organisation of labour, is the counterpart of the accumulation of capital'.[5] It is the fact that trade unions can exercise power which makes the process of collective bargaining operate effectively. To quote Sir Otto Kahn-Freund again, '[t]he conflicting expectations of labour and of management can be temporarily reconciled through collective bargaining: power stands against power'.[6]

The crucial issue, of course, concerns the source of the power which trade unions possess. The power of the trade unions stems from their ability to take collective action in the form of strikes, blacking work, etc., which will cause the employer loss. The calling of such action, however, in the absence of statutory intervention, would involve the trade union in a clear breach of the common law. For the essence of a strike is the withdrawal of labour on the part of the employees involved. Such a withdrawal inevitably means that those who have failed to provide their labour will be in breach of their contracts of employment by their refusal to work. The illegality does not stop here, however. The trade union is equally acting unlawfully by inducing this illegal conduct on the part of the strikers. In other words, although the exercise of trade union power will cause the employer loss, the unlawful source of this power provides relief to him since he can take action in the courts to prevent or end it.

As Wedderburn has put it:

> 'In calling out workers on strike or in procuring them to take other industrial action (e.g. blacking work), [trade unions] often induce inevitable breaches by the men of their contracts of employment and become liable in damages to the other contracting party - the employer'.[7]

THE PRESENT STATUTORY POSITION

Parliament has recognised that it is in the public interest to enact legislation which moderates the position at common law. It has sought, therefore, to provide trade unions with certain immunities from legal action.[8] The present immunities are contained in section 13 of the Trade Union and Labour Relations Act 1974 (as amended) although the basis of the modern law can be traced back to legislation of 1871, 1875 and 1906,[9] in particular section 13(1) is of importance in defining the present immunities given to trade unions. It provides as follows:

> 'An act done by a person in contemplation or furtherance of a trade dispute shall not be actionable in tort on the ground only -
>
> (a) that it induces another person to break a contract or interferes or induces any other person to interfere with its performances; or
> (b) that it consists in his threatening that a contract (whether one to which he is a party or not) will be broken or its performance interfered with, or that he will induce another person to break a contract or to interfere with its performance'.

It should be noted that the terms of section 13(1) make it clear that the immunities only exist where the act in question is taken 'in contemplation or furtherance of a trade dispute'. Section 29(1) of the 1974 Act explains what, for the purposes of this statute, constitutes a trade dispute. According to section 29(1) a trade dispute:

> 'means a dispute between employers and workers, or between workers and workers, which is connected with one or more of the following, that is to say -
>
> (a) terms and conditions of employment, or the physical conditions in which any workers are required to work;
> (b) engagement or non-engagement, or termination or suspension of employment or the duties of employment, of one or more workers;
> (c) allocation of work or the duties of employment as between workers or groups of workers;
> (d) matters of discipline;
> (e) the membership or non-membership of a trade union on the part of a worker;
> (f) facilities for officials of trade unions; and
> (g) machinery for negotiation or consultation ...'

The provisions of section 13(1) provide immunity not only for inducing breaches of contracts of employment, but for inducing a breach of any contract. Section 3 of the Trade Disputes Act 1906 provided immunity for inducing breaches of contracts of employment only. The original provisions of section 13 used similar language to that of the 1906 statute despite attempts by the Labour Government to extend the scope of trade union immunity to cover all types of contract.[10] It was not until the Trade Union and Labour Relations (Amendment) Act 1976, however, that the provisions of section 13(1) were amended to ensure that all types of contract were within the ambit of the immunities.[11]

LORD DENNING'S REACTION

The present nature and extent of trade union immunity has been the subject of severe criticism by Lord Denning in a series of extra-judicial statements. He has claimed that the trade unions have become 'far too powerful for the nation's well-being'.[12] It is his view that the 1974 Act has given trade unions 'virtual immunity from legal action'.[13] Lord Denning regards '[t]he power of the great trade unions as perhaps the greatest challenge to the rule of law ...'[14] It is they who '... take away the liberty of our individual'.[15] It is this regularly expressed view that trade unions are now virtually above the law which has undoubtedly coloured Lord Denning's own approach to the interpretation of the present legislation. Lord Denning provides an interesting insight into the working of the judicial mind when he says that '... when the question arises, as it does, what is the interpretation of the words 'in furtherance of a trade dispute' I think the natural instinct of the judge is to see that immunity is not carried too far ...'[16]

THE REASON FOR THE PRESENT LAW

For the largest part of the twentieth century[17] the ruling provisions on trade union immunity were contained in section 3 of the Trade Disputes Act 1906. This section provided protection for trade unions not only for inducing breaches of contracts of employment but also for '... interference with the trade, business or employment of some other person or with the right of some other person to dispose of his capital or his labour as he wills'. No specific immunity was provided, however, for inducing breaches of commercial contracts.

The second limb of section 3 seemed to render this unnecessary. A trade union which takes industrial action obviously interferes with the business of the employer involved. Such interference, however, was specifically catered for in the second limb of section 3. In any case, as the law stood in 1906, it appeared very difficult for a trade union to be guilty of inducing breaches of commercial contracts by taking strike action or any other type of action. A number of decisions before 1906, such as Lumley v Gye[18] had required that for there to be an unlawful inducement to break a contract there had to be knowledge of the terms of the contract as well as an intention to bring about a breach of it. This view seemed to be confirmed in the area of trade disputes by the subsequent decision of the Court of Appeal in D.C. Thomson & Co. v Deakin.[19] In that case, one of the grounds of decision was that the trade union had not induced breaches of the employer's commercial contract with a third party because the trade union did not have actual knowledge of the employer's contract with that party. The application of these two decisions, however, was to be very much restricted by a series of decisions in the 1960s.

(a) The cases

The first case where a new strategy towards inducement of breaches of commercial contracts was articulated was Stratford & Sons Ltd. v Lindley.[20] In this case, the House of Lords made considerable inroads on the test for inducement as laid down in Lumley v Gye and followed in D.C. Thomson & Co. v Deakin.[21] Their Lordships declared that in order for a trade union to induce a breach of contract it was not necessary for the union to know all its terms. A trade union would be taken to have unlawfully induced breaches of third party contracts where it was reasonable to infer that the union knew that its action would cause breaches of commercial contracts. As Lord Pearce put it:

> 'It is no answer to a claim based on wrongfully inducing a breach of contract, to assert that the respondents did not know with exactitude all the terms of the contract. The relevant question

> is whether they had sufficient knowledge to know that they were inducing a breach of contract'.[22]

In the subsequent case of Emerald Construction Co. v Lowthian[23] Lord Denning, himself, further limited the strict requirement for inducement as laid down in the earlier cases. In this case, which involved the blacking of a labour-only sub-contractor, Lord Denning opined that it was enough to constitute inducement if the officers of the trade union had the means of knowledge of the terms of the contract which they deliberately disregarded. It was not necessary to know the actual terms of the contract, itself. Lord Denning also made it clear that the test for unlawful inducement would be satisfied where recklessness could be attributed to the union involved. It was his view that '... if the officers deliberately sought to get this contract terminated, heedless of its terms, regardless whether it was terminated by breach or not, they would do wrong'.[24] As Lord Wedderburn has claimed, '[t]his was a far cry from the old cases which demanded real knowledge and intent'.[25]

The erosion of the tests for inducement was taken several stages further by the Court of Appeal's decision in Torquay Hotel Co. Ltd. v Cousins.[26] In that case, Lord Denning took the opportunity to examine the requisite elements of unlawful inducement:

> 'First, there must be interference in the execution of a contract. The interference is not confined to the procurement of a breach of contract. It extends to a case where a third person prevents or hinders one party from performing his contract, even though it be not a breach. Second, the interference must be deliberate. The person must know of the contract or, at any rate, turn a blind eye to it and intend to interfere with it. Third, the interference must be direct'.[27]

It has been claimed that '[a]uthority for this proposition is virtually non-existent'.[28] The effect of it, however, was to ensure that trade unions were liable in circumstances where no breach of contract actually took place, but where its performance was hindered as a result of direct deliberate acts. Lord Denning's judgment, therefore, meant that the tort of unlawfully inducing breaches of contract no longer required that any breaches should ever take place.

Up to this point the cases which have broadened the circumstances where unlawful inducemement has been held to exist involved situations where there was direct interference by the union with the third party contracts. It must be asked, however, what if the inducement should take place indirectly? In other words, is it unlawful if the third party contract is affected without there being any direct contact between the trade union and the third party? In Daily Mirror Newspapers v Gardner[29] Lord Denning went so far as to suggest that there was no difference between direct and indirect inducement. Both types were unlawful if there was no sufficient justification for the interference.[30] He retreated from this extreme position in his judgment in the Torquay Hotel case. Lord Denning accepted that there must be a distinction between direct interference with a contract and indirect inducement of it '... else we should take away the right to strike altogether'.[31] It was his view that '[i]ndirect interference is only unlawful if unlawful means are used'.[32] No guidance was given as to what constituted 'unlawful means'. It was uncertain how extensively this phrase would be interpreted. Grabiner, in the Modern Law Review, has suggested that the test for 'unlawful means' would be broad enough to cover disputes where the employees of the third party contractor refused to deliver to the employer in dispute and, thus, were technically in breach of their employment contracts.[33] The point was moot whether it was unlawful merely for a trade union to call a strike which, as a result, rendered it impossible for an employer to fulfil the terms of his commercial contracts. It has been suggested by Grabiner that the third party contractor would have a right of action in such circumstances.[34]

In terms of the diminution of the right to strike, an answer to the question of how extensive 'unlawful means' would be interpreted, was really unnecessary. Lord Denning's assertion that the courts should not take away the right to strike altogether must be looked at in light of his own judicial pronouncements on direct inducement.[35] The net result of these was to severely limit a trade union's right to take industrial action. As Lord Wedderburn has suggested, it is a fact of life that trade union officials:

> '... are bound to approach other persons 'directly' - employers, customers, suppliers, and so on, persons whom they surely ought to inform of impending strike action which clearly has the object of 'hindering' execution of contracts. This is the very object of trade unions' industrial action ... They have no other weapon to balance management power. Yet now it is said they can be liable when no breach of such contracts has been caused and all their actions have been lawful'.[36]

It is no wonder that Lord Wedderburn further claimed that '[s]tatutory intervention is urgently needed against this wild new swing of the pendulum'.[37]

This is the real reason for the statutes of 1974 and 1976. It is not that the Labour Government conspired to put trade unions above the law. Rather, the legislation was a reaction to a series of decisions, many of them penned by Lord Denning, which had severely restricted the parameters of trade union immunity as they had been laid down in the 1906 Act.[38] The effect of these decisions was to render unlawful many types of activity which the 1906 Act had originally appeared to cover. When one also considers that other decisions, such as Rookes v Barnard,[39] which had 'developed' the tort of intimidation, had also limited the extent of trade union immunity, it cannot be denied that some response was required from Parliament to return the law to its original state.

(b) The Donovan Report

There is another reason why Parliament sought to redefine the immunities provided to trade unions. As well as those decisions which we have just discussed severely restricting the circumstances in which industrial action was lawful, the net result of these cases was to create much uncertainty about what types of industrial action fell within the ambit of the legislation. The Donovan Commission[40] considered this point when it presented its Report to Parliament in 1968. It considered that the law on inducement as it had been interpreted by the courts created a 'legal maze'.[41] The complicated nature of the law posed 'an almost insoluble problem for the trade union official seeking to 'advise' a customer of the employer in dispute ... Employers themselves apparently misunderstand the law'.[42] Donovan believed that '... the law upon the subject ought not to be left in such a state that all persons, whether they be employees, employers or trade union officials should be so uncertain of their position'.[43] As a result, Donovan recommended that the protection provided to trade unions should be extended to cover all contracts. This recommendation was made in the belief that the provisions of the 1906 Act allowed:

> '... trade unions or other persons to take action leading to a breach of commercial contracts without incurring any liability for damages, and that such liability is incurred only if a complicated state of the law is either unappreciated or misunderstood'.[44]

If anything, it was this particular recommendation which formed not only the basis but the rationale for the 1976 amendments to the 1974 Act.

LORD DENNING'S INTERPRETATION OF THE PRESENT LAW

Since the 1976 amendments to the Trade Union and Labour Relations Act 1974, there have been a number of cases where employers have sought to challenge the legality of industrial action taken by trade unions. Most of these cases have reached the Court of Appeal, and all the important cases that have reached this Court have been heard by a bench of judges which included Lord Denning. Lord Denning, therefore, has been in a particularly strong position to decide upon the extent of the new provisions on trade union immunity. He, above any other judge, has been given the greatest opportunity to shape and develop the new law.[45]

(a) The motive test

The first case to come before the Court of Appeal in the period post-1976 which merits discussion was BBC v Hearn.[46] In that case, the Association of Broadcasting Staff intimated to the BBC that unless steps were taken to prevent the FA Cup Final being televised in South Africa industrial action would be taken to achieve this result. The BBC refused to comply with this request. When the trade union continued to make it clear that it would take industrial action to prevent the proposed broadcast, the BBC sought an injunction. The application for injunction was refused by Pain J.[47] On appeal, however, the decision of Pain J. was reversed by an unanimous Court of Appeal.[48]

Lord Denning's finding that the trade union activity contemplated in this case was outwith the scope of the 1974 Act, hinged upon his definition of a trade dispute. As we know, section 29(1) lists the types of dispute which are protected by the legislation as trade disputes. The Court of Appeal was asked to hold that the dispute between the BBC and the ABS was a trade dispute because it concerned 'terms and conditions of employment'. This is a type of dispute which is protected by section 29(1). In the opinion of Lord Denning, however, this dispute did not concern terms and conditions of employment. As a consequence, he held that the dispute was not a trade dispute:

> 'It never reached the stage of there being a trade dispute. There was not a trade dispute 'in contemplation'. It was coercive interference and nothing more'.[49]

To assist him in this conclusion, Lord Denning turned to an analogy involving a trade union which informs a newspaper that if it does not withdraw a particular article on a political issue, the trade union will not print the paper. It was his view that a dispute in this case was about the publication of the article and not about the terms and conditions of employment.[50] For Lord Denning, the issue was the same in the present case. The dispute was not about terms and conditions of employment, it was over a political matter. The motive behind the dispute was to protest against the policy of apartheid, not to promote any legitimate trade object.[51] As a consequence, the impugned activity in this case was not protected by the 1974 Act.[52]

The question of motive was also considered by Lord Denning in the subsequent case of Star Sea Transport Corporation v Slater[53] where a more extensive version of the motive test was applied. This case concerned attempts by the International Transport Workers' Federation to secure that the wage rates paid on a Liberian vessel, the 'Camilla M', were in line with recognised ITF minima. The 'Camilla M' although registered in Liberia, was crewed by Greek officers and Indian seamen. The ITF, therefore, considered that it flew a 'flag of convenience'. It is the ITF's policy to discourage flags of convenience because ships flying such flags usually paid badly and provided poor conditions of employment. As a result, the ITF made demands on the owners of the 'Camilla M' that the Indian seamen should be paid ITF rates. If this did not happen the ITF promised to black the ship. The shipowners agreed to meet the demands, but the members of the crew, themselves, refused to sign new articles based on the ITF rates. The ITF continued to insist on blacking the ship. The shipowners therefore sought injunctive relief. The application for injunction was refused by Donaldson J. This decision, however, was reversed by the Court of Appeal.[54]

In considering whether the activity of the ITF was carried out 'in contemplation or furtherance of a trade dispute', Lord Denning had this to say:

> 'If one gives those words their full and literal meaning, they would seem to cover the differences here. They were connected with the terms of employment of the Indian crew ... They would seem also to cover the demands made by the ITF. But there are decisions of the Courts [55] ... which have put a limit on those words. They show that the Courts will look at the motive for which the action is taken. If the action is taken, not bona fide for a legitimate trade object, but for an extraneous motive, such as to punish an individual ... then it is not done in contemplation or furtherance of a trade dispute'.[56]

Turning to the present dispute, Lord Denning considered that the ITF's demands were 'impossible', because the members of the crew did not wish to accede to them. Furthermore, the demands were 'so unreasonable that it stamps the ITF as intermeddlers and may put them outside the pale of immunity'.[57] Since the ITF were making demands which could not reasonably be fulfilled and because of the ITF's dislike for 'flags of convenience', Lord Denning considered that they were acting for 'some extraneous motive' and not for any legitimate trade object. The ITF was, therefore, not acting in furtherance of a trade dispute. In reaching this conclusion, of course, Lord Denning was forced to ignore the natural meaning of the words 'in contemplation or furtherance of a trade dispute'. Equally, he had to ignore the fact that the dispute was clearly 'connected with' terms and conditions of employment as provided for in section 29(1), since the effect of the dispute would be to improve the terms and conditions of employment of the Indian seamen.

As Brian Doyle has suggested:

> '[n]ot for the first time in such matters ... their Lordships eschewed the normal rules of construction and sought to put a limit upon the otherwise unambiguous effect of the legislation'.[58]

(b) The remoteness test

In Beaverbrook Newspapers v Keys[59] Lord Denning applied a somewhat different approach to his interpretation of the relevant legislation. This particular case arose out of a strike by journalists at the 'Daily Mirror'. Express Newspapers decided to print more copies of their newspaper in order to take up the slack caused by the non-appearance of the 'Daily Mirror'. The Society of Graphical and Allied Trades sought to prevent the 'Daily Express' publishing its extra copies. To ensure that this would happen SOGAT ordered its members at the Express not to handle or distribute any more papers than normal. The employers thereupon sought injunction in the High Court. This was refused before Cusack J., but awarded by the Court of Appeal.[60]

In his judgment in this case, Lord Denning introduced the question of remoteness in deciding whether a dispute was a trade dispute. Lord Denning accepted that there was certainly a trade dispute at the 'Daily Mirror'. It was a different matter, however, at the 'Daily Express'. The activities of SOGAT at the 'Daily Express' were too remote from the original dispute at the 'Daily Mirror' to be done in furtherance of a trade dispute. Lord Denning questioned whether it could '... fairly be said that the acts done by [SOGAT] were in 'furtherance' of the 'Daily Mirror' dispute?'[61] He answered this question as follows:

> 'The acts done were a consequence of a trade dispute, but not in 'furtherance' of it. As I read the statute, in order that an act should be done in furtherance of a trade dispute, it must be directly in furtherance of it. You cannot chase consequence after consequence after consequence in a long chain and say everything that follows a trade dispute is in 'furtherance' of it'.[62]

Lord Denning, therefore, made it clear that in order for the statutory immunity to apply the activity in question had to be more than merely in furtherance of the dispute; it had to be directly in furtherance of it. The Act, itself, does not require that the activity has to be directly in furtherance of the dispute. Yet, Lord Denning introduced this requirement which he and other judges have applied in subsequent cases.[63] The justification for this requirement has been doubted by at least one academic writer.[64] Regardless of the justification for this requirement, the consequence of it is '... to undermine secondary action by trade unions'.[65] In writing about this decision, Simpson has observed that '... the doubtful validity of the view that legislation since 1974 has almost totally excluded the law from the area of industrial conflict has been fully exposed'.[66]

Lord Denning returned to the remoteness test in <u>Associated Newspapers Group</u> v <u>Wade</u>.[67] In that case, the National Graphical Association, in pursuit of recognition at the 'Nottingham Evening Post', had instructed its members to black the advertisements of organisations who had taken up advertising space in the 'Evening Post'. The blacking was to apply to all national and provincial newspapers and all magazines and periodicals. The purpose of the blacking was to discourage any organisation advertising in the 'Evening Post'. In this way it was hoped that the owners of the paper would accede to the NGA's claims for recognition because of the loss of advertising revenue which they would suffer. Once again, Lord Denning recognised that '[s]ome acts are so remote from the trade dispute that they cannot properly be said to be 'in furtherance' of it'. Looking to the present dispute, Lord Denning considered that the trade union's activities were too remote to be protected. The trade union was directly injuring the organisations who advertised in the 'Evening Post', and not the employers who owned the paper. Lord Denning put it this way:

> '... when trade unions choose not to cause damage or loss to the employer himself, but only to innocent third persons - who are not parties to the dispute - it is very different. The act done may then be so remote from the dispute itself that it cannot reasonably be regarded as being done 'in furtherance' of it. The trade union may believe it to be in furtherance of it, but their state of mind is by no means decisive. It is the fact of 'furtherance' that matters, not belief in it'.[68]

The application of the remoteness test in this case ensured that the NGA's actions were found to be unlawful. It has been argued that this test ignores both the intention behind and the effect of the trade union's action.[69] What Lord Denning's test does ensure, however, is that any secondary activity, will be outwith the statutory immunities.[70] Lord Denning, himself, declared in Wade that 'secondary picketing is unlawful at common law and is so remote from the dispute that there is no immunity in regard to it'.[71]

(c) The objective test

Lord Denning relied upon another test concerning the meaning of the phrase 'in furtherance' in Express Newspapers Ltd. v McShane.[72] This case arose out of a dispute between the National Union of Journalists and the proprietors of local newspapers over a pay claim. The NUJ had already called a strike at the local newspapers. In order to ensure that its action was more effective, however, the NUJ sought to ensure that the local newspaper proprietors did not have access to Press Association copy. The NUJ, therefore, called out its members at the Press Association. On top of this, the NUJ ordered its members at the 'Daily Express' and other national newspapers to black Press Association copy. It was this particular facet of the dispute which came before the courts.[73] When the case came before the Court of Appeal, the issue again concerned whether the trade union's action in calling out the national newspaper journalists was 'in furtherance' of a trade dispute. All three judges[74] of the Court considered that the NUJ's action was not in furtherance of the trade dispute and was, therefore, unprotected by the 1974 Act. Lord Denning's analysis was as follows:

> 'It is said on behalf of the trade union leaders that 'furtherance' depended on their state of mind. If they genuinely and honestly believed that the 'blacking' would advance the cause of the provincial journalists, then their acts were done 'in furtherance' of the dispute ... 'Furtherance' is not a merely subjective concept. There is an objective element in it ... It seems to me that, for an act to be done 'in furtherance' of a trade dispute, it must be reasonably capable of doing so, or have a reasonable prospect of it in this way, that it must help one side or the other to the dispute in a practical way by giving

> support to the one or bringing pressure to bear on the other'.[75]

The NUJ had claimed that the purpose behind the blacking of Press Association copy, was to improve the morale of the strikers. Lord Denning, however, could not accept that the need to improve morale legitimately furthered the dispute. In his view, since the blacking did not appear to have any practical effect on the dispute, it was not done 'in furtherance' of it. As in other cases, Lord Denning applied a narrow construction of the appropriate words of section 13(1) in order to reach his conclusion. He agreed with the trial judge that the words required a 'narrower construction'. 'A wide construction would confer too wide an immunity'.[76]

It must be admitted that the terms of the statute are silent on what is the proper test to apply for when a particular type of trade union activity is 'in furtherance' of a trade dispute. To this extent the McShane case is a much more difficult case than any of the others, since it does require the judges to consider difficult questions of language. Lord Denning's decision, therefore, to apply an objective test is certainly tenable. Indeed, an objective approach was also adopted by Lawton and Brandon L.J J. in the Court of Appeal, since both these judges required that the action had to be 'reasonably capable' of furthering the objective. Their test, however, did not go as far as Lord Denning's because theirs did not demand that the action had actually to achieve the objective. Lord Wilberforce, in the House of Lords, also applied an objective test.[77] The problem in this case, therefore, is not that Lord Denning should have chosen to apply an objective test. Rather, it is the nature of the test which Lord Denning applied which is open to criticism.[78] Lord Denning's test required that the action of the trade union should further the dispute in some 'practical way'.[79] The question is, of course, what types of action actually help the dispute in some practical way? Lord Denning's answer to this question was to suggest that the action had to give support to one side or bring pressure on the other. This, surely, is to judge the lawfulness of a particular form of action by the effect it produces. As Lord Wilberforce put it:

> 'This I think with respect goes too far: it involves judging the matter by results (at what time?) a very uncertain process in the

> complex and sometimes irrational world of industrial relations. He did, as I read his judgment, take into account the actual effect of the action as he saw it. But one cannot use hindsight to interpret or apply the expression; the act must be appraised when it is done'.[80]

In any case, Lord Denning's reasoning in this case creates two further problems. First, it requires that for any trade union action to be protected as being 'in furtherance of a trade dispute', that action must in some way provide practical assistance in the resolution of the dispute. It is for the courts, of course, to decide when a specific form of industrial action practically assists the union in the dispute. Such a test, therefore, creates a wide discretion in the courts in deciding when industrial action furthers a dispute. As a corollary, it makes it difficult for a union to decide when a particular type of action actually objectively furthers the dispute.

Second, the test in the form in which Lord Denning applied it in this case, further reduces the circumstances where industrial action is lawful. The fact that Lord Denning demanded that the action had to help the dispute in some practical way before being protected, meant that he had to show a distinction between action of a practical nature and strikes which merely improved morale or promoted the confidence of the strikers. These latter types of action,[81] according to Lord Denning, were unprotected by the legislation. If strikes which improve morale are unlawful then certainly some sympathetic strikes must be unlawful since their purpose is to show solidarity with those in dispute.[82] It has been suggested that such a result is contrary to the intention of Parliament.[83]

(d) Conclusion

In deciding these cases which we have just discussed, Lord Denning has relied upon three major tests for discovering when the provisions of the 1974 Act actually apply. The tests, the motive test; the remoteness test; and the objective test;[84] all ensure that the provisions of the 1974 Act will be interpreted restrictively.[85] The first two tests require that changes be made in the natural meaning of the words 'connected with' in section 29(1) and 'in furtherance' in section 13(1). The third test, as Lord Denning has applied it, defies the intention of Parliament.

The Labours of Lord Denning

In the introduction to this essay we noted that Lord Denning claims that in all cases he interprets statutes in a way which will 'promote the general legislative purpose'. It is very difficult to see how the tests we have described can 'promote the general legislative purpose' of the 1974 Act given the fact that their application ensures a restrictive interpretation of the legislation. Indeed, Lord Denning's claim about following the purpose of the legislation does not bear close scrutiny in this field. If anything, his approach to trade disputes appears to defy the policy of the legislation rather than implement it. His overriding philosophy is to ensure that trade union immunity is 'not carried too far'. Such a philosophy, however, requires him not only to flout the intention of Parliament, but in fact to do damage to the literal words of the statute. So, in relation to trade union immunity, Lord Denning goes further than merely failing to apply the purpose behind the legislation, he actually fails to implement what the words of the statute plainly mean. This is the single most important feature of Lord Denning's performance in this field. He claims that trade unions are virtually above the law. Yet, as has been suggested in 'New Society', 'his own court decisions in case after case over the past three years have severely qualified that sweeping observation'.[86] It would seem that the cautionary words of Lord Devlin are apt here. Lord Devlin has claimed that the words of a statute '... must be taken to mean what they say and not what their interpreter would like them to say; the statute is the master and not the servant of the judgment'.[87] Surely this is the approach to be preferred particularly in such a sensitive area as industrial disputes.

THE HOUSE OF LORDS AND TRADE DISPUTES

Lord Denning's approach to the question of trade union immunity has been the subject of discussion and criticism in two decisions of the House of Lords. In NWL Ltd. v Woods and Nelson,[88] a case which once again involved the blacking of a ship, the House considered Lord Denning's motive test as it was laid down in the 'Camilla M' case.[89] In Express Newspapers v McShane[90] the question of what activity was 'in furtherance' of a trade dispute was considered.

In the Woods case, the House unanimously overruled[91] the decision of the Court of Appeal in 'Camilla M'. Lord Diplock declared that the 'Camilla M' decision was '... an embarrassment by which your Lordships are not affected'.[92] Lord Scarman suggested that in interpreting section 29(1) all that is required:

> '... is that the dispute be connected with one or more of the matters it mentions. If it be connected, it is a trade dispute, and it is immaterial whether the dispute also relates to other matters ...'[93]

In the McShane case, the House of Lords by a four to one majority,[94] declared that the test for 'in furtherance' was subjective. If a trade union acts with the purpose of helping parties to the dispute to achieve their objectives in the honest and reasonable belief that it will do so, that activity is protected. In McShane, Lord Scarman criticised Lord Denning's test for what is 'in furtherance' of a trade dispute, Lord Scarman believed that:

> 'It would be a strange and embarrassing task for a judge to be called upon to review the tactics of a party to a trade dispute and to determine whether in the view of the court the tactic employed was likely to further, or advance, that party's side of the dispute ... It would need very clear statutory language to persuade me that Parliament intended to allow the courts to act as some sort of back-seat driver in trade disputes'.[95]

Both cases are full of references about what is the proper interpretation of the 1974 Act. In the Woods case, Lord Scarman suggested that '[i]t is wrong to attempt to construe any section or subsection of these Acts without reference to their legislative purpose'.[96] The legislative purpose according to Lord Scarman was '... to exclude trade disputes from judicial review by the courts'.[97] As far as he could discover, the 1974 Act put the law back '... to what Parliament had intended when it enacted the Act of 1906 - but stronger and clearer than it was then'. All this led Lord Scarman to the conclusion that:

> 'Judicial decision cannot impose limitations upon the language of Parliament where it is clear from the words, context and policy of

the statute that no limitation was intended'.[99]

Lord Diplock was equally forthright in the McShane case. He perceived an assumption apparent in the decisions of the Court of Appeal construing the words 'in furtherance' '... that Parliament cannot really have intended to give so wide an immunity',[100] to trade unions in sections 13 and 29. Lord Diplock was of the view that this was not '... a legitimate assumption on which to approach the construction of the Act'.[101] For him, the policy of the legislation was '... to strengthen the role of recognised trade unions in collective bargaining ...'[102] As a consequence, it was Lord Diplock's belief that the words of sections 13 and 29 should be given their plain and ordinary meaning. It is submitted that these views constitute the most appropriate way of interpreting the relevant provisions of the 1974 Act.

THE HOUSE OF LORDS' DECISIONS AND LORD DENNING

Despite these observations about the proper interpretation of sections 13 and 29 of the 1974 Act, Lord Denning has persisted in applying his own individual approach to the interpretation of these sections. In Duport Steels Ltd. v Sirs[103] where the Iron and Steel Trades Confederation sought to extend their dispute with British Steel into the private sector of the industry, Lord Denning held that such an extension was not protected by the 1974 Act.[104] As far as Lord Denning was concerned, the extension of the dispute into the private sector created a second dispute.[105] This second dispute was not between workers and employers, but between the union and the Government. Its purpose was to put pressure on the Government. Accordingly, Lord Denning held that this extension of the dispute was not in furtherance of a trade dispute.

It is difficult to perceive any difference between the facts in this case and those of the McShane case. Both cases involved an attempt by a trade union to extend the dispute away from the primary employer. In both cases the purpose behind the extension of the respective disputes was to bring them to a speedier conclusion. When one takes into account the House of Lords ruling in McShane - that the test for when particular activity is 'in furtherance' of a trade dispute was a subjective test requiring only that the trade union honestly believed the activity would further the dispute - Lord Denning's decision becomes all the more puzzling. Professor Zander[106] believed that this decision appears to be 'blatantly in defiance' of the House of Lords decision in McShane. It certainly cannot be reconciled in any other way. To quote Professor Zander again, the decision in Duport Steels can only be described as 'legally and intellectually indefensible'. Yet it does illustrate the determination of Lord Denning to continue to apply his own philosophy about the dangers as he perceives them of extending trade union immunity too far.

The effect of the Court of Appeal's decision, of course, was short-lived. Within one week it had been reversed by the House of Lords.[107] Like Professor Zander, the House of Lords could see no difference between the present case and the McShane decision. Indeed, all five judges[108] who heard the case were each of the opinion that the only possible conclusion to reach was one which applied the law as laid down in McShane. A number of their Lordships,[109] however, did take the opportunity to explain what they considered to be the proper function of a judge when interpreting legislation such as the 1974 Act. Lord Diplock suggested, for example, that:

> '... where the meaning of the statutory words is plain and unambiguous, it is not for the judges to invent fancied ambiguities as an excuse for failing to give effect to its plain meaning, because they themselves consider that the consequences of doing so would be inexpedient, or even unjust or immoral'.[110]

Lord Scarman declared that in areas where the law has been made by Parliament:

> '... the judge's duty is to interpret and apply the law, not to change it to meet the judge's idea of what justice requires'.[111]
>
> 'Unpalatable statute law may not be disregarded or rejected, merely because it is unpalatable'.[112]

As the above quotations suggest, there was also a general recognition by their Lordships that the present legislation on trade union immunity had created a number of consequences which were both distasteful and detrimental to the public interest. Their Lordships believed, however, that any necessary changes in the law had to come about through the operation of 'democratic processes'.[113] As Lord Diplock put it '... it is for Parliament not for the judiciary to decide whether any changes should be made in the law as stated in the Acts ...'[114] The reason why the House of Lords favoured this approach is that to act in any other way would be to involve the judges in 'political controversy'.[115] Such an involvement would endanger '... continued public confidence in the political impartiality of the judiciary, which is essential to the continuance of the rule of law ...'[116]

These opinions expose the fundamental weakness of Lord Denning's approach. Regardless of how beneficial or otherwise the results of Lord Denning's judgments in this field may be, they do tend to blur the crucial distinction between judicial creativity and political decision-making. This point has clear and obvious dangers for the neutrality and independence of the judiciary. The problem is best summed up by Lord Scarman in the Duport Steels case. He said that:

> '... if people and Parliament come to think that the judicial power is to be confined by nothing other than the judge's sense of what is right ... confidence in the judicial system will be replaced by fear of it becoming uncertain and arbitrary in its application'.[117]

GENERAL CONCLUSION

This essay has sought to examine Lord Denning's performance in construing the present legislation on trade union immunity. We have examined some of the reasons for the present shape of the legislation;[118] we have examined Lord Denning's recent decisions on it; and we have examined the reaction of the House of Lords to those decisions. The conclusion is inescapable. Lord Denning has persistently attempted to place a particularly narrow construction on the words of the 1974 Act. He has applied a series of tests which not only involve a restrictive interpretation of the relevant legislation, but also create a great deal of discretion in the courts for deciding when a particular type of action is unlawful. It may be that this is the principal reason for Lord Denning's restrictive approach. As Keith Ewing has suggested:

> '[t]he development of narrow and difficult distinctions and the gratuitous qualification of the statutory language by concepts of reasonableness, directness and remoteness have enabled the courts to assert a high level of discretion and control over the circumstances in which industrial action may be lawfully conducted'.[119]

If this is Lord Denning's reason it makes his approach to the subject of trade union immunity all the more indefensible. For surely the decision about what types of industrial action are lawful is one for the legislature alone. As we have suggested, it is not a decision to be made by a judge acting upon his own particular view about the benefit of trade unions in our society. To return to the words of Lord Devlin:

> 'If a judge leaves the law and makes his own decisions, even if in substance they are just, he loses the protection of the law and sacrifices the appearance of impartiality which is given by adherence to the law'.[120]

KENNETH MILLER

NOTES

(1) Lord Denning, The Discipline of Law, Butterworths, London, 1979.
(2) Lord Denning, ibid, pp.15-17.
(3) [1978] ICR 336, p.344
(4) Ibid, at p.344. See also Lord Denning's statement in 'Person to Person', BBC TV, 12 July 1979. 'When Parliament enacts a statute we must follow it and we do'.
(5) O. Kahn-Freund, Labour and the Law, 2nd ed., Stevens, London, 1977, p.6.
(6) Kahn-Freund, ibid, p.51.
(7) K.W. Wedderburn, The Worker and the Law, 2nd ed., Penguin, London, 1971, p.349.
(8) One of the problems in discussing this area of the law is that it is littered with such terms as 'immunity' and 'privilege'. These terms could be taken to suggest some sort of arbitrariness in the

statutory definition concerning the lawfulness of trade union action. Such a suggestion undoubtedly has repercussions for any debate about the scope and extent of trade union law. This point is discussed by J.A.G. Griffith in 'Unequal before the Law', Spectator, 2 February 1980 at p.12 where he contrasts the constitutional guarantees given to trade unions in other western democracies, with the British predilection for exempting trade unions from the operation of particular sections of the common law.

(9) Trade Union Act 1871 which dealt with trade unions in restraint of trade; Conspiracy and Protection of Property Act 1875, which abolished many of the criminal offences trade unions could commit; Trade Disputes Act 1906, which created the 'golden formula' for when trade unions were acting lawfully when engaged in trade disputes.

(10) For a discussion on these attempts, see Lord Wedderburn, 37 MLR, 1974, 525, p.540.

(11) Discussed by G. England and W.M. Rees, 39 MLR, 1976, 698. See particularly, pp.703-6.

(12) Daily Express, 21 April 1979.

(13) Lord Denning, ibid. Some of his reported decisions have also contained statements to this effect. See, for example, BBC v Hearn [1977] ICR 691, where in discussing the present statutory framework, Lord Denning remarked that 'All legal restraints have been lifted so as [trade unions] can now do as they will'. (At p.691).

(14) Quoted by David Dimbleby in 'Person to Person', BBC TV, 12 July 1979.

(15) Lord Denning, 'The Freedom of the Individual Today', 45 Medico-Legal Journal, 1977, p.49. It is not only the trade unions that take away our liberty. According to Lord Denning, the new statutory commissions do this as well. See, for example, his comments about the Equal Opportunities Commission in Science Research Council v Nasse [1978] ICR 1124. In considering the powers of the EOC, Lord Denning remarked that they went back to 'the days of the Inquisition' and 'the days of the General Warrants' (p.1139). See also, his comments about ACAS in United Kingdom Association of Professional Engineers v Advisory, Conciliation and Arbitration Service [1979] ICR 303 that ACAS could become a '... tool of powerful trade unions'.

(16) 'Person to Person', supra.

(17) In the years from 1906 to 1971. In the period between 1971 and 1974, the question of trade union immunity was

dealt with in the Industrial Relations Act 1971. The 1974 Act has brought the law back to the position of creating negative immunities in favour of trade unions (the 'golden formula').

(18) (1853) 2 E & B 216.

(19) [1952] Ch. 646.

(20) [1965] AC 269.

(21) The House of Lords also found against the trade union on other grounds - for example, that the dispute was only undertaken to enhance the prestige of the union. The issue of the motive behind the industrial action is a matter which will be considered _infra_.

(22) _Supra_, p.351. It is interesting that when this case was before the Court of Appeal, Lord Denning found for the trade union. On the question of inducement, Lord Denning held that there had been no inducement to breach commercial contracts because of a lack of intention. He also doubted whether any breaches of the contracts, if they did take place, were the necessary consequence of the trade union's action. See [1965] AC 276, particularly p.288.

(23) [1966] 1 WLR 691. In _The Discipline of Law_, Lord Denning refers to this case as '[t]he first way in which the law about 'inducing a breach of contract' was extended ...', p.178. See, generally, pp.175-193.

(24) _Ibid_, pp.700-1.

(25) K.W. Wedderburn, _The Worker and the Law_, 2nd ed., Penguin, London, 1971, p.351.

(26) [1969] 2 Ch. 106.

(27) _Ibid_, p.138.

(28) A.S. Grabiner, 'There is a Tort of Interference with Contractual Relations', 32 _MLR_, 1969, 435, p.436.

(29) [1968] 2 QB 768.

(30) See, Lord Denning's judgment, particularly p.781.

(31) [1969] 2 Ch. 106, p.138.

(32) _Ibid_, p.139.

(33) A.S. Grabiner, _supra_, p.437.

(34) Grabiner based his view on the unlawfulness of the individual employees in actually breaching their contracts of employment. See, Grabiner, _supra_, p.437. His footnote 20 canvasses what little authority there was on this point.

(35) Other judges followed similar lines to Lord Denning. See, for example, the judgments of Russell and Winn L.JJ. in the _Torquay Hotels_ case, _supra_, p.305 and 308. The House of Lords was also in favour of restricting trade union immunity. See, _Stratford_ v _Lindley_, _supra_.

See also, Rookes v Barnard [1964] AC 1129, a decision dubbed by Otto Kahn-Freund as a 'frontal attack upon the right to strike'.

(36) Lord Wedderburn, supra, p.378.

(37) Lord Wedderburn, ibid, p.379.

(38) As Lord Scarman has said, the purpose of the present law is to put the position of the law back to what Parliament had intended in 1906. See, Lord Scarman, in NWL Ltd. v Woods and Nelson [1979] 1 WLR 1294, discussed infra.

(39) [1964] AC 1129. For a critical examination of this decision, see Lord Wedderburn, supra, pp.361-373.

(40) Royal Commission on Trade Unions and Employers' Associations 1965-68, Cmnd 3623.

(41) It should be remembered that this view was adopted by the Donovan Commission prior to the decision of the Court of Appeal in Torquay Hotels. This decision would surely only have strengthened Donovan's view.

(42) Donovan Report, para. 892.

(43) Ibid, para. 892.

(44) Ibid, para. 893.

(45) Lord Denning has, in effect, admitted as much himself. In 'Person to Person', he stated that the day to day law is moulded in the Court of Appeal especially in many urgent cases. Most of the cases which we are about to discuss were urgent cases where Lord Denning and his colleagues had to speedily consider the legality of granting an injunction to an employer in order to prevent real or threatened industrial action.

(46) [1977] ICR 685.

(47) Reported at [1977] IRLR 269.

(48) Lord Denning M.R. and Roskill and Scarman L.JJ.

(49) [1977] ICR 685, p.693. As Lord Wedderburn has pointed out, most industrial disputes involve 'coercive interference' by someone. See, 'Labour Injunctions and Trade Disputes', 41 MLR, 1978, 80, p.83.

(50) See his judgment at pp.692 and 693. The difficulty with this analogy for Lord Denning was that he was forced to accept that had the trade union sought to include as a term and condition of employment of its members, a right not to be involved in broadcasts to South Africa, this might make the dispute a trade dispute. The flaws in this approach are exposed by Lord Wedderburn, ibid, pp.83-5.

(51) The question of the motive behind the dispute is one we have already noted. See the decision of the House of Lords, Stratford v Lindley, supra. Lord

Denning was to use it again in subsequent cases. See, Star Sea Transport Corporation v Slater, infra. in particular.

(52) This is despite the fact that section 29(1) requires that the dispute only has to be 'connected with' one of the several heads to be protected. This point is discussed by Keith Ewing in 'The Golden Formula: Some Recent Developments', ILJ, 1979, 133, p.137.

(53) [1979] 1 Lloyd's Rep. 26.

(54) Lord Denning M.R., Stephenson and Brandon L.JJ.

(55) The authority Lord Denning cited here was Conway v Wade [1909] AC 506 where a union official had sought to induce an employer to sack a worker for non-payment of a union fine. The court had held that there was no trade dispute here, merely a personal dispute between Wade and Conway. The House of Lords have since said about Conway.v Wade that 'it would be unwise to treat what was said 70 years ago ... in Conway v Wade as still authoritative', per Lord Diplock in NWL Ltd v Woods and Nelson [1979] 1 W.L.R. 1294, p.1304. Discussed infra.

(56) [1979] 1 Lloyd's Rep. 26, p.30.

(57) Ibid, p.31. The fact that the trade union had to show that its demands were capable of being fulfilled before being protected, added a further restriction to trade union activity. This restriction has been criticised by Brian Doyle in 'Trade Disputes and the Labour Injunction Yet Again', 42 MLR, 1979. 458, particularly, p.459. He believes that the attempt in this case "... to limit the legitimacy of the trade dispute by reference to some vague and undefined standard of what might be reasonable or possible for the employer to concede in response to industrial action ... has extended yet again the categories of labour disputes which fall outside the 'golden formula'".

(58) Doyle, ibid, p.459.

(59) [1978] ICR 582.

(60) Lord Denning M.R., Goff and Cumming-Bruce L.JJ.

(61) [1978] ICR 582, p.586.

(62) Ibid, p.586.

(63) See, for example, Lord Denning in Associated Newspapers v Wade, discussed infra and Ackner J's decision in United Biscuits (UK) Ltd v Fall [1979] IRLR 110.

(64) See, R.C. Simpson, 'Trade Disputes and the Labour Injunction Again', 41 MLR, 1978, 470, particularly p.472. Simpson believes that '... there is no more justification for reading 'directly' into this

part of the [Act] than there is for reading it into the trade dispute definition before the words 'connected with'". (This, of course, was the result of Lord Denning's interpretation of section 29(1) in the Hearn case, supra).

(65) Ewing, supra, p.139.

(66) Simpson, supra, p.474.

(67) [1979] ICR 664.

(68) Ibid, p.695. The reasoning here also contains elements of the objective test which Lord Denning developed in Express Newspapers v McShane [1979] ICR 210 discussed infra.

(69) Ewing, supra, p.142. Ewing also believes that the remoteness test '... cannot readily be reconciled with the language of the statute' (p.142).

(70) Ewing argues that it is inconsistent with the intention of Parliament to interpret the legislation in such a way that it restricts secondary activity. In support of this argument he quotes a statement by Michael Foot when the 1974 Act was at Committee Stage that 'a secondary boycott is a legitimate way for trade unions to bring pressure on an employer with whom they are in dispute'. See, Ewing, ibid, p.142.

(71) [1979] ICR 664, p.695. Lord Denning's judgment also contains comments about trade union interference with the freedom of the press. 'A trade union has no right to use its industrial strength to invade the freedom of the press. They have no right to interfere with the freedom of editors to comment on matters of public interest ... These freedoms are so fundamental in our society that no trade union has any right to interfere with them' (p.691). It has been claimed that Lord Denning's view would deprive a trade union of any protection under section 13 where press freedom was an issue. See R.C. Simpson, 42 MLR, 1979, 701, p.703.

(73) Decision of Lawson J. affirmed.

(74) Lord Denning M.R., Lawton and Brandon L.JJ. Both Lawton and Brandon L.JJ. believed that trade union activity was only 'in furtherance' of the dispute if it was reasonably capable of achieving the union's objectives. See their judgments, pp.220 and 222 respectively.

(75) [1979] ICR 210, p.218.

(76) Ibid, p.220.

(77) Express Newspapers Ltd. v McShane [1980] 2 WLR 89, 90. In R. v Sheffield Crown Court, ex parte Brownlow 'The Times', 4 March 1980, Lord Denning has commented that of the total of nine judges who were involved in the McShane case, five favoured an objective test and four a subjective test. In his view, the selection of the appropriate test was '... one of the policy of the law, or of public policy'. In Lord Denning's view '... subsequent events and comments had shown convincingly' that the majority in the House of Lords was wrong in selecting a subjective test. The author finds it difficult to understand on what basis Lord Denning makes this claim.

(78) It must be stated, however, that Lord Denning has been prepared to apply a subjective test in other fields of labour law. In the area of unfair dismissal law, for example, Lord Denning has stated that in deciding whether an employer acted reasonably in treating a specific reason as sufficient reason for dismissal of a particular employee, the test to be applied is subjective. In Taylor v Alidair Ltd. [1978] IRLR 82 in construing para. 6(8) of Schedule 1 of the Trade Union and Labour Relations Act 1974 (now s.57 of the Employment Protection (Consolidation) Act 1978) Lord Denning declared that if the employer '... honestly believed on reasonable grounds that the [employee] was lacking in proper capability ... this was a good and sufficient reason to determine the employment' (p.84).

(79) At first blush, this form of the objective test would protect any type of action which provided practical assistance. This test, however, must be read in conjunction with the remoteness test which requires that only acts which are directly 'in furtherance' of the dispute are protected.

(80) Supra, p.95.

(81) Lord Wilberforce in the House of Lords in the McShane case, disagreed with Lord Denning that the improvement of morale could not be a legitimate objective of a trade dispute. See [1980] 2 WLR 89, p.96. Lord Wilberforce declared that '[m]orale is a vital factor in all confrontations, whether at Alamein or in Fleet Street ...' (p.96).

(82) This is an argument which Ewing also makes. He supports it by stating that the outlawing of certain sympathetic action '... is inconsistent with the weight of authority, both judicial and otherwise'. Ewing, supra, p.141.

(83) Ewing, *ibid*, p.141, who again quotes Michael Foot that 'the Government are prepared to say that the sympathy strike must be permitted ...'

(84) A possible fourth test was applied by Lord Denning in *Meade* v *Haringey London Borough Council* [1979] ICR 494. In that case, Lord Denning asserted that a trade union had no immunity when its action would cause a breach of statutory duty on the part of a public authority.

(85) Both the remoteness test and the objective test were applied by Ackner J. in *United Biscuits* v *Fall* [1979] IRLR 110. There is a danger that judges will apply the tests which have been created rather than examine the relevant words as contained in the statute.

(86) *New Society*, 31 January 1980, p.239.

(87) Lord Devlin, 'Judges and Lawmakers', 39 *MLR*, 1976, 1, p.13.

(88) [1979] 1 WLR 1294.

(89) *Star Sea Transport Corporation* v *Slater* discussed *supra*.

(90) [1980] 2 WLR 89.

(91) Lord Diplock, Lord Fraser of Tullybelton and Lord Scarman.

(92) [1979] 1 WLR 1294, p.1302. When the two cases of *Woods* and *Nelson* came before the Court of Appeal, Lord Denning had distinguished the '*Camilla M*' case from the present case on the basis of the 'unreasonable demands' which were made by the ITF in that case, but which were not present in this case. See [1979] ICR 744 and [1979] ICR 755. Lord Diplock could not distinguish the '*Camilla M*'case from the *Woods* case.

(93) *Ibid*, p.1313.

(94) Lord Wilberforce sought to apply an objective test that the act done should be reasonably capable of achieving its objective. See his judgment, *supra*, p.95. See also *supra*. In applying his test to the facts, Lord Wilberforce held that the circumstances of the *McShane* case were protected by the 1974 Act.

(95) *Ibid*, p.104.

(96) [1979] 1 WLR 1294, p.1311.

(97) *Ibid*, p.1312.

(98) *Ibid*, p.1312.

(99) *Ibid*, p.1314.

(100) [1980] 2 WLR 89, p.96.

(101) *Ibid*, p.96.

(102) Ibid, p.97.
(103) [1980] 1 WLR 142; 148.
(104) Concurring judgments to that of Lord Denning were issued by Lawton and Ackner L.JJ. in the Court of Appeal.
(105) The two disputes argument was not one which was put forward by counsel in argument. It seems to have originated from a suggestion made by one of the judges in the Court of Appeal during the hearing of the case. When the case was heard before the House of Lords, counsel for Duport Steels did not even use the two disputes argument in support of his case. It appears that he considered that this argument could not be 'rationally' supported. The matter is discussed at some length in Lord Diplock's judgment reported at [1980] 1 WLR 156. See particularly p.161.
(106) The Guardian, 28 January 1980.
(107) [1980] 1 WLR 142; 156.
(108) Lord Diplock, Lord Edmund-Davies, Lord Fraser of Tullybelton, Lord Keith of Kinkel and Lord Scarman.
(109) See particularly, Lord Diplock at p.157; Lord Edmund-Davies at pp.164-5; Lord Keith of Kinkel at p.167 and Lord Scarman at pp.168-9.
(110) Ibid, p.157.
(111) Ibid, p.168.
(112) Ibid, p.168.
(113) Per Lord Keith at p.167.
(114) Ibid, p.157.
(115) Per Lord Keith at p.168.
(116) Ibid, p.157.
(117) Ibid, p.169.
(118) The state of the present law on trade union immunity is likely to be substantially affected by the provisions of the Employment Bill 1980. The Conservative Government's Working Paper on Secondary Industrial Action which was published on 19 February 1980 to allow for consultation prior to changes in the Bill being made, contains proposals which would certainly reduce the circumstances where industrial action is lawful. Amongst other things, the proposals would introduce the twin tests that the action must be (a) reasonably capable of furthering the trade dispute in question; and (b) taken predominantly in pursuit of that trade dispute and not principally for some extraneous motive before being protected by the law. These two tests, of course, are based on decisions such as BBC v Hearn and 'Camilla M' dis-

cussed *supra* and the judgments of Lawton and Brandon L.JJ. and Lord Wilberforce in *McShane*.

(119) Ewing, *supra*, p.135.

(120) Lord Devlin, *supra*, p.4.

Developing a System of Administrative Law?

"Lord Denning indicated in the course of his judgment that the Courts were not the slaves of words, but their masters. This was the approach of Humpty Dumpty. 'When _I_ use a word', Humpty Dumpty said in rather a scornful tone, 'it means just what I choose it to mean - neither more nor less.' 'The question is', said Alice, 'whether you _can_ make words mean so many different things.' 'The question is', said Humpty Dumpty, 'which is to be master - that's all.'" - 'Justinian' in the _Financial Times_.

INTRODUCTION

In few areas of the law has development been as rapid in recent years as in administrative law. 'Natural justice is being applied more widely and is producing more case law than ever before ... Discretionary power is subject to strict judge-made limits and the notion of unfettered discretion is rejected. Preclusive clauses no longer protect excess of jurisdiction, and the doctrine of _ultra vires_ is now so wide that most administrative illegalities are jurisdictional. Quashing for error on the face is a thriving industry. The citadel of Crown privilege has been overturned ... As for controlling the executive generally, the courts are probably more active in this respect than at any previous time, and they have finally shaken off their timidity.'[1]

In all of these important developments Lord Denning has played a leading role - it would probably be true to say that no judge since the war has had a greater influence upon the way in which administrative law has developed. The outstanding feature of that development has been the great extension of the scope for judicial review of administrative action. The courts have, in effect, asserted, or conferred upon themselves, very wide powers to interfere with the decisions of administrative bodies. Whether such intervention powers are in fact exercised in any particular case would frequently appear, however, to be a matter for the court's discretion, and it is the main contention of this essay that it is in this respect that Lord Denning has had most influence upon the development of administrative law.

NATURAL JUSTICE

The development of the rules of natural justice has been described as 'one of the law's most notable achievements'.[2] The rules require the observance, in the making of certain types of decision, of 'fair' procedures. Following the decision in Ridge v Baldwin,[3] the courts have come to insist that the principles of natural justice should be followed in very many areas of decision-making. Lord Denning has played a major part in extending the scope of natural justice.

Prior to the decision in Ridge v Baldwin, it appeared that the rules of natural justice applied only to 'judicial' and not to 'administrative' proceedings. Lord Denning has rejoiced in the scotching of that 'heresy',[4] but has himself made the applicability and content of natural justice depend on such nebulous distinctions as that between a 'right' and a 'privilege'.[5] In Breen v Amalgamated Engineering Union,[6] for example, he declared: 'If a man seeks a privilege to which he has no particular claim ... then he can be turned away without a word. He need not be heard.'

However, in cases involving expulsion from trade unions, Lord Denning has stretched the meaning of 'right' to include for the purpose of deciding whether natural justice is applicable, the 'right to work'. This 'right' the court will then protect by requiring the trade union to observe the principle of natural justice before taking action. In one or two cases, Lord Denning has expressed the view that an applicant for a mere privilege has a right to be fairly treated; in the Liverpool Taxi case,[7] for instance, he was prepared to hold that where a local authority proposed to increase the number of taxi licences, the holders of existing licences were entitled to be heard in that they 'would be greatly affected by the decision'.

On the other hand, in Schmidt v Secretary of State for Home Affairs,[8] Lord Denning held that the rules of natural justice did not apply where an alien student of Scientology sought permission to extend his stay in Britain in order that he might complete his studies. The Home Secretary was, it was held, entitled to refuse the extension without giving the student an opportunity to be heard.

The fact of the matter is that there are, as Lord Denning said in the Gaming Board case, 'no rigid rules as to when the principles of natural justice are to apply ... Everything depends on the subject-matter.'[9] This lack of rules means that the courts are often free to decide, as a matter of policy, whether or not the rules of natural justice are to apply in a particular case.

Even if the court decides that the rules of natural justice are applicable, there are, as was also pointed out by Lord Denning in the Gaming Board case, no rigid rules as to their content. Here, too, everything depends on the subject-matter and it is for the court in each case to decide, as a matter of judicial policy, what will satisfy natural justice. Sometimes the judges appear concerned to compel administrative authorities to adopt procedures very similar to those followed in the courts. As a recent example of this approach, one might instance Lord Denning's judgment in Bushell v Secretary of State for the Environment[10], concerning the right of objectors at a motorway inquiry to cross-examine departmental witnesses on traffic forecasts.

In other cases, however, Lord Denning has been very easily satisfied as to the fairness of the procedure adopted by decision-making bodies. In Ward v Bradford Corporation,[11] for example, he was prepared to uphold the expulsion of a student from a teacher - training college even though the procedures followed in connection with the expulsion were in several respects very deficient. As H.W.R. Wade says: 'Had the court been sympathetic to the plaintiff, it could easily have found in her favour.'[12] Lord Denning might also be felt to have been very easily satisfied in the Selvarajan case.[13] In that case, four of the seven members of a committee which had to determine whether a complaint of unlawful discrimination was justified, were not in possession of the full papers on the case; they only had a report which described the case as 'clearly predictable' and which recommended a finding of 'no discrimination'. Lord Denning said: 'It may reasonably be inferred that these four were not in a position to form an opinion of their own', yet he was able to conclude that the committee's decision was 'manifestly correct' and that the applicant had been 'most fairly treated'.

It is clear that Lord Denning wishes the courts to have very wide powers to control the procedures of administrative authorities and trade unions. He takes the view, contrary to logic though it may be, that natural justice cannot be excluded by agreement; 'public policy' demands that the law should, for example, refuse to recognise any provision in the rules of a voluntary association or trade union which would have the effect of excluding natural justice.[14] It seems equally clear, however, that Lord Denning wishes to enforce natural justice as a matter of discretion rather than as a matter of law. A further example of this desire to enlarge judicial discretion is to be seen in R. v Secretary of State for the Environment, ex parte Ostler,[15] in which Lord Denning expressed the view that breach of natural justice would make a decision voidable rather than void.[16] The result of such an approach (which is again, perhaps, contrary to logic) is that the court need only quash a decision if it feels there has been substantial injustice. As Wade says: 'This policy is open to the objection that it would introduce dangerous uncertainty - one might say, palm-tree injustice.'[17]

It has been said that certain aspects of the law relating to natural justice have become endowed with a 'kaleidoscopic unpredictability'. The present writer would submit that that description could aptly be applied to a very large part of the law on the subject and that Lord Denning, in his concern to achieve a just result in the case before him, has had much to do with the law's development in that direction. It is, of course, desirable that 'right' should be done in the individual case, but consistency and principle are also important. In the end of the day, those who, from whatever motive, show a want of consideration for principle 'do only disservice to the true cause of justice.'[18]

APPROACHES TO LEGISLATION

Since the powers and duties of public authorities derive almost entirely from statute, judicial attitudes to legislation are of special importance in administrative law.

In a speech to Justice in 1977, Lord Denning said that 'the judges always loyally obey what Parliament has laid down.'[19] His Lordship expressed similar sentiments in the Hosenball case[20] and in that case was prepared to accept that even cherished concepts like natural justice must give way to Parliament's clear intention. He believes that the court should, if need be, put a strained construction on the words of a statute to give effect to what it perceives to be the intention of Parliament.

It is one thing to seek to ascertain and apply the intention of Parliament; it is perhaps a rather different matter to specifically 'depart from the literal words' of the Act (as Lord Denning conceded he was doing in R v Local Commissioner for Administration, ex parte Bradford City Council[21]) 'on the ground that it will 'promote the general legislative purpose' underlying the [statutory] provision'. That case perhaps illustrates that the purposive approach to statutory interpretation (for the acceptance of which Lord Denning has fought hard and long and with a measure of success) can be used to get around a clear statutory provision - simply to substitute for the straightforward words of the Act the judge's view of what Parliament should have said.[22] One might feel some sympathy for the Parliamentary draftsman; how, as one writer asked, does the draftsman make statutory provisions proof against the effect which 'Lord Denning's big heart has on his respect for what Parliament actually says?'[23]

Administrative authorities too must attempt to give effect to Parliament's intention. One of Lord Denning's important contributions to administrative law was his dissenting judgment in Padfield[24] (the basis of which was accepted by the House of Lords), declaring that it was not enough for an administrative authority which is exercising a discretionary power to act within the strict letter of the statute; if administrative action runs counter to the policy and purposes of the Act, that action will be declared to be unlawful.

The underlying 'legislative purpose' of a statutory provision is therefore important. How is a judge to discover the policy of an Act? He cannot look at Parliamentary debates (Lord Denning's efforts in that direction having, for the moment at least, failed[25]). Once a judge goes beyond the actual words of a statute, he becomes, in effect, a legislator and the only basis on which he can legislate is his own conception of what the 'public interest' demands.[26] Not infrequently Lord Denning's decisions on the meaning of legislation appear to be founded in his view of the public interest.

In R. v Sheffield Crown Court, ex parte Brownlow[27] Lord Denning openly suggested that the choice between two possible meanings of a statutory provision should not be made on the basis of the words used in the statute; the choice should, as a matter of 'the policy of the law, or of public policy', be made on the basis of the judge's view of the interpretation which gave 'the more sensible result'. In advocating this approach, Lord Denning appears to have been influenced by the fact that in a number of recent cases, particularly those concerned with trade union immunities, several judges expressed the view that they would have liked to come to a decision different from that to which they felt driven by the actual words of the statute. A leader in The Times was critical of Lord Denning's approach.[28] 'He does not', said The Times, 'suggest that such a result should conform to what Parliament intended or that it should follow the natural and obvious meaning of the words in issue; it would be, under his formula, for the majority of judges to determine the sensible result. That would be to usurp Parliament's function, and give judges a power which the vast majority of them neither seek nor are capable of exercising'.

Lord Denning has been described as 'restive' under the supremacy of Parliament.[29] One might go further and suggest that there are circumstances in which Lord Denning will simply disregard the will of Parliament. In The Discipline of Law Lord Denning tells the story of his efforts to 'oust' statutory provisions which attempt to restrict judicial control of administrative action.[30]

Although he is in no doubt as to Parliament's intention - ouster clauses were, he says, 'set up by Parliament in order to stop the High Court interfering' with the actions of various sorts of administrative bodies - he sees such provisions merely as 'obstacles' to be 'cleared' or 'overcome' by the courts. Lord Denning's approach to such statutory provisions is perhaps summed up in his statement that 'We [the judges] have lots of tricks up our sleeves to get round [ouster clauses].'[31]

In The Discipline of Law, Lord Denning recounts first of all how finality clauses and 'no certiorari' clauses were rendered ineffective. 'So far so good', he says, 'but those who frame 'ouster' clauses were not to be outdone. They invented a new 'ouster' clause which they thought would be foolproof - or shall I say proof against interference by the courts.' This too was overcome. It now appears, Lord Denning says, that the result of the decision in Pearlman[32] is that 'notwithstanding any 'ouster' clause which Parliament may insert' into an Act, the courts will always be able to intervene for error of law. The basis of Lord Denning's decision in Pearlman is that 'no court or tribunal has any jurisdiction to make an error of law on which the decision of the case depends.' Any such error takes the court or tribunal outside its jurisdiction. Its decision is therefore a nullity and cannot be protected by an ouster clause. As a result, 'ouster clauses' have, says Lord Denning, 'themselves been ousted.'[33] Thus, in Re a Company,[34] for example, the Court of Appeal was able to allow an appeal from the decision of a High Court judge in the face of a statutory provision declaring that a decision of this nature should 'not be appealable'. 'We could not', states Lord Denning in The Due Process of Law, 'allow such a clause to prevent us hearing an appeal ...'[35]

Lord Denning's judgments in several cases show that he takes an extremely broad view of what constitutes an error of law.[36] 'We have', he said on one occasion, 'often managed to turn a question of fact into a question of law.'[37] His Lordship's view that a court can intervene whenever an inferior body makes 'an error of law on which the decision of the case depends' means, therefore, that despite any ouster clause that Parliament may insert in a statute, the court will, if it wishes, almost always be able to intervene.

Developing a System? Lord Denning and Administrative Law

In Freedom Under the Law Lord Denning declared that any talk of 'judicial sabotage' of legislation was 'an unfair criticism of the judges.' 'The judges of England', he said, 'always carry out the intentions of Parliament ...'[38] The 'ousting' of ouster clauses would appear to have been done in furtherance of what Lord Denning conceives to be a higher principle, but is it anything other than 'judicial sabotage'?

It is interesting to notice that Lord Denning will not invariably ignore ouster clauses. In the case of statutory provisions which declare compulsory purchase orders and certain ministerial decisions to be unchallengeable after a specified period, Lord Denning takes the view that after the expiry of that period the courts should not intervene. Not, however, because such challenge is specifically excluded by statute. Lord Denning clearly believes that the courts could intervene if they wished, but he considers that they should not do so because, as soon as the specified time has elapsed, 'the authority will take steps to acquire property, demolish it and so forth. The public interest demands that they should be safe in doing so.'[39] The question whether the courts will 'loyally obey' Parliament's intention comes to depend, therefore, on whether the court considers the legislation to be in the public interest or not.

There are many other respects in which the judges' view of 'the public interest' appears to inform their attitude to legislation. Procedural requirements are sometimes treated as mandatory, sometimes as directory.[40] 'May' is sometimes taken to mean 'must'.[41] Sometimes, a statutory provision imposing an apparently absolute obligation is treated in effect as if it merely conferred a power. That there are no very clear legal principles underlying such decisions may perhaps be illustrated by consideration of one or two of Lord Denning's judgments in cases involving the enforcement of statutory duties.

In R. v Bristol Corporation, ex parte Hendy[42] Lord Denning had to consider s.36(1) of the Land Compensation Act 1973, which provides that where, as a result of the activities of a public body, 'a person is displaced from residential accommodation ... it shall be the duty of the relevant authority to ensure that he will be provided' with suitable alternative residential accommodation. Lord Denning reduced this seemingly absolute obligation to little more than a discretion to rehouse displaced occupiers. He said: 'I think that the corporation fulfil their duty when they do their best, as soon as practicable [neither of these phrases appears in the Act] to get [the tenant] other accommodation.'[43] Hostel accommodation would suffice even if it meant frequent moves and the splitting up of a family. The dispossessed occupier's name might go to the bottom of the housing waiting list. The authority did not, his Lordship thought, owe to a '1973 Act' claimant a duty higher than that owed to other persons on the waiting list. Since persons on the housing waiting list have no enforceable right to a house, Lord Denning's judgment would seem to mean that the 1973 Act confers no rights at all on displaced householders.

In other cases, Lord Denning has taken a markedly different approach to duties imposed on local authorities. Bradbury v Enfield L.B.C.[44] arose out of an authority's failure to give public notice of a scheme for the introduction of comprehensive education. Holding that the duty on a local authority to 'maintain' a school meant that the authority had to ensure that the school retained its 'fundamental character', Lord Denning declared: 'If a local authority does not fulfil the requirements of the law, this court will see that it does fulfil them ... Even if chaos should result, still the law must be obeyed.'[45] It might be suggested that the duty about which these strong words were used was less clear-cut than the duty considered in Hendy's case.

Ministers are commonly given powers to take remedial action where a local authority fails in its statutory duties. Sometimes the courts will treat such default powers as excluding any other remedy for enforcement of the duty. In Southwark L.B.C. v Williams,[46] Lord Denning held that homeless families who alleged breach on the part of a local authority of the duty to provide temporary accommodation for persons in urgent need of accommodation were not entitled to any remedy in the courts, his reason for reaching such a conclusion being that the Act gave the Minister power to enforce the duty. The families should, said his Lordship, 'approach the Minister and ask him to make an order ...';[47] they must, he said, 'make their appeal for help to others, not to us.'[48]

One might contrast the decision in Southwark with the decisions in Meade v London Borough of Haringey[49] and A.G., ex rel. McWhirter v Independent Broadcasting Authority.[50] In the former case, it was held that an education authority which had closed its schools because of industrial action was in breach of its statutory duty to 'secure that there shall be available ... sufficient schools for providing full-time education'. Although the Education Act provided a remedy by way of complaint to the Minister, that did not, in Lord Denning's view, exclude other remedies. The courts, as 'the last resort available to the beleaguered citizen', would provide a remedy if necessary.

In McWhirter an attempt was made to prevent the showing on television of a film which was alleged to offend against public decency. The broadcasting of the film would, it was claimed, involve a breach of the statutory requirements on broadcasting. Lord Denning was prepared in this case to ignore the statutory powers available to the appropriate Minister. The possibility that the Minister might exercise his powers did not seem to Lord Denning to be a remedy that was 'reasonably available'; it was not 'so accessible', 'so speedy or effective' or 'so independent as the courts of law.'[51]

In the course of his judgment in McWhirter Lord Denning said that the first point was 'whether Mr. McWhirter had any locus standi to come to the court at all.' 'This', said Lord Denning, 'is a point of constitutional significance. We live in an age when Parliament has placed statutory duties on government departments and public authorities - for the benefit of the public - but has provided no remedy for the breach of them. If a government department or a public authority transgresses the law laid down by Parliament, or threatens to transgress it, can a member of the public come to the court ...?'[52] In this case, Lord Denning was prepared to hold that any member of the television-viewing public had sufficient interest to draw a threatened breach of the broadcasting legislation 'to the attention of the courts of law and seek to have the law enforced.' In the Southwark case, however, his Lordship simply declared: 'It cannot have been intended by Parliament that every person who was in need of temporary accommodation should be able to sue the local authority for it.'[53]

In relation to statutory interpretation (as in other areas of the law) the present writer would suggest that Lord Denning allows his determination to achieve what he conceives to be a just result to get in the way of adherence to any very clear principles. It is important that people should have some idea of where they stand without having to resort to litigation. Even more importantly, whatever the defects of the legislative process, they are not so great as to justify Lord Denning's apparent reluctance to accept the supremacy of Parliament. Social policy should, as one writer said, 'be shaped by elected representatives in Parliament.'[54] In relation to statutory interpretation, there can, in Lord Devlin's words, 'be no general warrant authorising the judges to do anything except interpret and apply.'[55]

EXECUTIVE DISCRETION

In The Discipline of Law, Lord Denning tells how the courts have taken action 'to curb the abuse of power by the executive powers.'[56] An important theme of this part of the book is that no matter how wide a discretionary power may appear to be, it is always open to challenge in the courts; if, on examination by the courts, it is found 'that the power has been exercised improperly or mistakenly so as to unjustly impinge on the legitimate rights or interests of the subject, then these courts must so declare.'[57]

In support of this proposition, Lord Denning includes in the book extracts from his judgments in well-known cases such as Padfield,[58] Tameside,[59] Laker[60] and Congreve[61] (relating respectively to ministerial action concerning an agricultural marketing scheme, a local education scheme, the designation of airlines and the licensing of television sets). It can, of course, be argued that in some or all of these cases the courts were over-ready to intervene and that the judgments are no more than thinly-disguised policy decisions. J.A.G. Griffith is particularly critical of the Padfield and Tameside cases, saying that 'in both these cases the courts took it upon themselves to tell Ministers that they had acted wrongly, not because they had taken decisions which were ultra vires in substance or in procedure, but because they had taken policy decisions on grounds which the courts disapproved of.'[62]

It does not seem unreasonable to expect that a judge will, if he is going to interfere with the exercise of an apparently wide administrative discretion, make clear the legal basis on which he is acting. Lord Denning does not, in this writer's view, always do that. His judgment in Congreve was, for example, described as amounting to little more than 'a dogmatic allegation of unfairness and injustice by the minister', there being 'little in the judgment which goes further than simply criticising the minister's style of play in taking an unsporting advantage of the rules. It remains unclear that the minister had actually acted in breach of them.'[63]

The judgments selected for inclusion in The Discipline of Law show Lord Denning as very ready to assert judicial control over the exercise of discretionary powers. On some occasions Lord Denning has, however, shown a marked reluctance to interfere with executive discretion. In Azam,[64] for example, his Lordship declared that the power to send back illegal immigrants was 'entirely a matter for the Secretary of State.' 'Parliament has', he said, 'entrusted this decision to the Home Secretary and not to the courts. It has left it to his discretion. It is better left there ... This is not a justiciable matter for the courts. It is an administrative matter for the Secretary of State.' In Schmidt[65] Lord Denning said of a refusal by the Minister to extend an alien's stay in Britain: 'I think that the Minister can exercise his power for any purpose which he considers to be for the public good or to be in the interests of the people of this country.'

In Hosenball[66] there was, said Lord Denning, 'a conflict between the interests of national security on the one hand and the freedom of the individual on the other.' 'The balance between the two is not', he said, 'for a court of law. It is for the Home Secretary. He is the person entrusted by Parliament with the task.' He expressed great confidence in the good faith of ministers, saying that 'successive Ministers have discharged their duties to the complete satisfaction of the people at large ... They have never interfered with the liberty or freedom of movement of any individual except where it is absolutely necessary for the safety of the state.' Since the court upheld the Minister's refusal to reveal why he had invoked his powers, it is difficult to see how Lord Denning could make this assertion with such confidence.

Professor Griffith says of the courts' decisions in cases concerning review of executive discretion that 'little attempt is made to treat like situations in a like manner or to act consistently within a framework of judicial analysis.'[67] That statement could, it is submitted, be applied to Lord Denning's judgments in many of the leading cases in this field. One or two illustrations of apparent inconsistencies are given below.

In _Azam_[68] Lord Denning said: 'The statute places no limit on [the Minister's] discretion. If he exercises it honestly, I do not think that the court can interfere with his discretion.' On the other hand, for claiming in _Padfield_ that the courts had no power to interfere with an honest exercise of ministerial discretion, the Minister was, in Lord Denning's words, 'roundly rebuked ... for his impudence.'[69]

In cases like _Congreve_ and _Tameside_ the actions of the Minister were subjected to minute examination (and, even at that, the present writer is unsure that anything clearly unlawful was discovered). However, in the _ASLEF_ case[70] concerning the exercise of a ministerial power to require a ballot of workers before industrial action was taken, Lord Denning refused to interfere with the Minister's discretion, saying that the Minister's decision was not to be 'conned over word by word, letter by letter, to see if he has in any way misdirected himself.'

In _Sagnata Investments_ v _Norwich Corporation_[71] Lord Denning would not have interfered with the decision of a local authority to refuse a permit for the provision of amusements with prizes, saying that if the local authority 'think that an amusement arcade is socially undesirable, they are entitled to say so. They do not require evidence for the purpose ... Their decision should be supported if possible.' In _Tameside_, on the other hand, Lord Denning's conclusion that the Minister's action was unreasonable was based in part upon the view that there was no evidence before the Minister on which he could declare himself satisfied that the local education authority was proposing to act unreasonably.[72]

Even if a Minister is under no statutory obligation to give reasons for a decision, Lord Denning has said that the court is entitled to infer from the absence of reasons that the Minister had no good reason and was acting arbitrarily (see, for example, Padfield); lack of reasons will not, however, always lead his Lordship to draw such an inference (see, for example, ASLEF and Soblen).[73] Sometimes Lord Denning has no hesitation in interfering with ministerial decisions on policy matters (see, for example, Laker and Tameside); in Azam, on the other hand, his Lordship declared that 'the matter is one of policy, which the courts cannot handle.'[74]

All of the cases mentioned above involved consideration of a statutory power but the justification for judicial intervention in some cases and not in others is not to be found in differences of statutory language; there does not, therefore, appear to be any clear legal basis for holding in some cases that Parliament intended the Minister to be left as judge of his own powers and for holding in other cases that the exercise of ministerial powers is to be judged by objective standards.

A clue to the explanation of the apparent contradictions is perhaps to be found in Lord Denning's statement in ASLEF that the scope for challenge of ministerial action 'depends very much on the subject-matter with which the Minister is dealing.'[75] The decision as to whether or not to intervene is, it would seem, made on policy rather than legal grounds. The cases in which the courts have quashed decisions of Ministers represent, says Professor Griffith, 'the judicial desire ... to protect the individual against political policies which are seen by the judiciary to be contrary to the public interest.'[76] Where, on the other hand, a Minister is seen to be acting in a way which accords with the judiciary's conception of the public interest, the court will not intervene.

'THE ORDINARY MAN'S DEFENCE'

Reviewing The Discipline of Law, Lord Scarman suggested that Lord Denning's 'steadfast purpose has always been to strengthen the ordinary man's defence against abuse of power.'[77] Many of Lord Denning's judgments demonstrate a concern to protect what he has described as 'the freedom of the individual as against the state and the bureaucrats.'[78] 'There is', he said in a speech to Justice in 1977, 'one mistake which the judges have never made. They have never abandoned the freedom of the individual.'[79]

The anxiety to protect liberties threatened by public powers, to be discerned in cases like Congreve, Tameside and Laker, is perhaps to be seen at its strongest in the Rossminster case.[80] Here a search warrant granted to the Inland Revenue was quashed because it did not specify exactly what evidence was being sought or what offence was suspected. Although Lord Denning was, in 1969, prepared to accept as a settled principle of the common law that if, in the course of searching a man's house for material relating to a suspected crime, police officers 'come upon any other goods which show him to be implicated in some other crime, they must take them ...',[81] he took the view in Rossminster that the powers of search conferred by Parliament upon the Inland Revenue should be very narrowly construed; although the warrant granted to the Revenue incorporated the words of the relevant statutory provision, the statutory power was, in Lord Denning's view, 'drawn so widely that in some hands it might be an instrument of oppression', and he considered that it was, therefore, the duty of the courts 'so to construe the statute as to see that it encroaches as little as possible upon the liberties of the people of England.'[82]

One might perhaps contrast Lord Denning's hostile attitude to the Inland Revenue's powers of search with the fairly sympathetic comments made in The Due Process of Law[83] on 'Anton Piller' orders - orders which are granted by the courts to private individuals and which are almost equivalent in effect to search warrants.[84]

In Hubbard v Pitt[85] Lord Denning, in a dissenting judgment, was not prepared to see the courts interfere on technical grounds with the right of tenants to demonstrate outside an estate agent's office. This, as Professor Griffith says, 'is the voice of freedom under the law.'[86] A similar view might well be taken of certain of Lord Denning's comments in R. v Sheffield Crown Court, ex parte Brownlow.[87] In that case, Lord Denning expressed the view that it was unconstitutional for the police authorities to engage in 'jury vetting'. 'If that sort of thing was allowed, what,' he asked, 'becomes of a man's right to privacy?' A man summoned to serve on a jury 'should not thereby be liable to have his past raked up and handed on a plate to prosecuting and defending lawyers.' On occasion, Lord Denning's concern for individual freedom might even be felt to be excessive; in Congreve,[88] for example, he expressed the somewhat remarkable view that the Minister's power to licence television sets was 'a very special kind of power' in that it 'invades a man in the privacy of his own home.'[89]

'Freedom' does not, however, invariably win through in Lord Denning's judgments. Although it is sometimes, and perhaps justifiably, suggested that judges tend to be unduly protective of the freedom of landowners, Lord Denning's decisions in, for example, cases under the town planning legislation - legislation which interferes very considerably with common law property rights - do not generally show such a tendency; in accordance with what he conceives to be the policy of the legislation, many of his judgments in this field are anything but restrictive of the powers of local planning authorities.[90] Similarly, although the Race Relations legislation restricts what Lord Diplock described as 'the liberty which the citizen has previously enjoyed at common law to differentiate between one person and another',[91] Lord Denning was not on that account persuaded in the Charter case or the Dockers Labour Club case[92] to place a narrow construction on the legislation, but interpreted it instead in such a way as to widen its sphere of operation.

Individual liberty was, however, subordinated to other considerations in the ASLEF case (in which the freedom of workers to take industrial action was mentioned but was, in the context of 'a grave threat to the national economy', accorded almost no weight by Lord Denning). In several important cases in which Lord Denning took a leading part, individual freedom has taken second place to national security or government policy on aliens or immigrants (see, for example, the Hosenball, Soblen, Schmidt, and Azam cases). It should, of course, be said that Lord Denning is not alone in this approach to such cases; the judiciary as a whole has, as H.W.R. Wade says, 'shown a marked reluctance to extend to aliens the same principles of procedural protection and fair play that apply to citizens of this country.'[93]

It does not, of course, follow that because a decision protects certain freedoms or is couched in the language of freedom, the decision is necessarily worthy of support. Not all 'freedoms' are equally worthy of protection. Although Lord Denning, in an address in 1977, cited the Congreve, Laker and Tameside cases as showing that the judges 'do their best to protect the liberty of the individual in our time under the rule of law,'[94] it might be asked whether the freedoms involved in those cases (freedom not to pay an increased TV licence fee, freedom to operate 'Sky Train' and the freedom of a local authority to modify an educational scheme) were more worthy of protection than the freedoms at stake in the ASLEF, Soblen and Hosenball cases. Some of the 'liberties' upheld by Lord Denning might even be thought unworthy of any protection at all. It was, for example, said of the decision in Congreve: 'To elevate tax avoidance into a liberty of the subject protected by the Bill of Rights is a complete inversion of moral values'; the decision simply 'epitomises the courts' laissez-faire philosophy of every man for himself at the expense of the community.'[95]

It might also be suggested that in his concern to protect 'freedom' against state power, Lord Denning may, as was said in the context of the Rossminster decision, run the risk of undermining the important principles 'that the law shall uphold the will of the people expressed through Parliament' and that the law shall 'apply equally to all.'[96]

In the course of his Hamlyn Lectures, Lord Scarman said: 'It is no longer sufficient for the law to provide a framework of freedom in which men, women and children may work out their own destinies; social justice, as our society now understands the term, requires the law to be loaded in favour of the weak and exposed ...'[97] Whereas in many of his judgments, Lord Denning can clearly be seen to favour the individual citizen whose liberties are threatened by state power, his Lordship's judgments in cases involving the state in its role of provider for or protector of the individual citizen do not appear to demonstrate any great anxiety to favour the citizen who is at odds with authority. In particular, statutes which impose on public authorities duties to provide for the 'weak and exposed' - attempts to 'load' the law in favour of certain categories of citizen - have not always been rigorously enforced by Lord Denning.

In the Southwark and Hendy cases,[98] for example, statutory provisions which imposed upon public authorities certain duties to make housing provision for the homeless were treated by Lord Denning as imposing no enforceable obligation. In Liverpool City Council v Irwin[99] Lord Denning expressed the view that council tenants, occupying flats in a tower block 'at very low rents', should not be allowed to recover damages for the discomfort and inconvenience they had suffered as a result of the council's failure to keep the lifts and stairs of the block reasonably fit for use; if the tenants were to be allowed to recover damages, they would be able to off-set the damages against their rents and 'would be able to stay in these flats for years without paying anything.' 'That', said Lord Denning, 'does not seem to me to be right.' Given the admittedly appalling conditions in which the tenants had to live, it might not be thought to be self-evidently wrong.

Allegations of discrimination on grounds of race or sex can be extremely difficult to prove and Parliament has conferred wide investigatory powers on the Equal Opportunities Commission and the Commission for Racial Equality. In Science Research Council v Nasse[100] the Court of Appeal had to undertake the difficult task of attempting to balance the need not to frustrate anti-discrimination legislation against the desirability of preserving confidentiality for personal reports. What is remarkable about Lord Denning's judgment in the Science Research Council case is the hostility evinced towards the Commissions' statutory powers - powers designed to assist in the vindication of individual rights. The Commission's requests to see documents which the employers regarded as confidential were, he said, 'presumptuous'. Their powers to require disclosure of information (which are in fact subject to quite substantial safeguards) were in Lord Denning's view such that it might be thought 'we were back in the days of the Inquisition' or 'the days of the general warrant.'

In R. v Preston Supplementary Benefits Appeal Tribunal, ex parte Moore[101] Lord Denning was at pains to emphasise that the courts should not generally afford their assistance to claimants seeking to challenge adverse decisions by supplementary benefit appeal tribunals - judicial intervention in such cases might mean, he said, that 'the courts would become engulfed with streams of cases.'[102] One might contrast his Lordship's statement in Bradbury:[103] 'Even if chaos should result, still the law must be obeyed.' And what of the view expressed in The Discipline of Law that the citizen who 'complains that the law is not being enforced as it should' ought to be able to seek the assistance of the courts? If Lord Denning was right to hold, as he did, that the National Federation of Self-Employed and Small Businesses has a sufficient interest to entitle it to take action against the Inland Revenue over a 'tax amnesty' granted to certain printing workers;[104] if any citizen who considers that post office workers are threatening unlawful industrial action is to be allowed to take action in the courts;[105] if a member of the public who complains that the television authorities intend to show an allegedly offensive film,[106] or that the police are not enforcing the law on pornography[107] or gaming,[108] is to be afforded the assistance of the courts,[109] it seems rather hard to refuse such assistance to the supplementary benefit claimant on the ground that the courts could not cope.

In the Preface to The Discipline of Law, Lord Denning declares it to be his theme that 'the principles of law laid down by the judges in the nineteenth century ... are not suited to the social necessities and social opinion of the twentieth century', and that the law should be 'moulded and shaped to meet the opinions of today'. While it is clear that in some areas of the law Lord Denning has endeavoured to shape the law in accordance with those sentiments, it might be suggested that his Lordship's approach to the duties of the welfare state is still that of the nineteenth century and laissez-faire.

JUDICIAL POLICY

It has been suggested at several points above that policy plays an important part in judicial decisions as to whether or not to intervene in particular types of case. If the court does decide to intervene, judicial policy may also have a part to play in the court's decision on the merits of the case. Lord Denning has, on quite a number of occasions, openly asserted the court's right and duty to decide cases on policy grounds or on the basis of 'the public interest.'[110] The courts ought, he has said, to decide cases 'according to the reason of the thing' or, even on the basis of 'the law as it should be.'[111] 'Nowadays', said Lord Denning in Dutton, 'we direct ourselves to considerations of policy.'[112] It might be suggested that here, as elsewhere, Lord Denning is perhaps more open about his views than other judges tend to be.

In Enderby Town Football Club v Football Association[113] Lord Denning said: 'I know that over 300 years ago Hobart C.J. said that 'Public policy is an unruly horse' ... So unruly is the horse, it is said, that no judge should ever try to mount it lest it run away with him. I disagree. With a good man in the saddle, the unruly horse can be kept in control.' His Lordship appears not to be impressed by the argument that 'public policy' decisions should be made by elected representatives in Parliament rather than by judges, and apparently entertains no doubts as to the judiciary's ability to make decisions on the basis of 'the public interest'.[114] In the Preface to The Due Process of Law Lord Denning says that time and again, when the Court of Appeal has ventured out on a new line, it has been rebuffed by the House of Lords on the ground, as Lord Denning puts it, 'that the legislature - advised by this body or that - can see all round, whereas the Judges see only one side.' 'This', his Lordship states, 'I dispute. The Judges have better sight and longer sight than those other bodies ...'

When politically sensitive issues have come before him, Lord Denning has, however, sometimes been at pains to disclaim an interest in the political or social consequences of the proceedings.[115] The court is, in such cases, declared to be merely the agent of Parliament; here there is little talk of discretion to intervene or of decisions based on policy. In The Discipline of Law, however, Lord

Denning declares that he will, in demonstrating how the courts have curbed the 'abuse of power by the executive authorities', 'show that previous decisions have been departed from; that long-accepted propositions have been overthrown; that 'ouster' clauses have themselves been ousted; and that literal interpretation has gone by the board.' If the law is not to be found in earlier decisions or established principles or in the literal words of statute, and if, as Lord Denning makes clear in Pearlman, the judges frequently have a choice as to whether or not they should intervene, the only basis for decision would appear to be the judge's own values, his view of what public policy demands.[116]

If it is right that many of the courts' decisions in the field of administrative law are policy decisions, it must then be asked whether the courts are adequately equipped to determine questions of administrative and political expediency Somewhat ironically, it would seem that although the courts are quite ready to invalidate a minister's decision if it is shown that he has failed to take account of all relevant considerations, the policy decisions of the courts are of necessity based on very inadequate material. 'The judicial system does not', as one writer said, 'enable the judge to be informed of policy considerations (whether by pressure groups or any other source). It does not allow issues to be thrashed out in public debate.'[117] The policy decisions which Lord Denning is, it is submitted, very ready to make, appear to be based on little more than his Lordship's conception of what justice and fairness demand, his ideas of which values deserve protection, or simply his reaction against the exercise of powers he instinctively dislikes.[118]

This instinctive approach can, it is submitted, be discerned in many of Lord Denning's judgments. His Lordship's main reason for denying a remedy to the student teacher in Ward, for example, would seem to have been his disapproval of the plaintiff's behaviour and morals ('She would never make a teacher. No parent would knowingly entrust their child to her care.') His refusal to lend assistance in the Gaming Board case seems to stem, in part at least, from a disapproval of gambling. ('What they are really seeking is a privilege - almost, I might say, a franchise - to carry on gaming for profit, a thing never hitherto allowed in this country.') In Laker the

Minister's action was preventing 'a man of enterprise' putting an 'exciting project' into operation. In Dutton v Bognor Regis U.D.C. the local authority's shoulders were, Lord Denning said, 'broad enough to bear the loss.' Readers of Lord Denning's judgment in Hosenball might, as was said in an editorial in the New Law Journal, 'be pardoned for supposing that it was Mr Mark Hosenball's conduct, rather than that of the Home Secretary, that was in issue.'[119]

One might well have considerable doubts about the effect in practice of some of the policy decisions in which Lord Denning has been involved. Examination of this question would be a very large task but it might be suggested that the results of decisions such as those in Lever Finance[120] and Dutton,[121] both of which have had very important effects upon the liabilities of local authorities, have not been entirely beneficial.[122] Lord Denning's 'away with bureaucratic technicalities' approach in Lever Finance may well mean that developers will not suffer where an official of a local planning authority makes a mistake - an erroneous or unauthorised statement may well be treated as binding upon the authority. On the debit side, however, planning officials are, because of the possibility that an unguarded statement may be held binding, likely to be less open and helpful in their dealings with developers and the public generally.[123] The decision in Lever may also have the undesirable consequence of prejudicing the position of 'third parties' such as neighbours 'in that a decision may become binding without compliance with statutory procedures designed to protect them.'[124] Other judges have taken a rather different view of what policy demands in this matter and their reluctance to follow Lever Finance has resulted in very considerable confusion in this area of the law.[125]

In very broad terms, might it be asked whether (in contrast to the ombudsmen's activities, which would generally seem to have the effect of imposing high standards of conduct upon administrators) the result in practice of judicial intervention in administrative action is frequently no more than to slow down the decision-making process or to place obstacles in the way of efficient administration?[126] Judicial control may, for example, inhibit communication between central departments and local authorities. It can even have the effect of making it difficult for an administrative body to alter a view it has previously taken in the exercise of its administrative discretion.[127]

In general, policy decisions should, it is submitted, be left to politicians.[128] It is not that policy decisions made by judges are necessarily any worse or any more illiberal than those made by the executive. The important point is that whatever criticisms can be made of the relationship between the executive and Parliament, the executive is in some measure answerable to Parliament and ultimately to the electorate, whereas judges are virtually irremoveable and are accountable to no one. Most importantly, where policy decisions are made by the judiciary there will generally be little opportunity for prior public debate on the issues involved.[129]

A DEVELOPED SYSTEM?

In Breen v AEU,[130] Lord Denning said: 'It may truly now be said that we have a developed system of administrative law.' Griffith, on the other hand, declares that it is 'a tribute both to the ingenuity of judges and their consistency that they have managed, during the course of handing down hundreds and hundreds of decisions' since the time of Dicey 'to maintain that purity which Dicey so admired', i.e. the absence of a system of administrative law. 'Partly', he says, 'the device has been, as soon as anything like a system of legal principle appeared to be forming ... to abort it at once. This has not been done by any method so crude as refusing to recognise the principles. It has been done much more simply by encouraging counter-principles to arise.'[131] Whether it is right to suggest, as Griffith appears to do, that the present condition of the law is the result of conscious efforts on the part of the judges may be open to some doubt, but his description seems much closer to reality than Lord Denning's.

Lord Denning's influence on administrative law has, it is submitted, been very considerable. He has been a major force in widening the scope for judicial intervention in relation to the activities of administrative bodies. As a result, however, of the increased discretion which the courts have taken to themselves, it has become more and more difficult to predict when and how judicial control will be exercised. Little progress has been made towards a principled system of administrative law. Lord Denning's efforts to 'do justice', to achieve results which 'the right-thinking members of the community believe to be fair',[132] may well have taken us further than ever from a 'developed system' of administrative law.

In his readiness to intervene when intervention seems desirable, in his anxiety to achieve a just result, in his readiness to throw off the past, Lord Denning has, it is suggested, contributed to the creation of a body of law for which Tennyson's phrase 'a wilderness of single instances' is almost apt. In The Discipline of Law Lord Denning declares that the courts' actions to 'curb the abuse of power by the executive authorities' have been taken 'in support of the rule of law'. 'The rule of law' is, of course, a remarkably elastic concept, but it does imply government conducted, in Wade's words, 'within a framework of recognised rules and principles.'[133] Arbitrary exercises of judicial power do not provide an answer to arbitrary exercises of executive power. Whatever the inadequacies (and they would seem to be many) of present methods of political control over administrative bodies, the move, under the influence of Lord Denning, towards giving the judges an unfettered discretion to decide when and how to intervene in administrative action does not represent a satisfactory solution to the question of how to control the activities of public authorities.

ERIC YOUNG

NOTES

(1) Schwartz B. & Wade H.W.R., Legal Control of Government, Clarendon Press, Oxford, 1972, p.320.
(2) Wade H.W.R., Administrative Law, 4th ed., Clarendon Press, Oxford, 1977, p.40.
(3) [1964] AC 40.
(4) See R. v Gaming Board for Great Britain, ex parte Benaim and Khaida [1970] 2 QB 417, 430.

(5) See, for example, R. v Gaming Board (supra).
(6) [1971] 2 QB 175.
(7) R. v Liverpool Corporation, ex parte Liverpool Taxi Fleet Operators Association [1972] 2 QB 299. See too R. v Gaming Board (supra).
(8) [1969] 2 Ch. 149.
(9) [1970] 2 QB 417, 430.
(10) (1979) 123 Sol. Jo. 605 (reversed by the House of Lords - See The Times, 8 February 1980).
(11) (1972) 70 LGR 27.
(12) Administrative Law, 4th ed., p.413.
(13) R. v Race Relations Board, ex parte Selvarajan [1975] 1 WLR 1686.
(14) See, for example, Lee v Showmen's Guild of Great Britain [1952] 2 QB 329. See too Lord Denning, The Discipline of Law, Butterworths, London, 1979, Part Four.
(15) [1977] QB 122.
(16) Lord Denning has advocated a similar approach in other contexts - see, for example, R. v Paddington Valuation Officer, ex parte Peachey Property Corporation (No.2) [1966] 1 QB 380; and Director of Public Prosecutions v Head [1959] AC 83.
(17) Administrative Law, 4th ed., p.449.
(18) Bennion F., Want of Consideration (1953) 16 M.L.R. 441.
(19) Reported in The Times, 29 June 1977. See too Denning, Sir A., Freedom under the Law, Stevens, London, 1949, p.84.
(20) R. v Secretary of State for Home Affairs, ex parte Hosenball [1977] 1 WLR 766.
(21) [1979] QB 287, 313.
(22) It might also be suggested that strenuous efforts to 'promote the general legislative purpose' are not invariably to be discerned in Lord Denning's judgments. See, for example, United Kingdom Association of Professional Engineers v Advisory, Conciliation and Arbitration Service [1979] 1 WLR 570. (Reversed by the House of Lords - see The Times, 15 February 1980).
(23) Bennion F., Legislative Technique, (1979) 129 New L.J., 1170.
(24) Padfield v Minister of Agriculture, Fisheries and Food [1968] AC 997.

(25) Lord Denning has, however, suggested means by which judges might evade the effect of the House of Lords' ruling on this matter - see R. v Local Commissioner, ex parte Bradford Council [1979] QB 287, p.311.
(26) See Ganz, G., Caravans and Judicial Law-Making, (1964) 27 MLR 611.
(27) The Times, 4 March 1980.
(28) 4 March 1980.
(29) Bennion, F., Legislative Technique (1980) 130 New L.J. 243.
(30) See, in particular, pp.69-78 and 106-109.
(31) Lord Denning, The Freedom of the Individual Today, 45 Medico-Legal Journal (1977), p.56.
(32) Pearlman v Keepers and Governors of Harrow School [1979] QB 56.
(33) The Discipline of Law, p.62.
(34) (1979) 123 Sol. Jo. 584.
(35) Lord Denning, The Due Process of Law, Butterworths, London, 1980, p.80.
(36) See, in particular, Ashbridge Investments v Minister of Housing and Local Government [1965] 1 WLR 1320; and Coleen Properties v Minister of Housing and Local Government [1971] 1 WLR 433.
(37) The Freedom of the Individual Today, 45 Medico-Legal Journal, (1977) p.56.
(38) p.84.
(39) R. v Secretary of State for the Environment, ex parte Ostler [1977] QB 122.
(40) In Bradbury v Enfield London Borough Council [1967] 1 WLR 1311, for example, one statutory provision was held to be mandatory while another provision was held to be merely directory.
(41) See, for example, Congreve v Home Office [1976] QB 629.
(42) [1974] 1 WLR 498. See Young E., Rehousing Displaced Householders (1979) 32 SCOLAG Bulletin, 76.
(43) Ibid, p.501.
(44) [1967] 1 WLR 1311.
(45) Ibid, p.1324.
(46) [1971] Ch. 734.
(47) Ibid, p.743.
(48) Ibid, p.744.
(49) [1979] ICR 494.
(50) [1973] QB 629.
(51) Ibid, p.649.

(52) Ibid, p.646.
(53) [1971] Ch. 734, 743.
(54) Bennion F., Legislative Technique,(1980) 130 New L.J. 243.
(55) Devlin, P., The Judge, Oxford University Press, Oxford, 1979, p.9.
(56) p.61.
(57) Laker Airways v Department of Trade [1977] QB 643, 708.
(58) Supra.
(59) Secretary of State for Education and Science v Tameside Metropolitan Borough Council [1977] AC 1014.
(60) Supra.
(61) Congreve v Home Office [1976] QB 629.
(62) Griffith, J.A.G., Administrative Law and the Judges, Haldane Society, London, 1979, p.16.
(63) Judicial Refereeing : Unheard Whistles,(1979) 24 J.L.S.S., 113.
(64) R. v Governor of Pentonville Prison, ex parte Azam [1974] AC 18, 31.
(65) Supra, p.169.
(66) R. v Secretary of State for Home Affairs, ex parte Hosenball [1977] 1 WLR 766, 783.
(67) Griffith, J.A.G., The Politics of the Judiciary, Manchester University Press/Fontana, London, 1977, p.129.
(68) Supra, p.31.
(69) Breen v AEU [1971] 2 QB 175, 190.
(70) Secretary of State for Employment v Associated Society of Locomotive Engineers and Firemen (No.2) [1972] 2 QB 455, 493.
(71) [1971] 2 QB 614, 628.
(72) See too Coleen Properties v Minister of Housing and Local Government [1971] 1 WLR 433.
(73) R. v Governor of Brixton Prison, ex parte Soblen [1963] 2 QB 243.
(74) [1974] AC 18, 34.
(75) [1972] 2 QB 455, 493.
(76) The Politics of the Judiciary, p.211.
(77) (1979) 95 LQR 445.
(78) The Freedom of the Individual Today, 45 Medico-Legal Journal (1977), p.49.
(79) Reported in The Times, 29 June 1977.
(80) R. v Inland Revenue Commissioners, ex parte Rossminster Ltd. [1980] 2 WLR 1.

(81) Ghani v Jones [1970] 1 QB 693, 706.
(32) [1980] 2 WLR 1, 19.
(83) See pp.123-130.
(84) Anton Piller KG v Manufacturing Processes Ltd. [1976] Ch. 55 ('So useful are these orders that they are in daily use.') See too Ex parte Island Records Ltd. [1978] Ch. 122. In Re a Company (1979) 123 Sol. Jo. 584, Lord Denning was prepared to give a wide construction to what he described as the 'important and desirable' powers, analogous to a search warrant, granted by s.441 of the Companies Act 1948.
(85) [1976] QB 142.
(86) The Politics of the Judiciary, p.146.
(87) The Times, 4 March 1980.
(88) [1976] QB 629, 649.
(89) See too Attorney General v Independent Broadcasting Authority [1973] QB 629 in which Lord Denning said that when the plaintiff switched on his television set 'he was entitled to expect that the programme would comply with the statutory requirements. There were thousands like him sitting at home watching. All were entitled to have their privacy respected.'
(90) See, for example, Miller-Mead v Minister of Housing and Local Government [1963] 2 QB 196; and Newbury District Council v Secretary of State for the Environment [1978] 1 WLR 1241.
(91) Charter v Race Relations Board [1972] 1 QB 545.
(92) Dockers' Labour Club v Race Relations Board [1974] QB 503.
(93) Administrative Law, 4th ed., p.483.
(94) The Freedom of the Individual Today, 45 Medico-Legal Journal (1977), p.49.
(95) Ganz, G., TV Licences and the Bill of Rights, (1973) P.L. 14.
(96) Sunday Times, 18 November 1979.
(97) Scarman, Sir Leslie, English Law - The New Dimension, Stevens, London, 1974, p.29.
(98) Supra.
(99) [1975] 3 WLR 663, 668.
(100) [1978] ICR 1124.
(101) [1975] 1 WLR 624, 631. See too R. v Industrial Injuries Commissioner, ex parte AEU [1966] 2 QB 21.
(102) In the course of his judgment, Lord Denning said: 'The courts should hesitate long before interfering ... with the decisions of appeal tribunals ... They should leave the tribunals to interpret the Act in a

broad reasonable way according to the spirit and not the letter: especially as Parliament has given them a way of alleviating any hardship.' As Professor Griffith says: 'These generous words with their emphasis on the alleviating of hardship sound well until it is realised that they are used to prevent a claimant from challenging an adverse decision by the tribunal.' (Administrative Law and the Judges, p.15).

(103) Supra.

(104) R. v Inland Revenue Commissioners, ex parte National Federation of Self-Employed and Small Businesses, The Times, 28 February 1980.

(105) Gouriet v Union of Post Office Workers [1977] 2 WLR 310 (reversed by the House of Lords [1978] AC 435).

(106) A.G. ex rel. McWhirter v Independent Broadcasting Authority [1973] QB 629.

(107) R. v Police Commissioner, ex parte Blackburn [1973] QB 241.

(108) R. v Commissioner of Police of the Metropolis, ex parte Blackburn [1968] 2 QB 118.

(109) And see The Discipline of Law, Part Three.

(110) See, for example, Lee v Showmen's Guild [1952] 2 QB 329; Faramus v Film Artistes Association [1963] 2 QB 527; Science Research Council v Nasse [1978] ICR 1124; and Enderby Town Football Club v Football Association [1971] 1 Ch. 591.

(111) See Dutton v Bognor Regis U.D.C. [1972] 1 QB 373, 397; and Liverpool City Council v Irwin [1975] 3 WLR 663, 672.

(112) Dutton v Bognor Regis U.D.C. (supra).

(113) [1971] Ch. 591.

(114) A leader in The Times of 4 March 1980 expressed the view that the great majority of judges would not be capable of exercising such a power.

(115) See, for example, Tameside and Gouriet (supra).

(116) See The Politics of the Judiciary, ch.9.

(117) Bennion, F., Politics and Law, (1979) 129 New L.J. 201.

(118) See Griffith, J.A.G., Administrative Law and the Judges, p.12

(119) (1977) 127 New L.J. 325.

(120) Lever Finance Ltd. v Westminster (City) London Borough Council [1971] 1 QB 222.

(121) Supra.

(122) The series of decisions which began with Dutton was, for example, criticised by Mr Michael Heseltine, the

Secretary of State for the Environment, as having had certain undesirable consequences and as having placed upon local authorities liabilities which were neither foreseen nor intended by the legislature. (See Local Government Chronicle, 14 December 1979, p.1330). On Dutton, see too (1978) 41 MLR 87.

(123) See Brooks & Burton v Secretary of State for the Environment (1976) 75 LGR 285, 296.

(124) Alder, J., Development Control, Sweet & Maxwell, London, 1979, p.37.

(125) See, in particular, Western Fish Products v Penwith District Council (1979) 77 LGR 185.

(126) See, for example, Payne, P., Planning Appeals (1971) Jo. RTPI, 114 on the practical consequences of increased judicial control over ministerial decisions on planning appeals.

(127) See HTV Ltd. v Price Commission [1976] ICR 170.

(128) See Griffith, J.A.G., The Political Constitution (1979) 42 MLR 1.

(129) Where judges make decisions on the basis of policy, or simply on the basis of what they consider to be right, criticism of that policy or the rightness of a particular decision would not seem to be unfair. Lord Denning has, however, suggested that those who cast doubt on the good sense or fair-mindedness of the judges are 'undermining the confidence of the people in the judges' and are thus striking 'at the very root of law and order.' (Speech to Justice, reported in The Times of 29 June 1977).

(130) [1971] 2 QB 175.

(131) Administrative Law and the Judges, p.2.

(132) It was in these terms that Lord Denning defined 'justice' in an address to the Law Society of Scotland on 14 May 1978 (see the Scotsman, 15 May 1978).

(133) Administrative Law, 4th ed., p.23.

Sabotaging the Rent Acts

In his study of the political role of the British judiciary,[1] John Griffith observes that '[t]he attitude of the judiciary to legislation which seriously interferes with rights to the enjoyment of property ... has traditionally been one of suspicion'.[2] While this observation is undoubtedly accurate, it does little to convey the antipathy of the judiciary towards the series of enactments which collectively have come to be known as 'The Rent Acts'. Since the first of these Acts was introduced in 1915, to prevent the escalation of social unrest on the Clyde which threatened to cripple the war-time munitions industry,[3] the judiciary have indulged in a particularly pernicious form of judicial sabotage. At times stopping just short of squeezing the life from the policy.[4] Yet, it is one thing for the judiciary to restrict the ambit of social policy by adopting a literal and formalistic approach to statutory interpretation, and quite another for a judge to refuse to implement the will of the legislature. And that, in effect, is what Lord Denning has done. A trenchant opponent of substantive formalism,[5] Lord Denning is quite open about the lengths to which he is willing to go to ensure that landlords retain unfettered control of their properties:

> 'It must be remembered that at common law the landlords would have had a clear, indisputable right to turn the defendant out; and, even if they did allow her to stay on and accepted rent from her, the consequences would not be serious because the landlord could always get rid of her by giving her a week's notice to quit. In that state of affairs, it was very proper to infer a tenancy at will, or a weekly tenancy, as the case may be, from the acceptance of rent. <u>But it is very different when the rights of landlords are obscured by the Rent Restriction Acts</u> ... the consequences of granting her a contractual tenancy would be very far-reaching, because she would then be clothed with the valuable status of irremovability conferred by the Rent Restriction Acts

> ... In these circumstances, it is no longer proper for the courts to infer a tenancy at will, or a weekly tenancy, as they would previously have done from the mere acceptance of rent ...'[6]

This study attempts to trace how Lord Denning created, and subsequently widened, a hole in the Rent Acts through which, in his own words, an articulated vehicle could be driven.[7]

THE COMMON LAW

At common law the position of a person entering onto land was relatively straightforward. If his entry was unlawful then, broadly speaking, he was a trespasser. However, if his entry was lawful, and he was not the owner of the land, the status of his possession of the land depended upon the circumstances of his entry. If he was not granted actual possession, he was a mere licensee, e.g. a lodger or a guest. In the words of Vaughan C.J. the classic distinction at common law between a tenancy and a licence was that 'a dispensation or licence properly passeth no interest nor alters or transfers property in anything, but only makes an action lawful, which without it would be unlawful'.[8]

If, on the other hand, he was granted and entered into actual possession of the land, he could be said to be either a tenant at will or a licensee. In these circumstances, the crucial matter to determine whether the parties intended to create the relationship of landlord and tenant or licensor and licensee was the clear and unambiguous test of exclusive possession. Whilst the judiciary created a number of exceptions to accommodate family arrangements and situations where it was thought to be unjust to infer that a tenancy had been created, the test of exclusive possession, nevertheless, remained decisive. However, in a series of decisions in the early fifties, Lord Denning clearly stated that, in his opinion, the common law approach was not suited to the needs of the twentieth century and therefore was no longer to be regarded as decisive:

> 'In distinguishing between (leases and licences), a crucial test has sometimes been supposed to be whether the occupier has exclusive possession or not. If he was let into exclusive possession, he was said to be a tenant, albeit only a tenant at will ... whereas if he had not exclusive possession he was only a licensee ... This test has, however, often given rise to misgivings because it may not correspond to realities ... The test of exclusive possession is by no means decisive'.[9]

THE INTENTION OF THE PARTIES

In ascertaining the intention of the parties, it has been frequently emphasised that their relationship is not to be determined by the label which the parties themselves attach to it, but by the law, and that the courts will look beyond the form of the agreement to its substance.[10] However, the nature of the agreement itself is a matter of some importance. For in the absence of a written agreement, the courts have tended to infer the intention of the parties from the circumstances and the conduct of the parties, whereas if the parties have expressed their purpose in entering into a transaction in a formal document, that document is, at least, *prima facie* evidence of their common intention.[11] Given the fundamental differences in judicial approaches towards formal and informal occupancy agreements, we have chosen to deal with the cases where no formal agreement existed separately from those where the parties had entered into written agreements. The division, it should be noted, is not a rigid but heuristic one.

INFORMAL AGREEMENTS

> 'In all the cases where an occupier has been held to be a licensee there has been something in the circumstances, such as a family arrangement, an act of friendship or generosity or such like, to negative any intention to create a tenancy'.[12] (Lord Denning)

It would appear that the above exceptions to the exclusive possession test were initially established by the judiciary to enable the courts to hold that a lease had not been created in circumstances where to do so would have been 'unjust'.[13] The willingness of the judiciary to infer that a 'possessory licence',[14] rather than a lease had been created, however, has not been constant. And we shall attempt to demonstrate that as rent control has been extended, judges have adopted Lord Denning's arguments and have become increasingly unwilling to infer the existence of a lease. Lord Denning's role has been, itself, crucial.

FAMILY ARRANGEMENTS

> 'In most of these cases the question (of the legal effect of family arrangements) cannot be solved by looking to the intention of the parties, because the situation which arises is one which they never envisaged, and for which they made no provision. So many things are undecided, undiscussed, and unprovided for that the task of the courts is to fill in the blanks. The court has to look at all the circumstances and spell out the legal relationship. The court will pronounce in favour of a tenancy or a licence, a loan or a gift ... according to which of these legal relationships is most fitting in the situation which has arisen; and will find the terms of that relationship according to what reason and justice require'.[15] (Lord Denning)

This frank acknowledgement by Lord Denning of the deficiencies of the amorphous test of 'the intention of the parties' is of paramount importance in attempting to reconcile the authorities on family arrangements. For in this area of law the decisions of the judiciary have been based on 'Kadi-justice', viz informal judgements rendered in terms of concrete ethical or practical valuations,[16] rather than any clearly articulated criteria known in advance. The test which Lord Denning put forward as preferable to the more straightforward test of 'exclusive possession' in Errington, in the final analysis, is based on intuition, or more on what Lord Denning euphemistically describes as 'according to what reason and justice require'.

CREATING A PRINCIPLE

The facts in the leading case on family arrangements, Errington v Errington,[17] in which Lord Denning cast doubt on the usefulness of the test of 'exclusive possession' and created a new form of tenure, were surprisingly straightforward. Briefly, a father wished to provide a home for his son and daughter-in-law. He purchased a dwelling-house through a building society, paying a lump sum and leaving the balance to be paid by weekly instalments. The property was conveyed to the father and he paid the rates, but promised that if the son and daughter-in-law continued to occupy the house and paid the mortgage instalments until the last one was paid, he would transfer the property to them. However, before the instalments had been fully paid the father died leaving all his property, including the house, to his widow. In the intervening period between his father's death and the raising of an action for repossession, the son deserted his wife. In a subsequent action for possession brought by the widow against her daughter-in-law, the county court judge held that the son and daughter-in-law were tenants at will. On appeal, however, the Court of Appeal were 'relieved' to find that the husband and daughter-in-law were licensees under a personal contract to occupy the house for so long as they paid the instalments to the building society. Lord Denning was 'glad to reach this result'. His enthusiasm was not shared by others. A.D. Hargreaves writing in The Law Quarterly Review in 1953 opined:

> '... the inconsistencies and incongruities of Errington v Errington are so manifest, the reasoning so demonstrably unsatisfactory, the number of cases overlooked or misunderstood so great, that it must surely be within the powers of at least the Court of Appeal to review the whole question. Let us hope that when the opportunity arises that court will boldly wield the axe'.[18]

Yet despite misgivings as to the correctness of Lord Denning's approach to distinguishing leases and licences, his reasoning in Errington was followed in subsequent Court of Appeal decisions on family arrangements. In the same year, Lord Denning was able to consolidate the doctrine of possessory licensees in Cobb v Lane.[19] In that case, holding that a brother was a licensee in the house bought by his sister for him to live in, Lord Denning pronounced that:

> 'Under the old cases there would have been some colour for saying that the brother was a tenant at will, but the old cases can no longer be relied on. Owing to the impact of the Rent Acts, the courts have had to define more precisely the difference between a tenant and a licensee'.[20]

RECENT DEVELOPMENTS

In recent years, however, the question of whether the legal effect of a family arrangement has been to create a lease or a licence has largely been concerned with the proprietary 'rights' of mistresses and deserted wives. In Tanner v Tanner,[21] Lord Denning held that, although the plaintiff's ex-mistress had no proprietary interest in the house provided by the plaintiff for her and their children, she did have a contractual right as a licensee to live there until the children were no longer of school age:

> 'It is said that they were only licensees - bare licensees - under a licence revocable at will; and that he was entitled in law to turn her and the twins out on a moment's notice. I cannot believe that this is the law. This man had a moral duty to provide for the babies of whom he was the father. I would go further. I think that he had a legal duty towards them. Not only towards the babies. But also towards their mother. She was looking after them and bringing them up. In order to fulfil his duty towards the babies, he was under a duty to provide for the mother too ... It is impossible to suppose that in that situation she and the babies were bare licensees whom he could turn out at a moment's notice'.[22]

Sabotaging the Rent Acts

The Court of Appeal using this intuitive approach dealt with two further cases on the proprietary interests of mistresses and deserted wives in 1978. Here, whilst one might applaud the notion of providing remedies to women deserted by husbands or whose support at law appeared to be restricted, the problem of the criteria to be applied in such an exercise was not assisted by the Lord Denning test and distinct treatment of wives and mistresses is one result.

In the first case on this vexed question, Hardwick v Johnson and Another,[23] the Court of Appeal held that a mother who had bought a house for her son and daughter-in-law to live in, the couple paying her the sum of £7 per week for the privilege, was not entitled to possession against her daughter-in-law. The arrangement was a licence to the son and daughter-in-law jointly to live in the house on condition that they paid her £28 monthly and the licence was not conditional on the marriage succeeding.

Therefore the wife and child of the marriage were not to be ejected from the house when the son went off with another woman. In the second case, Chandler v Kerley,[24] the Court of Appeal held that a mistress was a contractual licensee under a licence terminable on reasonable notice. Reasonable notice in this case amounted to twelve months. In holding that in the circumstances they were unable to infer that the plaintiff's mistress occupied the house under a licence for her life, the Court of Appeal said:

> '... the plaintiff [cannot be supposed, in the circumstances] in the absence of express stipulation to have frozen his capital for as long as (his ex-mistress) pleased or for the duration of her life ... it would be wrong, however, to infer, in the absence of an express promise, that the plaintiff was assuming the burden of housing another man's wife and children, and long after his relationship with them had ended'.[25]

On balance, it appears to us that the criteria used by the judiciary in these cases to determine the legal effect of a family arrangement and the length of security of tenure which such agreements provide are based on unarticulated assumptions as to the nature of the family and the obligations flowing therefrom. The problem is that the issue of the relative merits of specific personal relationships as seen by the judiciary is not unproblematic.

ACTS OF FRIENDSHIP AND GENEROSITY

> 'To suggest there is an intention there to create a relationship of landlord and tenant appears to me to be quite impossible. There is one golden rule which is of very general application, namely,that the law does not impute intention to enter into legal relationships where the circumstances and the conduct of the parties negative any intention of the kind'.[26] (Lord Greene M.R.)

The first case which Lord Denning argued in Errington showed that the test of exclusive possession could no longer be regarded as decisive, was Booker v Palmer. In that case a landowner agreed with a third party by telephone to permit evacuees to stay at an empty cottage on his estate rent free for the duration of the war. Later, the landowner required the cottage for one of his labourers and demanded possession. The occupiers refused and the landowner brought an action of repossession against them. In these circumstances, the Court of Appeal held that the proper view of the facts was that the occupiers were mere licensees and the landowner could revoke the licence at any time. The agreement to permit the evacuees to stay at the cottage was concluded, in fact, between the landowner and a third party and not the landowner and the evacuees. In view of this, it is somewhat strange to find Lord Denning citing the above dicta of Lord Greene M.R. as authority for the proposition that 'the test of exclusive possession is by no means decisive (in determining whether the relationship created between owner and occupier is that of landlord and tenant or licensor and licensee)'.[27]

Excluding requisitioned properties and such occupancies, other instances given by Lord Denning in support of his view that the test of exclusive possession was no longer to be regarded as decisive were Foster v

Robinson[28] and Marcroft Wagons.[29] It should be noted that the issue in Foster appeared to be quite unconcerned with the question of exclusive possession and that the doctrine in Marcroft Wagons was itself a creation of Lord Denning. In the Foster case, the point at issue was whether a statutory tenancy had been extinguished by a subsequent oral agreement whereby a former employee was allowed to continue to occupy a cottage without paying rent for the rest of his life. On his death, his daughter, who had lived with him during the nine years prior to his death, claimed that she was entitled to succeed her father as his statutory successor under the old tenancy protected agreement. The Court of Appeal, with some hesitation, held that the original tenancy had, as a result of the later agreement, been surrendered and the landlord was entitled to possession. It should be noted, however, that Lord Evershed M.R. emphasised that the case had been a difficult one and one which had turned on its own facts and therefore should not be regarded as of general application. The issue of exclusive possession does not, in fact, arise in the case.

In Marcroft Wagons, the daughter of the widow of a statutory tenant was permitted by the landlords to remain in possession of the house after her mother's death and to pay the rent for six months after that date. In these circumstances, she was nevertheless held to be a licensee, Lord Denning explaining:

> 'According to the common law as it stood before the Rent Restriction Acts, when the defendant stayed on with the consent of the landlords, she would become a tenant at will; and when she afterwards paid a weekly rent which was accepted by them, she would become a weekly tenant ... however, it is not correct to consider the common law separately from the new position created by the Rent Restriction Acts ...'[30]

This judgment was later followed in Dealex Properties v Brooks.[31] More recently, the courts would appear to have grown less accommodating towards acts of friendship or generosity, holding in Barnes v Barrat and

Another,[32] and Heslop v Burns[33] that, in spite of the fact that the occupiers were granted exclusive possession in each case, they were licensees. In the words of Lord Scarman '... social changes ... seem to show that less and less will the courts be inclined to infer a tenancy at will from an exclusive occupation of indefinite duration'.[34]

WRITTEN AGREEMENTS

The problem of 'blanks' is not so pressing where the parties enter a written contract. The difficulty which emerges is the extent to which the courts can take any writings at face value. The contract documents are normally drawn up by landlords' agents and in a situation of scarce accommodation the notion of a freely-entered bilateral agreement may not, at first sight, seem easy to sustain. The courts, again with Lord Denning in the van appear to both recognise these difficulties and to sweep them under the carpet, trusting to their skill in interpreting contract documents. The implications of this approach have been serious for tenants, particularly since 1974 as landlords have striven to avoid the Rent Acts.[35]

THE TRUE RELATIONSHIP

The most dramatic changes have occurred in the way in which the courts seem to examine agreements between commercial landlords and those wishing to occupy rented property. In 1952 in Facchini v Bryson, Lord Denning explained the basic goal of the courts in disputes where one party attempted to claim a lease and the other claimed the agreement was a mere licence. 'It is simply a matter of finding the true relationship of the parties'.[36]

Whilst this goal has never been abandoned, its context or rationale appears to have altered. Lord Denning explained why it was 'important that ... (the courts) adhere to this principle':

> 'Else we might find all landlords granting licenses and nottenancies and we should make a hole in the Rent Acts through which could

> be driven - I will not in these days say a coach - but an articulated vehicle ...'[37]

In the immediate postwar period, the judiciary appeared to be aware of the dangers of creating loopholes in the protection afforded to tenants. The problem before 1974 appears to have been minimal. Landlords who wished to avoid the Rent Acts tended to offer furnished tenancies - often with rudimentary, if not minimal, furniture - thus replacing security of tenure with Rent Tribunal extensions of notice to quit.[38] As the Francis Committee Report found, this was an effective barrier to longterm tenancies of furnished property - partly, of course, stemming from the transient nature of a number of occupants of furnished property. Attempts though to avoid the Rent Acts through the creation of licences appear to have been limited according to the Francis Report.[39]

The apparently purposive approach in Facchini with the courts on the trail of the reality of the situation was confirmed in a number of cases in the following decade. In Parikh[40] in 1957, the issue was whether an agreement that a Mrs Flynn should be a 'paying guest' with the Parikhs created a tenancy or merely gave a licence to occupy. The Lord Chief Justice, Lord Goddard, was quite adamant about the effect of the label and content of the agreement which permitted the landlady to enter the room let out 'at all times'.

> 'If the landlady thinks that by the use of certain words she can avoid the provisions of the Act [of 1946] she is mistaken ... I cannot think that the landlady by putting in words saying that she is to have access to Mrs Flynn's room has thereby excluded the Act or say that Mrs Flynn has not exclusive occupation. I think the test is whether Mrs Flynn has the exclusive right to use the room as a residence'.[41]

This, then, established that whilst exclusive occupation was not itself conclusive to create a tenancy, mere reservation of a right of access would not be taken to destroy this occupation. This is derived from the court's reading of what Lynskey J. called 'the true meaning of the agreement'.[42] This adherence to the agreement as the source of reality of the relationship had interesting repercussions.

THE ETHICS OF AVOIDING THE RENT ACTS

A rather more sympathetic approach was taken by the Court of Appeal to landlords wishing to avoid the Rent Acts in Samrose Properties[43] in 1957 where Lord Evershed accepted that:

> 'A landlord is entitled so to arrange his affairs that the legal result will bring him outside the statutory provisions ... If they fail, that does not, therefore, reflect on the ethics of their business methods'.[44]

This reflects an interesting shift in the courts in their attitude to the operations of 'avoiding' landlords. This, allied with the limited nature of the test applied to determine the reality of the relationship and agreement between the parties, left open gaps for subsequent exploitation. Thus we find in Samrose the notion of 'substance' expanded but shedding little light on matters.

> 'merely giving a label to a particular type of payment will not by any means necessarily have the effect indicated by the label; for the truth and substance, in cases of this kind, must be examined'.[45]

Here, the landlords had attempted to take advantage of the exclusion from the Rent Acts of properties where the rent was less than two thirds of the rateable value. Their scheme involved a low rent coupled with a lump sum for granting the tenancy. No deception was involved and the landlords were quite open in explaining that these arrangements were designed to keep the property outside the scope of the Rent Acts. The Court of Appeal were prepared to read the documents which dealt with the money side of the agreement together, which took the contract well above the two thirds exclusion level.

The notion of a sham was more easily perceived in such circumstances. Citing a number of judgments on 'shams' Morris L.J. explained his approach:

> 'It seems to me that, in a case of this kind, one can only seek to ascertain what was the true nature and effect of the transaction; what was the reality of it, not being guided unduly by any labels that may have been used ... One must consider all the facts and see whether they afford some pointers towards forming a conclusion as to what was the reality of the matter'.[46]

What must not be forgotten, though, is that the circumstances which the court was prepared to examine and which they had in mind were limited to the documents constituting the agreement.

COMMERCIAL LICENCES

Not all the cases which have had an impact on the question of 'lease or licence' have been concerned with the Rent Acts or even with residential property. However, the criteria are the same. The object in Addiscombe Garden Estates,[47] also in 1957, was to avoid the security of tenure provisions of the Landlord and Tenant Act 1954 for business premises. Jenkins L.J. reiterated the words of Lord Denning in Facchini explaining, 'it is simply a matter of ascertaining the true relationship of the parties'.[48] As we have noted this test appeals more to the heart than the brain and leaves the Court with the agreement itself to examine.

In a similar vein to Addiscombe Garden Estates a dispute arose on security of tenure on agricultural land rented out by the Air Ministry to Archibald Finbow in 1950.[49] For the security provisions of the Agricultural Holdings Act 1948 to apply, the agreement had to be a tenancy. McNair J. adopted the tests from Facchini and Addiscombe, namely:

> '(1) that the agreement must be construed as a whole and that the relationship is determined by the law and not by the label which the parties

> put upon it, though the label is a factor to be taken into account in determining the true relationship ...
> (2) that the grant of exclusive possession, if not conclusive against the view that there is a mere licence as distinct from a tenancy, is at any rate a consideration of the first importance ...'[50]

He also went on to cite with approval the section in Facchini in which Lord Denning suggested that the licensee cases all involved a special relationship. For himself he was content, however, to regard these tests as satisfactory for determining the question of licence or lease, but he did add an interesting gloss to the cases involving residential tenants where he distinguished between residential and commercial letting and a situation where a Government Ministry is the landlord:

> 'In the cases under the Rent Acts and the Landlord and Tenant Act, the courts, when they held that a document purporting to be a licence was in law a tenancy, were giving effect to the public policy embodied in those Acts of conferring security of tenure and preventing the evasion of those Acts'.[51]

A further business case adds a somewhat different dimension to the test to be applied in determining lease or licence. In Shell-Mex v Manchester Garages,[52] the occupiers of a filling station claimed that the licence on which they had occupied their premises for some four years was, in reality, a tenancy and that they were entitled to the benefit of the security of tenure provisions of the Landlord and Tenant Act 1954. Lord Denning, modifying the test of lease or licence which he himself had formulated twenty years earlier, stated:

> 'This does not depend on the label which is put on it. It depends on the nature of the transaction itself ... Broadly speaking, we have to see whether it is a personal privilege given to a person, (in which case it is a licence) or whether it grants an interest in land, (in which case it is a tenancy). At

> one time it used to be thought that exclusive possession was a decisive factor, but that is not so. It depends on broader considerations altogether. Primarily, on whether it is personal in its nature or not ...'[53]

Lord Denning was able to apply these tests by looking at the terms of the agreement from which he is able to infer provisions which seem to be 'personal in their nature'. And he was unimpressed by the fact that tenancy agreements for other garages contain the same clauses or that there is exclusive possession.

His colleague, Sachs L.J., reaffirmed the 'substance' test and put some flesh on the bare bones of this notion where he looks to overall aims of the contractual relationship:

> 'Upon looking at the substance of the matter as a whole, it becomes apparent that the dominant objective of the contractual relationship between the parties was to further the promotion of the sale of [the plaintiffs'] products'.[54]

In rejecting the claim to a tenancy, the Court of Appeal accepted the notion that if the parties arranged their affairs in such a way as to avoid the legislative protection for tenants, that itself was no bad thing. It would seem that the substance is to be inferred from the form.

IMPOSING THE TRUE RELATIONSHIP - AFTER THE RENT ACT 1974

Since 1974, landlords have attempted to avoid the net of the Rent Acts by refining licence agreements. And in the process of doing so they have exposed the deficiencies of the criteria for distinguishing leases and licences largely fashioned by Lord Denning. Previously, these were masked by the crudeness of landlords' attempts to draft licence agreements. Recently, however, the judiciary, confronted by carefully drafted non-exclusive occupancy agreements, have found that Lord Denning's test of 'substance' has itself turned out to be a sham.

Sabotaging The Rent Acts

The reaction that these documents have produced in the courts is not simply a crude 'siding' with the landlord and his embattled position under the Rent Acts, but a clarification of the approach of courts to interpreting the 'intention of the parties'. In the earlier cases, the court would examine the operative clauses and determine whether or not these were appropriate to a lease or licence. In Facchini, Lord Justice Somervell explained:

> "If looking at the operative clauses in the agreement one comes to the conclusion that the rights of the occupier .. are those of a lessee, the parties cannot turn it into a licence by saying at the end, 'this is deemed to be a licence'".[55]

However, with the closing off of the 'furnished let' loophole, Lord Denning was again to be found in the forefront of the judicial approval to the movement to restrict the ambit of the Acts. In the case of Marchant v Charters[56] in 1977, however, even Lord Denning seemed to be at a loss to explain adequately the nature of the test to be applied to determine the nature of occupancies:

> 'Gathering the cases together (on the distinction between leases and licences) what does it come to? What is the test to see whether the occupier of one room in a house is a tenant or licensee? It does not depend on whether he or she has exclusive possession or not. It does not depend on whether the room is furnished or not. It does not depend on whether the occupation is permanent or temporary. It does not depend on what label the parties put on it'.[57]

What, then, does the test depend on? The Master of the Rolls went on to explain:

> 'All these are factors which may influence the decision, but none of them is conclusive. All the circumstances have to be worked out. Eventually, the answer depends on the nature and quality of the occupancy'.[58]

With respect, this 'explanation' is tautologous. How can the test for determining the nature of an occupancy be 'the nature and quality of the occupancy'?

The respondent in Marchant occupied a furnished bed-sitting room, containing a gas ring and grill, cooking utensils, crockery, cutlery, sink and hot water supply; each of the seven bed-sitting rooms was individually let; in common with the occupants of the other bed-sitting rooms, he did his own cooking in his own room, and shared the bathroom and lavatory with the other occupants; there was a resident housekeeper who cleaned the rooms daily and provided fresh linen weekly. In these circumstances, Lord Denning remarkably found that the occupant was a licensee and not a tenant. Few cases show more clearly the deficiencies of Lord Denning's amorphous test of the intention of the parties. Like his purposive approach to statutory interpretation, at best it allows the judiciary to develop the law to meet changes in social needs, but at worst it permits judges to give full vent to their predilictions.

BUILDING ON SHIFTING SANDS - THE 'TEST' UNDER PRESSURE

Landlords and their agents after 1974 have set about constructing documents which were, in theory, internally unequivocal. In Somma in 1978, for instance, the wording of the licence agreement was so specific that the Court of Appeal commented:

> '... the document so repeatedly proclaims itself a licence, and the relationship it creates between the applicant and each respondent as being that of licensor and licensee, that it raises the question why it should be necessary to protest so much and whether so many labels clearly written all over it give a true or false description of its real content'.[59]

In spite of recognising these agreements were constructed to avoid the Rent Acts, the courts were unprepared to prevent landlords and their advisers from driving a hole through the Acts.

Rather, the courts appeared willing to accept that a landlord should not be prevented from returning to market rents if their agreements could be skilfully constructed.

> 'Owners of property are seeking, perhaps understandably in the circumstances, to get the maximum financial advantage from their properties and to avoid what they no doubt regard as the irksome fetters of the Rent Act'.[60]

Their approach to written agreements was clearly stated in Somma, '... we start from the basis that it is to the documents that we must look and to the documents alone'.[61] This was seen to form the real intention of the parties and the onus was on the tenants to establish that the contract was other than that recorded in the documents that they signed.

Thus, in two decades, the role of the court had dramatically shifted from one apparently seeking the true relationship to a passive acceptance that this is embodied in the written documents alone. Whilst the Court of Appeal has not restricted itself to documentary evidence it is significant that the courts accepted that true intention stems from the written licence unless the 'tenant' can prove otherwise. Since, in future, there are not likely to be 'slip ups' like those in Facchini,[62] the courts now seem to have restricted their investigation to matters which negative the prima facie agreement and true intention. This legalistic approach is expressed quite explicitly. The courts seem now only prepared to operate a limited judicial test of legal draftsmanship.

> 'Nor can we see why their (owner and occupier) common intentions should be categorised as bogus or unreal or as sham merely on the ground that the court disapproves of the bargain'.[63]

More recently still in the second major case supporting the avoidance of the Rent Acts, the same notion of sham and subterfuge is uppermost in the mind of Lord Justice Geoffrey Lane, '... there seemed ... to be nothing disguised as a licence no one was disguising exclusive possession to make it look like something else'.[64]

The 'avoidance' attitude outlined in Somma is echoed by Geoffrey Lane L.J., '... there seemed to be nothing wrong in trying to escape onerous provisions or increase one's profit if one could legitimately do so'.[65] However, Roskill L.J., at least, is aware that the court must have some regard to the policy of the Rent Acts, 'the court should be specially careful to see no wool was being pulled over its eyes'.[66]

This question, though, seemed to resolve itself into whether the agreement entered into amounted to some form of deception or sham. When one party exercised a greater degree of real power in the housing contract Roskill L.J. suggested, 'it was important that the court should hold a balance fairly between the two'.[67] However, no test is suggested by Roskill other than that the decision as to whether an agreement is lease or licence, 'must in every case depend on the factual background against which the agreement had to be construed.[68] With respect, this is of limited assistance.

SHAMS AND DUPLICITY

However, some light on the way in which the Court of Appeal will approach the problem of determining genuine licence agreements from shams is given in the case of O'Malley v Seymour.[69] In this case, and merely two weeks after Aldrington Garages, the Court of Appeal was again faced with the question whether a document constituted a non-exclusive licence excluding the application of the Rent Acts, or whether it created a tenancy within the Acts. In the course of his judgments, Stephenson L.J. outlined the questions which the court will ask when faced with these agreements:

> 'First, what on its true construction is the nature of the written agreement which the plaintiff relied and relies in his claim for possession against the background of the evidence? Secondly, does the evidence prove and entitle the judge to hold that the document on its proper construction, does not truly represent or reproduce the real transaction between the parties?'[70]

While satisfied that the written agreement in O'Malley did create a licence,[71] the Court of Appeal held that it did not record the oral agreement reached two days prior to the signing of the document which in their view established a tenancy. In reaching this decision, the Court of Appeal were aided by the plaintiff's answers in cross-examination:

> 'I told him I would want a month's rent in advance ... He said he wanted to move in that weekend. It was a firm verbal agreement ... I expressed in no uncertain terms that the tenancy was for six months only'.[72]

And Judge Dow's assessment of the relative credibility of the two parties:

> 'I am not dealing with an illiterate or an unsophisticated person. Mr Seymour has a good job and I found him an honest and straightforward witness'.[73]

However, although the Court of Appeal held on the particular facts of this case that the document was a sham, landlords are left in no doubt that, in the words of Lawton L.J., 'a property owner is entitled to arrange his affairs so as not to get his property enmeshed in the Rent Acts'.[74]

How a document is supposed to be shown to be a sham from its own terms is not clear in these decisions. In the subsequent case of Demuren and Adefope v Seal Estates[75] the courts hint at the basis of their approach. Here, whilst finding that an agreement to lease was made between the parties before the signing of a licence, the Court of Appeal indicated some concern at the actual document purporting to create the licence. Without specifically indicating what was wrong with the document, both Megaw L.J. and Roskill L.J. refer to the 'curious' nature of the document. What their criticism appears to come down to, however, is that the licence was one-sided and gave all the rights to the owner and few to the occupiers. However, although the document is criticised for being 'curious and ill-drawn' no substantial test for its rejection is put forward by the Court of Appeal. All they suggest is that something is so badly wrong with this agreement that one is bound to look at it with the gravest suspicion.[76]

This appears to have been prompted by the fact that the owner/landlord could give notice to quit during the term agreed whilst the occupier was bound for the full term. This might be harsh and leonine but one doubts whether or not Megaw L.J.'s suggestion that the two clauses were 'irreconcilable' has much substance.

Similarly, this perfectly understandable sentiment was expressed later where the same judge opined that he doubted whether the document is capable of being given any meaning at all, because:

> 'There is no provision in that agreement for the licensee to cease to be liable for payment up to 30 September 1977 (the term) merely because he chooses to leave his residence in room No. 1'.[77]

One may well wish to applaud the rejection of the purported licence, yet the grounds here seem to be so shaky that any help from this case may extend no further than Messrs Demuren and Adefope. The implication of the decision taken along with the other decision in 1978 was that where an owner draws up a licence in the form adopted in Somma v Hazelhurst then, provided that no other form of specific verbal agreement can be adduced by the occupiers, the intention of the parties will be taken from the licence documents alone. To assist in this, the licence is reproduced in full in the Somma case report.

The 1978 cases adopt a view having regard to the documents and their problems or lack thereof. All that has been adduced in addition is what could be called the oral agreement. Thus, in Demuren the parties were able to succeed because they were able to show that the circumstances of the granting of the licence were taken by them and represented by the landlord's agent as a simple contract to let. The fact that they were Nigerian postgraduate students recently arrived in Britain lent credence to the notion of a tenancy rather than a technical limited licence right. Mr Fielder was not so lucky with his assumption that the flat he leased with Miss Maxwell was covered by the Rent Acts nor was Martin Hazelhurst whose intelligence was taken to indicate a willingness to accept a licence. In these latter cases the notion of what was agreed was assumed to represent the mutual intentions independently.

> 'We can see no reason why an ordinary landlord ... should not be able to grant a licence to occupy an ordinary house. If that is what both he and the licensee intend and if they can frame any written agreement in such a way as to demonstrate that it is not really an agreement for lease masquerading as a licence, we can see no reason in law or justice why they should be prevented from achieving that object'. [78]

The problem is that the test of the so-called intention of the parties has driven a large hole in the Rent Acts and the judiciary, led by Lord Denning, have paved the way for landlords to escape through it.

CONCLUSION

In this essay, we have attempted to show how Lord Denning has, in twenty years, re-orientated the common law to emasculate the provisions of the Rents Acts. Under the mask of providing a more flexible approach to distinguishing between leases and licences, Lord Denning has slowly eroded the statutory rights of tenants until they are virtually deprived of the protection which Parliament introduced to prevent exploitation of shortages of supply in the housing market. In doing so, he may well have been guided by the earnest desire to redress a fundamental shift in power away from the property owner and in favour of the tenant, but the task of power allocation is more properly a Parliamentary one, rather than a judicial one. It may be the task of the judiciary to hold the scales of justice, but it is not their role to tip those scales in favour of any party.

PETER ROBSON and
PAUL WATCHMAN

Sabotaging The Rent Acts

NOTES

(1) Griffith, J.A.G., The Politics of the Judiciary, Fontana, London, 1977.
(2) Ibid, p.107.
(3) Watchman, P., 'The Origin of the 1915 Rent Act', Law and State, No.5, 1979, pp.20-50.
(4) Griffith, J.A.G., 'Rent Tribunals - A Slight Case of Judicial Murder', 16 Modern Law Review, 1953, pp.79-82.
(5) Stevens, R., Law and Politics: The House of Lords as a Judicial Body 1800-1976, Weidenfeld and Nicolson, London, 1979, p.490.
(6) Marcroft Wagons Limited v Smith [1951] 2 KB 496, pp.505-6 (our emphasis).
(7) Facchini v Bryson (1952) 1 TLR 1386, p.1390.
(8) Thomas v Sorrell 1673 Vaugh, 330.
(9) Errington v Errington and Woods [1952] 1 KB 290, 296-7.
(10) Samrose Properties Ltd. v Gibbard [1958] 1 WLR 235.
(11) Somma v Hazelhurst [1978] 1 WLR 1014.
(12) Facchini v Bryson, supra, p.1389.
(13) Ibid.
(14) Cullity, M.C., The Possessory Licence, 29 Conv., 1965. 336
(15) Hardwick v Johnston and Another [1978] 1 WLR 683, p.688.
(16) Max Weber, Economy and Society , Bedminster, New York p.976.
(17) Supra, note 9.
(18) Hargreaves, A.D., 'Licensed Possessors', 69 L.Q.R., 1953, 466, p.484.
(19) [1952] 1 TLR 1037.
(20) Ibid. 1041
(21) Tanner v Tanner [1975] 1 WLR 1346.
(22) Ibid, p.1350.
(23) Hardwick v Johnston, supra, note 15.
(24) [1978] 1 WLR 693.
(25) Ibid, p.698.
(26) Booker v Palmer [1942] 2 All E.R. 674, p.677 per Lord Greene M.R.
(27) Errington, supra, p.297.
(28) Foster v Robinson [1951] 1 KB 149.
(29) [1951] 2 KB 496.
(30) Ibid, p.505.
(31) Dealex Properties Ltd. v Brooks [1966] 1 QB 542.

(32) Barnes v Barratt [1970] 2 QB 657.
(33) Heslop v Burns [1974] 1 WLR 1241.
(34) Ibid, p.1253.
(35) Licences Made Easy, 40 Conv., (N.S.) 5; Rent Act Round-Up, [1978] Conv. 397.
(36) Facchini, supra, p.1390.
(37) Ibid, . .
(38) Rent Act 1968, s.2(3); but see Woodward v Docherty [1974] 1 WLR 966.
(39) Report of the Committee on the Rent Acts 1971, Cmnd 4609.
(40) R. v Battersea, Wandsworth, Mitcham and Wimbledon Rent Tribunal, ex parte Parikh [1957] 1 WLR 410.
(41) Ibid, p. 412, 414
(42) Ibid, p.415.
(43) Samrose Properties Ltd. v Gibbard, supra, note 10.
(44) Ibid. p. 239
(45) Ibid, per Evershed MR.
(46) Ibid.
(47) Addiscombe Garden Estates Ltd. v Crabbe [1958] 1QB 513.
(48) Ibid, p.528
(49) Finbow v Air Ministry [1963] 1 WLR 697.
(50) Ibid, p.706.
(51) Ibid, p.707.
(52) Shell-Mex & BP Ltd. v Manchester Garages Ltd. [1971] 1 WLR 612.
(53) Ibid, p.615.
(54) Ibid, p.616.
(55) Facchini, supra, p.1389.
(56) [1977] 1 WLR 1181.
(57) Ibid, p.1185.
(58) Ibid.
(59) Somma v Hazelhurst, supra, p.1022.
(60) Demuren, infra, p.444.
(61) Somma, supra, p.1024.
(62) Facchini, supra, where the word 'tenancy' was used as well as several clauses which were inconsistent with the limited right of licence.
(63) Somma, supra, p.1025.
(64) Aldrington Garages v Fielder (1978) 247 EG 557.
(65) Ibid, p.559.
(66) Ibid.
(67) Ibid.
(68) Ibid.

(69) (1979) 250 EG 1083.
(70) Ibid.
(71) Ibid, p.1087.
(72) Ibid, p.1088.
(73) Ibid, p.1085.
(74) Ibid, p.1088.
(75) (1979) 249 EG 440.
(76) Ibid, p.443.
(77) Ibid, p.444.
(78) Somma, supra, p.1024

PART III
Towards a Theory of Judicial Action

Digression on Denning

A number of difficulties present themselves at the apprehension of two books by a judge, both of which reached the Sunday Times bestseller list, neither of which is an autobiography, and neither of which reveals anything new or scandalous about the judiciary. In looking at Lord Denning's two books it is important to bear in mind the extent to which his individualist rhetoric is merely rhetoric. The claims he makes can be measured against the reality of what he has accomplished. But again, the limited capacity of judges to change things must be considered; and the nature of a social organisation which contains access to and intervention by, a part of the state, on necessarily inegalitarian lines, should be allowed for. If the judges do fail to enforce their own rules, and if their judgments contradict what appears to be the humane spirit of welfare legislation, we have to ask how secure a foundation that spirit had or has. It is ourselves of whom we speak.

The difficulties are chiefly over the level of criticism which it would be fair or sensible to aim at an old, undoubtedly astute and sincere man, but whose 'posing of the trade union versus the individual shows how close is (his) ... philosophy to that of the National Association for Freedom and the right wing of the Tory Party'.[3] It is not the posing, but the sustaining of the political viewpoint which presents a problem. To write non-politically about law is, I think, impossible. Lord Denning, however, writes about law without apparently departing from the judicial manner, the style in which the contentious and controversial are presented as if beyond contradiction. On the occasions when he offers justification for his pronouncements, he shows that he can be as cavalier with historical as with legal sources.[4]

However accurate a picture the books present of Denning the man - and only future biographical scholarship will reveal that - these books do less than justice to Denning the judge. Like all lawyers, of course, he suffers from the Appellate Court Relativism summed up in Lord Goddard's remark: 'Some of my judgments have been wrong, I know, because they have been reversed'.[5] With Lord Denning, the sentiment is more subtle, but in the end he has to accept, having argued earnestly that the correct legal answer is x, that it is y whenever a majority in the court says so, because if he does not collude in the implication that when judges speak judicially they speak for a greater than themselves, he deprives himself of the right to innovate, even to speak at all.[6]

That is to say, he colludes when he is on the Bench. In his books, Law is invoked then occluded.[7] Lord Denning the virtuoso justifies professionally his performance by reference to an orchestra and, somewhere, a score. From time to time we are permitted to hear the other players, but mostly in the books if our maestro is not blowing his trumpet and banging his drum he is humming the other parts so loudly that we can never have the opportunity of judging them for ourselves. The over-exuberance for which he is frequently criticised in the Court of Appeal is translated into egocentricity in the texts.

The conditions of the books' success are, perhaps, not a puzzle. Class relations in Britain, more especially in England, are changing. 'Economic crisis', 'late capitalism' and other phrases often used by the Left will not be invoked here, but must await a context in which they can be properly explicated. But an interpretation of the present as an augury of capitalism's imminent collapse is simply too apocalyptic. It is relevant to the expressions and the sudden popularity of Lord Denning, however, to note the changes in class relations.

We can denote by class conflict 'the effects of the structure are concentrated in the practices of those particular ensembles constituted by social classes'.[8] The notion of 'mode of production' implies that the totality of social relations can be constructed theoretically as produced by, but essential for the reproduction of, the means by which the social formation secures its material existence. In the study of a particular formation 'relative autonomy' means that the politics of social relations cannot be 'read off' from the economy. So we refer to the concept of, say, capitalist economy, a mode of production involving wage-labour and the separation of the labourer from the means of production, a particular form of exploitation and a particular method of production of value - we can do this and still not possess the precise details of class organisation. The concept simply is not so specific.[9]

The transition to capitalism is the rise to economic dominance of the bourgeoisie. Politically in England this has meant dominance by a fragment of the land-holding aristocracy,[10] followed by the reign of bourgeois financiers.[11] In the circumstances of the end of the British Empire, industrial capital never secured the conditions of its continued reproduction.[12] Following the economic crises consequent upon this, bourgeois dominance at the economic level has increasingly found political expression in a peculiarly petty-bourgeois form. The morality of the banker has been superseded by that of the accountant and the High Street solicitor. They are the successor to the small shopkeeper whom Marx detected in Bentham, but with a large number of important differences. The conventional wisdom with which such a political apparatus operates is not at all functional to industrial capitalism, and it is not at all similar to the regime of liberalism produced last during the political dominance of the aristocracy.[13]

Political freedom ceases to be associated with the language of civil rights or liberties and becomes identified with that of freedom of contract. The corporatist industrialism that developed in the 'thirties devolved a good deal of power on to the working class - or at least on to working class organisations. But welfare policies, the commitment to full employment and the use of collective bargaining, ideas converged upon, and sanctioned, by enlightened members of both the Conservative and Labour Parties in the vocabularies of intellectuals such as Keynes and Beveridge, depended for their successful implementation on a political control that was never attained. Neither Parliament nor 'the commanding heights of the economy' were sufficient to ensure adequate control.[14]

In other words, what took place was not an inevitable product of the operation of the economy, but must be apprehended in the concrete peculiarities of English politics. Control over vital variables such as the international status of sterling, the exchange rate and the direction of investment away from real property (to where it migrated with the declining rate of industrial profitability) remained beyond the grasp of industry and its suspect working class clients. The wind that continued to erode the industrial foundation was the same wind that continued to sustain the flame of City finance capital.

A new class configuration developed in which the trade unions were no longer the allies of the dominant class.[15] Unions and the working class itself became enemies, or at least, dubious friends who must continually prove themselves. This is the language of the popular press.[16] Driven into obstruction by a framework of industrial relations over which they have no control, unions became the terrain chosen by the politically dominant class for a series of battles. Their reformist language cannot be answered except in the terminology already possessed by the petty bourgeois. The antithesis of the organised labour half of the industrial 'dynamic duo' of corporate capital, is the religion which has sustained the solicitor and the accountant in his (or her, but chiefly his) upward mobility from obscure origins - the religion of Thrift, Individualism and Busyness. The Beast in its idiosyncratic Revelation consists of precisely trade union collectiveness.[17] Workers who resist labour-saving innovations are wreckers, and those who accept them and become redundant are scroungers, but none of these petty bourgeois worshippers minds absurdity, or even notices it, for each has long since parted company from the intellectuals.

The war of the petty bourgeois with the working class is without the patriarchal conventions of the struggle conducted by the aristocracy, and the self-interested restraints of the industrial bourgeois and its allies. Our new Church Militant of professional men is doctrinally indifferent to class compromise because its members have neither experience nor need for labour on a significant scale. If they had heard of Hobbes they would resent his evaluation of the state of nature, having first applauded it as their proper milieu.

At the end of this pursuit of an eccentric kind of freedom lies the police state, for, in the end, the only way of permitting collective financial power and preventing collective labour from reacting, is by the use of surveillance and suppression.[18] The alternative is re-industrialisation after the collapse of finance capital, but the signs point to a lingering Portuguese half-life.

The vocabulary Lord Denning uses, and what he appears to represent, reflect the requirements of this particular struggle. 'Freedom' on slight examination, appears to have been annexed to the political right;[19] the 'individual' whose stalwart defence of this freedom Lord Denning celebrates appears to be, not the scrounger, or the squatter, or the tyrant of organised labour, but the wealthy gentleman with the leisure and articulacy, moreover, to contemplate litigation.

But things are not so simple. The logic of the political position of such a vocabulary is the systematic demotion of the judiciary - that is to say that although its social prestige may be maintained, its political importance is devalued.[20] Government by administration, which means the transfer of discretion to hierarchies of officials who operate differently from judges, and from whom some issues never emerge as discrete decisions, is simply another way of performing government.[21]

If there is a lack of fit between what Lord Denning <u>is</u>, and what his popular following infer him to be from his utterances, there is also a lack of fit between what more traditionally-minded judges say and social democratic practice. Social democratic tradition criticises the judiciary for exercising political authority without being under the obligation to answer to an electorate.[22] The reason for the criticism, though not its substantive justification, is that English judges frequently affront the sensibilities of those who seek, however modestly, to redistribute social and political goods in favour of people whose stock of such goods is meagre.[23] Disappointed conservatives are equally capable of using the argument against judgments of too progressive a kind, and have done so in the United States as a part of the backlash against the perceived excesses of the Warren Court.[24]

In truth, the argument is a limited device, for the critic wields his own definition of what is political and therefore outwith the competence of the judge. If he is a segregationist he is unlikely to be persuaded by Dworkin that desegregation decisions are matters of individual rights, not policy. Extending the franchise, and educational facilities to the black man looks to the white supremacist like a political move of the first consequence. Similarly, to the tenants in Hubbard v Pitt,[25] the decision that they broke the law by holding a demonstration against their landlord outside the offices of his agent, looks like a piece of political bias, however it might be disguised as a vindication of the private rights of the agent.

An attack on the undemocratic status of the judiciary, moreover, addresses an absent other which is democratic, responsive and fitted to make political innovations. Legislatures in most social democracies are unlikely candidates for these accolades.[26] The process out of which their membership emerges generally has a fairly remote connection with the expression of popular will and the citizen's solitary and infrequent vote scarcely amounts to his calling the government to account for its acts.

Subterranean to the separation of powers critique of judicial innovation is a silent neo Lockean assumption that the end of government is to sustain political liberty and private property in accordance with an original agreement. The executive carries out mundane tasks on behalf of the citizens, and the judiciary exists to settle disputed claims - all within the delineated area of liberty and property. The rightness or wrongness of decisions taken in that area can be deduced from the constituting principles. Changes to those principles, however, can be justified only by reference to the citizens for whom government was and is constituted. Dworkin[27] refers to changes of such a kind as 'policy' decisions and they may be of an apparently trivial nature on occasion - for example, a governmental assumption of powers to direct the location of factories away from scenic countryside, or to regions of high unemployment: not prima facie steps of constitutional significance, perhaps. It is the quality of the measure which counts, though, in interfering with existing rights of liberty or property.

But the idea that such a distinction can be made is misleading. Carefully formulated demarcations of most kinds can be rationally defended in texts based on premises carefully chosen by their authors, but in the event of material conflict, idealist claims to an impartial wisdom reveal themselves to be the rhetoric of political propaganda. The technologists of such propaganda can produce as constitutionalist arguments - that, after all, is their job - to support political protagonists, but in the end the real issue for both conservatives and radicals is not _that_ the judge has decided, but _what_ he has decided.

Is it not, then, legitimate to regard the judge as an asset, a piece of ordance to be struggled for, seized and used? The literature on judicial backgrounds and predilictions becomes more than descriptively significant. Whatever taste and exigency dictate, shall be the territory of the judge, but whatever it is, he must be chosen for a background and personality apt for the production of congenial decisions. In the social democrats' meritocracy of equality of opportunity, sustained by 'an elite of unassuming experts who could make no claim to superior social status, but content themselves with exercising the power inherent in superior knowledge and wider social experience'[28] the judge should perhaps be selected by competitive process from comprehensive school students who went to redbrick universities.

However, for materialism it is the existence of the judge, not his biography, or what he does, which marks out the range of social possibilities. Specifically, the very possibility of the site from which Lord Denning proclaims equal protection of all by law is the suppression of equal protection. Courts exist in order to intervene in the operation of political directives, but if they are to do so effectively they need to ration applications for their services.

There is a rationality which supplies a hierarchy of importance: one axis has to do with means to pay, another with a concept of public interest, or public importance. A person without means cannot litigate without justifying the expenditure of public funds on his behalf, and in Britain test cases do not attract such funds. (A geography of lawyer distribution on the maps of Britain's land-surface and its social class structure generally would reveal in what way legal services are narrowly provided). A person who has the means, but fails to lift-off relative to the other axis, is a vexatious litigant.[29]

Digression on Denning's Discipline and Due Process

Nevertheless, the existence of a possibility of access to the courts tells us something about the political practice within which it occurs. Equal protection is not a political challenge because when the plane of abstract liberal justice is carefully moulded to the social topography of the liberal state, it designates and reflects the existing contours, although it may constitute and define a new landscape.[30] In the rationality which explains and justifies the rationing of courts' services is inscribed the social formation, in so far as it is constituted in one pattern of de facto loss-distribution rather than another, and one pattern rather than another of the distribution of goods, or gains.

The courts of common law developed historically to resolve disputes of a kind which most people would not have, in non-criminal law, and to perform a largely symbolic role in the criminal law. In both cases, they served to intercept and modify the course of political direction. That is why it is important to notice the conditions of limited access to the courts. Equally important is to ask whether there could be a more broadly based access to the courts, and if so, whether law could in such a way become the property of the people as, for example, the Levellers envisaged. In the context of Lord Denning, the questions have a significance because he does more than hint at the former without conceding the latter in his judgments. He has been associated with 'law for the little man', but in his more astonishing and most successful solutions, his law has been the 'equity'[31] of the judicial conscience, and the 'history' of his own imagining.[32]

General access to law is a contradiction at the heart of the law's promise. On the one hand, to be effective in even a narrow fashion, judicial intervention must be thorough - and costly - and relatively infrequent, but on the other hand, greater access means relatively cheaper and certainly more frequent court hearings.[33] Effective intervention requires the removal oflaw from the mundane of political administration: or put another way, the professional practice of lawyers has defined the substance of their practice as precious, even mysterious; the rhetoric of social democratic political practice concedes this, but within that practice there is no place from which a judge can operate in opposition to the state.

He is locked into an integrated structure, and that is the only condition on which the state can operate through law, permitting juridical interventions in a government's conduct of the state.

So law is a state practice as much as government is. But it is not a state practice in the same way as government. It is not a legitimate target for those who seek fundamental change, not because it is something other than a species of political practice, but precisely because it _is_ a species of political practice, and one which loses its distinct identity and effectiveness once the specific conditions of its mystery are penetrated.

Communists like Karl Renner, and radicals who seek significant social change through law, misidentify their object. In point are the civil liberties questions. The role of any judiciary here is defined for it by the political apparatus of which it forms a part. There is a built-in inequality in relation to access to adjudication, as we have seen, but subject to that, where the state is liberal, judicial intervention in favour of civil liberties will frequently be successful. But there is no possibility of _achieving_ civil liberties as against the 'strong state'[34] by means of litigation. The precise stipulations of the constitution - in the legalistic sense of the term - are probably not important for a theoretical evaluation of the general situation, although they do indicate past political practice.[35] In the erosion of civic freedom over the last decades in the UK, English judges have not sustained the state against the legal subject reluctantly, on the excuse of their own constitutional impotence. On the contrary, in cases like _Chic Fashions_[36] and _Hosenball_[37] Lord Denning is to be seen enthusiastically endorsing the law and order/state security point of view.

Arguably, the most humane and far-sighted of English judges this century was Lord Atkin. His dissenting judgment in _Liversidge_ v _Anderson_ is an able statement of liberal values. Interestingly, we find Lord Denning quoting[38] a judgment of his, in _Hosenball_, in which he invokes the speech of Lord Maugham in _Liversidge_ v _Anderson_.[39] This was one of the speeches which Lord Atkin compared to those of the judges in Charles I's time. The point is not to measure Lord Denning against an accredited Hero of liberalism. Lord Atkin was a lone dissentient and was ostracised by his colleagues.[40] Rather, if Althusser's[41] notion of 'relative autonomy' is accepted, it should not be thought that the level of judicial law-making is a level which is capable of being relatively autonomous of the level of politics. Scheingold's[42] tactical advice is good, not to use the courts except as a part of an overall political campaign.

The problem with focussing on a non-autonomous part of a whole is that one's search for the causes of consequences is restricted. In the context of the English state it is predictable that the '... posing of the trade union versus the individual shows how close is Denning's philosophy to that of the National Association for Freedom and the right wing of the Tory Party'.[43] It is not surprising that 'Denning's heroes', the 'fine citizens who come to the court as representatives of the public good' are, 'coincidentally, perhaps ... all ... on the Right'.[44] Lord Denning's 'grotesque' view of the nineteenth century - referred to by Griffith[45] - is one that some members of the current Conservative administration appear to share. Ideas which are taken by a ruling class to be important in explaining and justifying what its members do will appear, reappear and have effects. Lord Denning is an upholder of a ruling class albeit not in any simplistic way. His illiberalism is for the most part the illiberalism of the class through which that rule is sustained- in other words, it is not note-worthy that it happens to be Lord Denning who articulates them.[46]

What is surprising,[47] though, is that Lord Denning should invoke a libertarian rhetoric, for his undoubted improvements to the law - the deserted wife's equity, equitable estoppel and inequality of bargaining power in contracts - do not require it, and it merely underlines the illiberality of his other pronouncements. But then, upholders of the ruling class are not merely so.

IAN DUNCANSON

Digression on Denning's Discipline and Due Process

NOTES

(1) Lord Denning, The Discipline of Law, Butterworths, London, 1979.
(2) Lord Denning, The Due Process of Law, Butterworths, London, 1980.
(3) Jeremy Smith, New Statesman, 19 July 1979, p.78.
(4) J. Griffith, 42 MLR 1979, p.348.
(5) E. Grimshaw and E. Jones, Lord Goddard, Allen Wingate, London, 1958, cited in Cain, 'Necessarily Out of Touch', in P. Carlen (ed.) The Sociology of Law, Sociological Review, London, 1976, p.226.
(6) A right which Lord Denning claims more openly than other judges - cf. Lord Radcliffe, Law and Its Compass, Northwestern, Evanston, 1961 - hence his invocations of the statute, 28 Edw. III C 3, and of the 5th Amendment of the US Constitution, in order to indicate the meaning of his title, Due Process.
(7) Judith Williamson analyses the users of absent subjects in advertising in Decoding Advertisements, Marion Boyars, London, 1978, p.69.
(8) N. Poulantzas, Political Power and Social Classes, NLB, London, 1973, p.105.
(9) See, inter alia, L. Althusser, Reading Capital, NLB, London,1970; for a critique, see P. Hirst, B. Hindess and A. Hussain, Marx's Capital and Capitalism Today, (Vol. 1, part III especially), RKP, London, 1977; for a defence see, for example, B. Fine and L. Harris, Re-Reading Capital, Columbia U.P., 1979, p.146 et seq.
(10) P. Anderson, Lineages of the Absolutist State, NLB, London, 1975, Ch.5.
(11) P. Anderson, 'The Origins of the Present Crisis', in P. Anderson and R. Blackburn (eds.), Towards Socialism, Cornell U.P., 1961 (cf. E.P. Thompson, 'The Peculiarities of the English', in E.P. Thompson (ed.), The Poverty of Theory, Merlin, London, 1979. In support of Anderson is T. Nairn, The Breakup of Britain, NLB, London, 1977.
(12) E. Hobsbawm, The Age of Capital, Weidenfeld & Nicolson, London, 1975 and particularly E. Hobsbawm, Industry and Empire, 1968; also H. Perkin, The Origins of Modern English Society, RKP, London, 1969.
(13) Perkin, op cit.
(14) P. Addison, The Road to 1945, Cape, London, 1975 (on the watershed of 'Butskellism'); K. Middlemas, Politics in an Industrial Society: The Experience of

the British System since 1911 (on the failure of industry), Deutsch, London, 1979.

(15) S. Hall, Nicos Poulantzas, 'State, Power, Socialism', 119 New Left Review, 1980, p.60.

(16) See P. Beharrell and G. Philo, The Trade Unions and the Media, Macmillan, London, 1977.

(17) But, of course, many formerly independent professionals are now employees, and union members. Nevertheless, they have taken their attitudes with them. See - with reservations, M. Larson, The Rise of Professionalism, California U.P., 1978.

(18) See, S. Hall, et al, Policing the Crisis: Mugging, the State and Law and Order, Macmillan, London, 1978.

(19) The Epilogue to Due Process with its brief account of the Dennings at war is arguably symptomatic of a tendency to which Thompson drew attention in a series of New Statesman and New Society articles during 1979, to annexe patriotism and heroism in war to the Right, too - now collected in Sir, Writing by Candlelight, Merlin, London, 1980.

(20) This is precisely the end to which the Whig Constitution seems to consign the judiciary; see I. Duncanson, 'Balloonists, Bills of Rights and Dinosaurs', Public Law, 1978, p.391.

(21) The police and the civil service are obvious examples: D. McBarnett, 'The Legal Context of Policing', in S. Holdaway (ed.), The British Police, Edward Arnold, London, 1979; I. Gough, The Political Economy of the Welfare State, Macmillan, London, 1979. The operation of magistrates' courts is often overlooked, presumably on the ground that it is technically judicial. But, see P. Carlen, Magistrates' Justice, Martin Robertson, 1976.

(22) See Lord Devlin, 'Judges and Lawmakers', 39 MLR 1976, p.1; R. Dworkin, Taking Rights Seriously, Duckworth, London, 1977, Ch.4 and pp.137-149.

(23) J. Griffith, The Politics of the Judiciary, Fontana, London, 1978.

(24) See the argument in Wechsler, 'Toward Neutral Principles of Constitutional Law', 73 Harvard L.R., 1959, p.1; Pollak, 'Racial Discrimination and Judicial Integrity', 108 U.P. a L.R. p.1.

(25) [1975] 3 All ER 1.

(26) See, C. Pateman, Participation and Democratic Theory, Cambridge U.P., 1970.

(27) Dworkin, op cit.

(28) B. Webb, Diaries 1912-24, Cole (ed.), 1952, cited Middlemas, op cit, p.31.
(29) P. Lewis, P. Morris and R. White, Social Needs and Legal Action, Martin Robertson, London, 1972; M. Zander, Legal Services for the Community, Temple Smith, London, 1978. See also the references cited in Duncanson, op cit.
(30) The response of the legal profession, local government and others to the apparently 'radical' stance of some law centres, was predictably unfavourable. See Community Development Project Report, Limits of the Law, 1977; also, as an example of the response, the Royal Commission on Legal Services, 1979, Cmnd 7648, Ch. 8.
(31) For example, High Trees [1947] KB 130; Binions v Evans [1972] 2 All ER 70.
(32) Griffith, 42 MLR 1979 p.348.
(33) Duncanson, op cit.
(34) Here, by State is meant the institutions that represent the status of class relations.
(35) Thus, see in the United States, where there is an entrenched Bill of Rights, Cramer v US (1944) 325 US 1 and the use made of the Smith Act 1940 and the Internal Security Act 1950. See, generally, J. Stone, Social Dimensions of Law and Justice, Stevens, London, 1966, Ch.5.
(36) Chic Fashions (West Wales) Ltd. v Jones [1968] 2 QB 299.
(37) R. v Home Secretary, ex parte Hosenball [1977] 1 WLR 766.
(38) The Due Process of Law, p.87.
(39) [1942] AC 206.
(40) See, R. Stevens, Law and Politics: The House of Lords 1800-1976, Weidenfeld and Nicolson, London, 1979, p.287.
(41) L. Althusser, For Marx, Allen Lane, London, 1969; Reading Capital, NLB, London, 1970.
(42) S. Scheingold, The Politics of Rights, Yale U.P., New Haven, 1974.
(43) Jeremy Smith, ibid.
(44) Ibid.
(45) J. Griffith, 42 MLR 348.
(46) The argument above has not been that law reflects dominant class interests in any simple way. Interestingly, and, as I argued, in subversion of his own position, Lord Denning articulates in many instances the dominance of a ruling fragment whose

predominance has been several decades in developing.
(47) Although, see the preceding footnote.

Index

Case Index

Attorney General Ex Rel McWhirter v Independent Broadcasting Authority
[1973] Q.B. 629; [1973] 2 W.L.R. 344; [1973] 1 ALL E.R. 689 pp.82, 83, 166, 172, 175

Barnes v Barratt
[1970] 2 Q.B. 257; [1970] 2 W.L.R. 1085; [1970] 2 ALL E.R. 483 pp.195, 196

Barrington v Lee
[1972] 1 Q.B. 326; [1971] 3 W.L.R. 962; [1971] 3 ALL E.R. 1231 pp.2, 32

Beaverbrook Newspapers v Keys
[1978] I.C.R. 582; [1978] I.R.L.R. 34 pp.137, 138

Bendall v McWhirter
[1952] 2 Q.B. 466; [1952] 1 T.L.R. 1332; [1952] 1 ALL E.R. 1307 p.2

Beswick v Beswick
[1966] Ch 538; [1966] 3 W.L.R. 396; [1966] 3 ALL E.R. 1 p.2

Binions v Evans
[1972] Ch 359; [1972] 2 W.L.R. 729; [1972] 2 ALL E.R. 70 p.219

Birmingham and District Land Co v London and North Western Railway Co
(1888) 40 Ch.D 268 p.29

Bolam v Friern Hospital Management Committee
[1957] 1 W.L.R. 582; [1957] 2 ALL E.R. 118 p.101

Bonsor v Musicians' Union
[1954] Ch 479; [1954] 2 W.L.R.
687; [1954] 1 ALL E.R. 822 p.39n

Booker v Palmer
[1942] 2 ALL E.R. 674 p.194

Bourne v Norwich Crematorium Ltd
[1967] 1 W.L.R.
691; [1967] 2 ALL E.R. 576 p.20

Boys v Chaplin
[1968] 2 Q.B. 1; [1968] 2 W.L.R.
328; [1968] 1 ALL E.R. 283 p.32

Bradbury v Enfield London Borough Council
[1967] 1 W.L.R.
1311; [1967] 3 ALL E.R. 434 pp.164, 165, 175

Bravery v Bravery
[1954] 1 W.L.R.
1169; [1954] 3 ALL E.R. 59 pp.76, 77, 78

Breen v Amalgamated Engineering Union
[1971] 2 Q.B. 175; [1971] 2 W.L.R.
742; [1972] 1 ALL E.R. 1148 pp.2, 39n, 158, 169, 179

Bridge v Campbell Discount Co
[1962] A.C. 600; [1962] 2 W.L.R.
439; [1962] 1 ALL E.R. 385 pp.2, 28

British Movietonews Ltd v London and District Cinemas
[1952] A.C. 166; p.2, 40n, 43n

British Broadcasting Corporation v Hearn
[1977] I.C.R. 685; [1977] 1 W.L.R.
1004; [1978] 1 ALL E.R. 111 pp.2, 134, 135, 148n, 155n

British Movietonews Ltd v London and District Cinemas
[1952] A.C. 166; [1951] 2 ALL E.R.
617; pp.2, 16, 27, 28
reversing [1951] 1 K.B.
190; [1950] 2 ALL E.R. 390

Brooks and Burton v Secretary of State for the Environment
(1976) 75 L.G.R. 285; [1976] J.P.L.
574 p.178

Broome v Cassell & Co
[1971] 2 Q.B. 354; [1971] 2 W.L.R.
853; [1971] 2 ALL E.R. 187 pp.16, 26, 29

D and C Builders Ltd v Rees
[1966] 2 Q.B. 617; [1966] 2 W.L.R.
288; [1965] 3 ALL E.R. 837 p.2

H P Bulmer Ltd v J Bollinger S.A.
[1974] Ch 401 p.25

Burmah Oil Co v Lord Advocate
[1965] A.C. 75; [1964] 2 W.L.R.
1231; [1964] 2 ALL E.R. 348 p.56

Bushell v Secretary of State for the Environment
(1979)
123; S.J. 605 p.159

Candler v Crane Christmas & Co
[1951] 2 K.B. 164; [1951] 1 T.L.R.
371; [1951] 1 ALL E.R. 426 p.2

Carter v Bradbeer
[1975] 3 ALL E.R. 158 p.24

Cassell & Co v Broome
[1972] A.C. 1027; [1972] 2 W.L.R.
645; [1972] 1 ALL E.R. 801 pp.16, 26, 29, 60

Cassidy v Ministry of Health
[1951] 2 K.B. 343; [1951] 1 T.L.R.
539; [1951] 1 ALL E.R. 574 p.112n

Causton v Mann Egerton (Johnsons) Ltd
[1974] 1 W.L.R.
162; [1974] 1 ALL E.R. 453 p.2

Central London Property Trust Ltd v High Trees House Ltd
[1947] K.B. 130; pp.2, 28, 219

Chandler v Kerley
[1978] 1 W.L.R.
693; [1978] 2 ALL E.R. 942 p.193

Chapman v Rix - The Times, November 19
1959 p.106

Charter v Race Relations Board
[1972] 1 Q.B. 545; [1972] 2 W.L.R.
190; [1972] 1 ALL E.R 556 p.172

Chic Fashions (West Wales) v Jones
[1968] 2 Q.B. 299; [1968] 2 W.L.R.
201; [1968] 1 ALL E.R. 229 p.220

Clarke v Martlew
[1973] Q.B. 58; [1972[3 W.L.R.
653; [1972] 3 ALL E.R. 764 p.2

Cobb v Lane
[1952] 1 T.L.R.
1037; [1952] 1 ALL E.R. 199 p.192

Coleen Properties v Minister of Housing and Local Government
[1971] 1 W.L.R.
433; [1971] 1 ALL E.R. 1049 pp.2, 14, 163, 170

Re a Company
(1979) 123 S.J. 584 pp.163, 184n

Congreve v Home Office
[1976] Q.B. 629; [1976] 2 W.L.R. pp.2, 49, 164, 165, 167,
291; [1976] 1 ALL E.R. 697 168, 169, 171, 172, 173

Con-Mech (Engineers) v Amalgamated Union of Engineering Workers (Engineering Section)
[1973] I.C.R.
620 p.64

Conway v Rimmer
[1967] 1 W.L.R.
1031; [1967] 2 ALL E.R. 1260 pp. 2, 27, 32, 88

Conway v Wade
[1909] A.C.
506 p.151n

Crabb v Arun D.C. .
[1976] 1 Ch 179; p.2

Cramer v U.S.
(1944) 325; U.S. 1 p.224n

Crawford v Board of Governors of Charing Cross Hospital
The Times, December 8
1953 p.106

D v National Society for the Prevention of Cruelty to Children
[1978] A.C. 171; [1977] 2 W.L.R.
201; [1977] 1 ALL E.R. 589 pp.90, 91, 94,

Daily Mirror Newspapers v Gardner
[1968] 2 Q.B. 768; [1968] 2 W.L.R.
1239; [1968] 2 ALL E.R. 163 p.132

Davis v Johnson
[1978] 2 W.L.R.
182; [1978] 1 ALL E.R. 841 pp.2, 16, 20, 31, 32, 69

De Falco v Crawley Borough Council; Silvestri v Crawley Borough Council
[1980] 1 ALL E.R. 913;
The Times, December 13 1979 pp.122, 123

Dealex Properties v Brooks
[1965] 2 W.L.R.
1241; [1965] 1 ALL E.R. 1080 p.195

Demuren and Adefope v Seal Estates
(1978) 249; E.G. 440 pp.204, 206, 207

D.P.P. v Head
[1959] A.C. 83; [1958] 2 W.L.R.
617; [1958] 1 ALL. E.R. 679 p.160

Dockers' Labour Club v Race Relations Board
[1974] Q.B. 503; [1974] 2 W.L.R.
166; [1974] 1 ALL E.R. 713 p.172

Dorset Yacht Co v Home Office
[1969] 2 Q.B. 412; [1969] 2 W.L.R.
1008; [1969] 2 ALL E.R. 564 p.2

Drive Yourself Hire Co (London) Ltd v Strutt
[1954] 1 Q.B. 250; [1953] 3 W.L.R.
1111; [1953] 2 ALL E.R. 1475 p.2

Duncan v Cammell Laird & Co
[1942] A.C. 624; pp.87, 89

Duport Steels Ltd v Sirs
[1980] 1 W.L.R.
142; [1980] 1 ALL E.R. 529
[1980] I.C.R. 161
(CA) and (HL) pp.2, 3, 16, 18, 19, 25, 144, 145, 146

Dutton v Bognor Regis Urban District Council
[1972] 1 Q.B. 373; [1972] 2 W.L.R.
299; [1972] 1 ALL E.R. 462 pp.2, 176, 178

W & J B Eastwood v Herrod
[1968] 2 Q.B. 923; [1968] 3 W.L.R.
593; [1968] 3 ALL E.R. 389 pp.2, 26, 32

Eddis v Chichester Constable
[1969] 2 Ch 345; [1969] 3 W.L.R.
48; [1969] 2 ALL E.R. 912 p.23

Edwards v Society of Graphical and Allied Trades
[1970] 1 W.L.R.
379; [1970] 1 ALL E.R. 905 p.39n

Emerald Construction Co v Lowthian
[1966] 1 W.L.R.
691; [1966] 1 ALL E.R. 1013 p.131

Enderby Town Football Club v Football Association
[1971] Ch 591; [1970] 3 W.L.R.
1021; [1971] 1 ALL E.R. 215 pp.18, 176

Engineers' and Managers' Association v Advisory Conciliation and Arbitration Service
[1979] I.C.R. 637; [1979] 1 W.L.R.
1113; [1979] 3 ALL E.R. 223
(CA) [1980] 1 W.L.R.
302 (HL) p.15

Errington v Errington and Woods
[1952] 1 K.B. 290; [1952] 1 T.L.R.
231; [1952] 1 ALL E.R. 149 pp.28, 189, 190, 191, 194

Esso Petroleum Co Ltd v Mardon
[1976] 1 Q.B. 801 p.2

Evenden v Guildford Football Club
[1975] 1 Q.B. 917; [1975] 3 W.L.R.
251; [1975] 3 ALL E.R. 269 p.2

Eves v Eves
[1975] 1 W.L.R.
1338; [1975] 3 ALL E.R. 768 pp.69, 75

Express Newspapers v McShane
[1979] 1 W.L.R.
390; [1979] I.C.R. 210
[1979] 2 ALL E.R. 360 (CA)
[1980] 2 W.L.R.
89; [1980] I.C.R. 42
[1980] 1 ALL E.R. 65 (HL) pp.2, 139, 140, 141, 143, 144, 145

Facchini v Bryson
[1952] 1 T.L.R.
1386 pp.188, 189, 190, 196, 199, 200, 202, 204

Faramus v Film Artistes' Association
[1963] 2 Q.B. 527; [1963] 2 W.L.R.
504; [1963] 1 ALL E.R. 636 pp.39n, 176

Farnworth Finance Facilities v Attryde
[1970] 1 W.L.R.
1053; [1970] 2 ALL E.R. 774 p.2

Farrell v Alexander
[1976] Q.B. 345; [1975] 3 W.L.R.
642; [1976] 1 ALL E.R. 129 pp.2, 32

Fawcett Properties Ltd v Buckingham County Council
[1961] A.C. 636; [1960] 3 W.L.R.
831; [1960] 3 ALL E.R. 503 p.27

Finbow v Air Ministry
[1963] 1 W.L.R.
697; [1963] 2 ALL E.R. 647 pp.199, 200

Fisher v Bell
[1961] 1 Q.B. 394; [1960] 3 W.L.R.
919; [1960] 3 ALL E.R. 731 p.20

Foster v Robinson
[1951] 1 K.B.
149; [1950] 2 ALL E.R. 342 pp.194, 195

Gallie v Lee
[1969] 2 Ch 17; pp.2, 32

Ghani v Jones
[1970] 1 Q.B. 693; [1969] 3 W.L.R.
1158; [1969] 3 ALL E.R. 1700 p.171

Glasgow Corporation v Muir
[1943] A.C. 448 pp.100, 103

Gold v Essex County Council
[1942] 2 K.B. 293 p.110n

Gouriet v Union of Post Office Workers
[1977] 2 W.L.R.
310; [1977] 1 ALL E.R. 696
(reversed by HL [1978] A.C. 435) pp.28, 175, 176

Grant v Australian Knitting Mills
[1936] A.C. 85 p.100

Grosvenor Hotel, London. Re (no 2)
[1965] Ch 1210; [1964] 3 W.L.R.
992; [1964] 1 ALL E.R. 92 pp.2, 87, 88, 89

Grunwick Processing Laboratories v Advisory Conciliation and Arbitration Service
[1978] ICR 231; [1978] A.C. 655; [1978] 2 W.L.R.
277 p.15

Guppys (Bridport) Ltd v Sandoe
(1975) 30 P & C.R. 69 p.116

Hanning v Maitland (No 2)
[1970] 1 Q.B. 580; [1970] 2 W.L.R.
151; [1970] 1 ALL E.R. 812 pp.2, 32

Harbutts "Plasticine" Ltd v Wayne Tank and Pump Co Ltd
[1970] 1 Q.B. 447; [1970] 2 W.L.R.
198; [1970] 1 ALL E.R. 225 pp.2, 5, 28

Hardwick v Johnson
[1978] 1 W.L.R.
683; [1978] 2 ALL E.R. 935 pp.190, 193

H.T.V. v Price Commission
[1976] I.C.R. 170 p.179

Hatcher v Black, The Times, July 2 1954
pp.102, 104, 106, 107

Heslop v Burns
[1974] 1 W.L.R.
1241 p.196

Hillyer v St Bartholomew's Hospital
[1909] 2 K.B. 820 p110n

Hubbard v Pitt
[1976] Q.B. 142; [1975] 3 W.L.R.
201; [1975] 3 ALL E.R. 1 pp.28, 171, 217

Hucks v Cole
(1968) 112 S.J. 483;
The Times, May 9 1968 pp.106, 107, 109, 110

Hughes v Metropolitan Railway Co
(1887) 2 App Cas 439 p.29

Island Records, ex parte
[1978] Ch 122; [1978] 3 W.L.R.
23; [1978] 3 ALL E.R. 824 p.184n

Re Jebb
[1966] Ch 666 [1965] 3 W.L.R.
810; [1965] 3 ALL E.R. 358 pp.11, 12, 13

Jorden v Money
(1854) 5 M.L. Cases 185 p.28

Kamara v D P P
[1974] A.C. 104; [1973] 3 W.L.R.
198; [1973] 2 ALL E.R. 1242 p.58n

Kammins Ballrooms Co Ltd v Zenith Investments (Torquay) Ltd
[1971] A.C. 850 [1970] 3 W.L.R.
287; [1970] 2 ALL E.R. 871 p.23

Karsales (Harrow) Ltd v Wallis
[1956] 1 W.L.R. 936; [1956] 2 ALL E.R. 866 p.2

Laker Airways v Department of Trade
[1977] Q.B. 643; [1977] 2 W.L.R.
234; [1977] 2 ALL E.R. 182 p.2, 67, 167, 170, 171, 173, 177, 178

Langston v Amalgamated Union of Engineering Workers
[1974] 1 W.L.R.
185; [1974] I.C.R. 180; [1974] 1 ALL E.R. 980 pp.15, 28

Lee v Showmen's Guild of Great Britain
[1952] 2 Q.B. 329; [1952] 1 T.L.R.
1115; [1952] 1 ALL E.R. 1175 pp.160, 176

Lever (Finance) Ltd v Westminster (City) London Borough Council
[1971] 1 Q.B. 222; [1970] 3 WLR
732; [1970] 3 ALL E.R. 496 pp.2, 178

Lim Poh Choo v Camden and Islington Health Authority
[1979] Q.B. 196; [1979] 3 W.L.R.
44; [1979] 1 ALL E.R. 332 pp.16, 18, 85n, 112n

Liverpool City Council v Irwin
[1976] Q.B. 319; [1975] 3 W.L.R.
663; [1975] 3 ALL E.R. 658 pp.1, 2, 17, 174, 176

London Street Tramways Co v London County Council
[1898] A.C. 375 p.31

London and North Eastern Rail Co v Berriman
[1946] A.C. 278 p.20

London Transport Executive v Betts
[1959] A.C. 213; [1958] 3 W.L.R.
239; [1958] 2 ALL E.R. 636 pp.23, 27, 32

Lumley v Gye
(1853) 2 E & B 216 p.130

M v M
[1947] 63 T.L.R. 645 p.2

McCormack v Redpath Brown & Co
The Times, March 24 1961 p.106

McPhail v Persons, Names Unknown
[1973] Ch 447; [1973] 3 W.L.R.
71; [1973] 3 ALL E.R. 393 pp.11, 119, 120

Magor and St Mellons Rural District Council v Newport Borough Council
[1952] A.C. 189; [1951] 2 T.L.R.
935; [1951] 2 ALL E.R. 839 pp.3, 16, 21, 22

Mahon v Osborne
[1939] 2 K.B. 14 pp.101, 107

Marchant v Charters
[1977] 1 W.L.R.
1181; [1977] 3 ALL E.R. 918 pp202, 203

Marcroft Wagons v Smith
[1951] 2 K.B.
496; [1951] 2 ALL E.R. 271 pp.188, 195

Meade v London Borough of Haringey
[1979] I.C.R.
494; [1979] 2 ALL E.R. 1016 pp.154n, 166

Merricks v Nott-Bower
[1965] 1 Q.B. 57; [1964] 2 W.L.R.
702; [1964] 1 ALL E.R. 717 p.2

Midland Silicones v Scruttons Ltd
[1962] A.C. 446; pp.2, 17, 28

Miliangos v George Frank (Textiles) Ltd
[1975] 1 Q.B. 487; p.30

Miller-Mead v Minister of Housing and Local Government
[1963] 2 Q.B. 196; [1963] 2 W.L.R.
225; [1963] 1 ALL E.R. 459 p.172

Ministry of Housing v Sharp
[1970] 2 Q.B. 223; [1970] 2 W.L.R.
802; [1970] 1 ALL E.R. 1009 p.2

N W L Ltd v Nelson
[1979] I.C.R. 755; [1979]
2 Lloyd's Rep 317 (CA) p.154n

N W L Ltd v Woods
[1979] I.C.R. 744; [1979]
2 Lloyd's Rep 325 (CA) p.154n

N W L Ltd v Woods and Nelson
[1979] 1 W.L.R. pp.142, 143, 21, 150n, 151n
1294; [1979] I.C.R. 867; [1979] 3 ALL E.R. 614 (HL)

National Provincial Bank v Hastings Car Mart
[1964] Ch 665; [1964] 2 W.L.R.
751; [1964] 1 ALL E.R. 688 pp.2, 69, 75

Newbury District Council v Secretary of State for the Environment
[1978] 1 W.L.R.
1241; [1978] 1 ALL E.R. 243 p.172

Nothman v Barnet London Borough Council
[1978] I.C.R. 336; [1978] 1 W.L.R.
220; [1978] 1 ALL E.R. 1243 pp.16, 24, 126

O'Malley v Seymour
(1979) 250 E.G. 1083 pp.205, 206

Padfield v Minister of Agriculture Fisheries and Food
[1968] A.C. 997; [1968] 2 W.L.R.
924; [1968] 1 ALL E.R. 694 pp.2, 161, 167, 169, 170

Panchaud Freres S.A. v Et General Grain Co
[1970] 1 Lloyd's Rep 53; p.2

Pearlman v Keepers and Governors of Harrow School
[1978] 3 W.L.R.
736; (1978) 247 E.G. 1173 pp.2, 114, 163, 177

Re Pergamon Press Ltd
[1971] Ch 388; [1970] 3 W.L.R.
792; [1970] 3 ALL E.R. 535 p.2

Photo-Production Ltd v Securicor Transport Ltd
[1978] 1 W.L.R.
856; [1978] 3 ALL E.R. 146 pp.2, 6, 7, 16

Plasticmoda Societa per Azioni v Davidsons (Manchester) Ltd
[1952] 1 Lloyd's Rep 527 p.2

R v Battersea, Wandworth, Mitcham and Wimbledon Rent Tribunal ex p Parikh
[1957] 1 W.L.R.
410 [1957] 1 ALL E.R. 352 p.197

R v Bristol Corporation ex p Hendy
[1974] 1 W.L.R.
498; [1974] 1 ALL E.R. 1047 pp.164, 174

R v Commissioner of Police of the Metropolis ex p Blackburn
[1968] 2 Q.B. 118; [1968] 2 W.L.R.
893; [1968] 1 ALL E.R. 763 p.175

R v Commissioner of Police of the Metropolis ex p Blackburn (No 2)
[1968] 2 Q.B. 150 p.33

R v Commissioner of Police of the Metropolis ex p Black - burn (No 3)
[1973] 1 Q.B. 241; [1973] 2 W.L.R.
43; [1973] 1 ALL E.R. 324 pp.74, 81, 175

R v Coney
[1882] 8 Q.B.D. 534 p.78

R v Donovan
[1934] 2 K.B. 498 p.78

R v Gaming Board for Great Britain ex p Benaim and Khaida
[1970] 2 Q.B. 417; [1970] 2 W.L.R.
1009; [1970] 2 ALL E.R. 528 p.2, 158, 159, 177

R v Governor of Brixton Prison ex p Soblen
[1963] 2 Q.B. 243; [1962] 3 W.L.R
1154; [1962] 3 ALL E.R. 641 pp.38, 170, 173

R v Governor of Pentonville Prison ex p Azam
[1974] A.C. 18; [1973] 2 W.L.R.
949; [1973] 2 ALL E.R. 741 pp.10, 168, 169, 170, 173

R v Immigration Officer ex p Thakrar see R v Secretary of State for the Home Department ex p Thakrar

R v Industrial Injuries Commissioner ex p Amalgamated Engineering Union (No 1)
[1966] 2 Q.B. 21; [1966] 2 W.L.R.
91; [1966] 2 ALL E.R. 97 p.184n

R v Inland Revenue Commissioners ex p National Federation of Self Employed and Small Businesses, The Times 28 Feb 1980 p.175

R v Inland Revenue Commissioners ex p Rossminster
[1980] 2 W.L.R. 1 pp.171, 173

R v Liverpool Corporation ex p Liverpool Taxi Fleet Operators' Association
[1972] 2 Q.B. 299; [1972] 2 W.L.R. 1262; [1972] 2 ALL E.R. 589 pp.2, 158

R v Local Commissioner for Administration for the North and East Area of England ex p Bradford Metropolitan City Council
[1979] Q.B. 287; [1979] 2 ALL E.R. 881 pp.16, 20, 161, 162

R v Metropolitan Police Commissioner ex p Blackburn, The Times, March 7 1980 p.85n

R v Munks
[1964] 1 Q.B. 304; [1963] 3 W.L.R. 952; [1963] 3 ALL E.R. 757 p.20

R v National Insurance Commissioners
[1972] A.C. 914 p.42n

R v Paddington Valuation Officer ex p Peachey Property Corporation (No 2)
[1966] 1 Q.B. 380; [1965] 3 W.L.R. 426; [1965] 2 ALL E.R. 836 p.160

R v Police Commissioner ex p Blackburn
[1973] Q.B. 241; [1973] 2 W.L.R. 43; [1973] 1 ALL E.R. 324 p.175

R v Preston Supplementary Benefits Appeal Tribunal ex p Moore; R v Sheffield Supplementary Benefits Appeal Tribunal ex p Shine
[1975] 1 W.L.R. 624; [1975] 2 ALL E.R. 807 pp.114, 115, 116, 175

R v Race Relations Board ex p Selvarajan
[1975] 1 W.L.R. 1686; [1976] 1 ALL E.R. 12 pp.2, 159

R v Secretary of State for the Environment ex p Ostler
[1977] Q.B. 122; [1976] 3 W.L.R.
288; [1976] 3 ALL E.R. 90 pp.160, 164

R v Secretary of State for Home Affairs ex p Hosenball
[1977] 1 W.L.R.
766; [1977] 3 ALL E.R. 452 pp.2, 89, 90, 91, 92, 93, 95, 96, 161, 168, 173, 178, 220

R v Secretary of State for the Home Department ex p Choudhary
[1978] 1 W.L.R.
1177; [1978] 3 ALL E.R. 790 pp.10, 11

R v Secretary of State for the Home Department ex p Thakrar
[1974] Q.B. 684; [1974] 2 W.L.R.
593; [1974] 2 ALL E.R. 261 pp.7, 8, 9

R v Sheffield Crown Court ex p Brownlow
The Times, 4 March 1980 pp.17, 113, 153n, 162, 172

Rahimtoola v Nizam of Hyderabad
[1958] A.C. 379; [1957] 3 W.L.R.
884; [1957] 3 ALL E.R. 441 p.2

Ridge v Baldwin
[1964] A.C. 40; [1963] 2 W.L.R.
935; [1963] 2 ALL E.R. 66 p158

Robertson v Minister of Pensions
[1949] 1 K.B. 227; [1948] 2 ALL E.R. 767 pp.2, 28

Roe v Minister of Health; Woolley v Same
[1954] 2 Q.B. 66; [1954] 2 W.L.R.
915; [1954] 2 ALL E.R. 131 pp.101, 103, 104, 106

Rookes v Barnard
[1964] A.C. 1129; [1964] 2 W.L.R.
269; [1964] 1 ALL E.R. 367 pp.29, 133

Sagnata Investments v Nowrwich Corporation
[1971] 2 Q.B. 614; [1971] 3 W.L.R.
133; [1971] 2 ALL E.R. 1441 p.169

Salisbury (Marquess) v Gilmore
[1942] 2 Q.B. 38 p.29

Samrose Properties v Gibbard
[1958] 1 W.L.R.
235 [1958] 1 ALL E.R. 502 pp.189, 198, 199

Schmidt v Secretary of State for Home Affairs
[1969] 2 Ch 149; [1969] 2 W.L.R.
337; [1969] 1 ALL E.R. 904 pp.7, 159, 168, 173

Schorsh Meier GmbH v Hennin
[1975] Q.B. 416 p.30

Science Research Council v Nasse
[1978] I.C.R. 1124; [1978] 3 W.L.R.
754; [1978] 3 ALL E.R. 1196 pp.129, 174, 176

Scruttons Ltd v Midland Silicones Ltd
[1962] A.C. 446; [1962] 2 W.L.R.
186; [1962] 1 ALL E.R. 1 p.16

Seaford Court Estates Ltd v Asher
[1949] 2 K.B. 481; [1949] 2 ALL E.R. 155 p.21

Secretary of State for Education and Science v Tameside
Metropolitan Borough Council
[1977] A.C. 1014; [1976] 3 W.L.R.
641; [1976] 3 ALL E.R. 665 pp.2, 49, 67, 167, 169, 170,
171, 173, 176

Secretary of State for Employment v A.S.L.E.F.. (No 2)
[1972] 2 Q.B. 455; [1972] 2 W.L.R.
1370; [1976] 2 ALL E.R. 949 pp.2, 16, 169, 170, 172, 173

Shaw v D P P
[1962] A.C. 220 p.66

Shell-Mex & B P v Manchester Garages
[1971] 1 W.L.R.
612; [1971] 1 ALL E.R. 841 pp.200, 201

The Siskina [1977]
2 Lloyds Rep 230 pp.16, 17

Smith and Snipes Hall Farm Ltd v River Douglas Catchment Board
[1949] 2 K.B. 500; [1949]
2 ALL E.R. 179 p.2

Somma v Hazlehurst
[1978] 1 W.L.R.
1014; [1978] 2 ALL E.R. 1011 pp.189, 203, 204, 207, 208

The Case of James Sommersett
(1772) 20 State Trials 1 p.7

Southwark London Borough Council v Williams
[1971] Ch 734; [1971] 2 W.L.R.
467; [1971] 2 ALL E.R. 175 pp.118, 119, 121, 165, 166, 167, 174

Sparham-Souter v Town and Country Developments (Essex)
[1976] Q.B. 858 p.2

Spartan Steel & Alloys v Martin & Co (Contractors)
[1973] Q.B. 27; [1972] 3 W.L.R.
502; [1972] 3 ALL E.R. 557 p.2

Sydall v Castings Ltd
[1967] 1 Q.B. 302; [1966] 3 W.L.R.
1126; [1966] 3 ALL E.R. 770 pp.13, 14

Star Sea Transport Corporation v Slater
[1979] 1 Lloyd's Rep 26 (CA) pp.135, 136, 143, 155n

Stratford (JT) & Son v Lindley
[1965] A.C. 269 p.130

Suisse Atlantique Societe D'Armement Maritime S.A. v
NV Rotterdamsche Kolen Centrale
[1967] 1 A.C. 361 p.5

Tanner v Tanner
[1975] 1 W.L.R.
1346; [1975] 3 ALL E.R. 776 pp.69, 192

Taylor v Alidair Ltd
[1978] 1 C.R. 445; [1978] 1.R.L.R.
82 p.153n

Thomas v Sorrell
(1673) Vaugh 330 p.188

Thomson (DC) & Co v Deakin
[1952] Ch 646 [1952] 2 T.L.R.
105; [1952] 2 ALL E.R. 361 p.130

Thornton v Shoe Lane Parking Ltd
[1971] 2 Q.B. 163; (1971) 2 W.L.R.
585; (1971) 1 ALL E.R. 686 p.2

Tiverton Estates Ltd v Wearwell Ltd
[1975] Ch 146; (1974) 2 W.L.R.
176; (1974) 1 ALL E.R. 209 p.35n

Torquay Hotels Co Ltd v Cousins
[1969] 2 Ch 106; [1969] 2 W.L.R.
289; [1969] 1 ALL E.R. 522 pp.131, 132

UGS Finance v National Mortgage Bank of Greece
[1964] 1 Lloyd's Rep 446 p.2

United Biscuits v Fall
[1979] I.R.L.R. 110 pp.151n, 154n

United Kingdom Association of Professional Engineers v
Advisory Conciliation and Arbitration Service
[1979] 1 W.L.R.
570; [1979] I.C.R. 303; [1979] 2 ALL E.R. 478 (CA)
[1980] 2 W.L.R.
254; [1980] 1 ALL E.R. 612 (HL) pp.15, 129, 162

Re United Railways of the Havana and Regla Warehouses Ltd
[1961] A.C. 1007 p.30

Ward v Bradford Corporation
(1972) 70 L.G.R. 27;
115; S.J. 606 pp.79, 80, 81, 159, 177

Warwick University v De Graaf
[1975] 1 W.L.R.
1126; [1975] 3 ALL E.R. 284 p.120

Wednesbury Corporation v Ministry of Housing and Local
Government
[1965] 1 W.L.R.
261; [1965] 1 ALL E.R. 186 p.89

Wells v Minister of Housing and Local Government
[1967] 1 W.L.R.
1000; [1967] 2 ALL E.R. 1041 p.2

Western Fish Products v Penrith District Council
(1979) 77 L.G.R. 185 p.178